M000227008

HOUSE GODS

Strawbale home-building site, south of Rio Grande del Norte
National Monument. Photo by Jim Kristofic.

HOUSE GODS

SUSTAINABLE BUILDINGS AND RENEGADE BUILDERS

JIM KRISTOFIC

LIBRARY OF
CONGRESS
SURPLUS
DUPLICATE

UNIVERSITY OF NEW MEXICO PRESS | ALBUQUERQUE

© 2022 by Jim Kristofic
All rights reserved. Published 2022
Printed in the United States of America

ISBN 978-0-8263-6365-7 (cloth)
ISBN 978-0-8263-6366-4 (electronic)

Library of Congress Control Number: 2022932096

Founded in 1889, the University of New Mexico sits on the traditional homelands of the
Pueblo of Sandia. The original peoples of New Mexico—Pueblo, Navajo, and Apache—
since time immemorial have deep connections to the land and have made significant
contributions to the broader community statewide. We honor the land itself and those
who remain stewards of this land throughout the generations and also acknowledge our
committed relationship to Indigenous peoples. We gratefully recognize our history.

Cover illustration: *Navajo Hogan* by J. R. Willis
Designed by Felicia Cedillos
Composed in Huronia Navajo

For my grandfather, Richard E. Thompson,
and the many builders before and after him.

———————————————

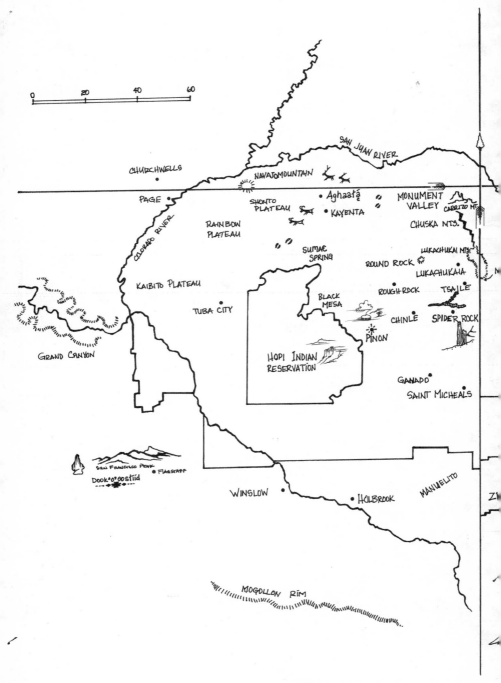

Map of Diné Bikéyáh, Navajo Country. Courtesy of Nolan Karras James.

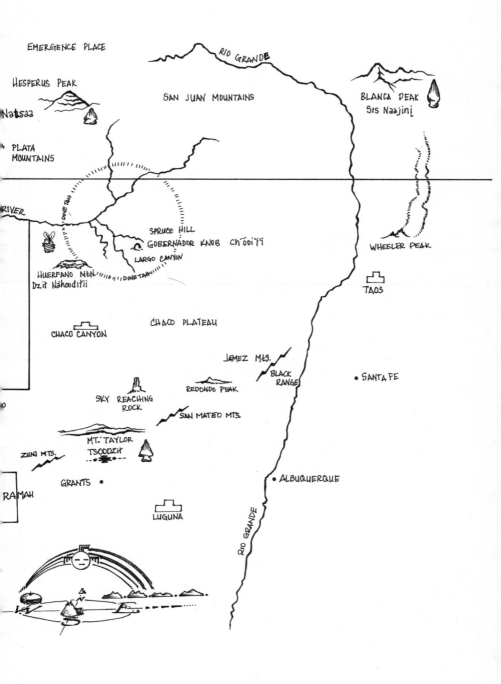

1/4" Masonite

Prologue | *The Endangering Species*

It is how we approach the door. At the door, we are not alone.

I grew up with *Diné* (Navajo) people, and when you are in their country, there is the *hoghan*. In the old ways, the *hoghan* was not a house; it was the area where you lived. There was a shelter where you slept. That shelter became the traditional Navajo home: a hexagonal or octagonal log cabin with *hogahn namaasí bighłeezh* (adobe mud) placed between the logs and domed on the roof. The fire burns at the center and the smoke rises from the *yá'há'hoo'tį́* (center hole). It is a place where women weave, where children read books or play their video games, where old men sing to the gods.

At the door of the *hoghan*—or at any house—lives *Haashch'ééhoghan*. Calling God. House God.

See his face. His eyes like an owl. His face descends like an owl. His hair spills out like sagebrush. His collar splays out in spruce boughs. The eagle feathers rise behind his head. *Haashch'ééhoghan*. House God. He is Strength. Wisdom. Good Health. Integrity. The thoughts that keep you away from that thing—drink, casinos, that illicit affair—that keeps you sleeping until noon.

In every *hoghan* there is an area of the door that faces east. *Haashch'ééhoghan* is in that area in the dawn, when the stars still shine before the sun has risen. There are many beings standing around the door, like an army of good essence. *Haashch'ééhoghan* is their leader. He is there, waiting in the door. You go to it. You move through it. You breath it in. You take in his essence. And that becomes your character. Your actions. You step through the door and you are made into something every day. Something that can live in your home—your *hoghan*—and on the Earth. Forever.

This book started when I went to work as a park ranger in my home country, Navajo country—*Diné Bikéyáh*. I was there to tour visitors through an old trading post, to tell stories of men who had once enslaved each other, then learned to dig wells, cut stone, and raise roof beams together. They built new kinds of doorways into what they believed were better worlds.

Then those men died and the world moved on.

The small log-and-mud *hoghans* became processed slabs of gypsum wallboard screwed to wooden boards hewn in faraway forests. Wooden wagon wheels became rubber tires for automobiles. Horses became blocks of tunneled steel that channel explosions into the motion of the axle and the wheel. This new world ran on petroleum. And now the petroleum is running out.

There is a price for this kind of world. I understood something about it.

My grandfather was an engineer and logistics specialist for Chemical Waste Management in the late 1980s. He was on the team that traveled to Alaska in the spring of 1989 to clean up the Exxon Valdez oil spill. An oil tanker got in the wrong lane and ran aground on a reef near Bligh Island and washed over 10 million gallons of oil into Prince William Sound. It was Exxon's fault. No one has ever doubted this. My grandfather was in Alaska for over a year, designing and building giant screws that would mix skimmed oil, beach sand, and cardboard into a sticky mass that could be safely trucked to landfills and buried.

He brought home photographs of sea otters entombed by oil, black blood coating their teeth. My grandmother said he shouldn't show me the pictures. My mom made him.

It was all part of a larger story.

People cutting down the rainforest at a rate of 150 acres every minute. They had a counter that recorded this at the local zoo.

People harpooning and gutting whales at a rate of ten thousand per year.

The sea otter. The bald eagle. The humpback whale.

So beautiful.

They died in their own blood. And in our oil. The horror.

And how could we help them? What does House God have to say? These animals—many of whom are millions of years older than humans—are what were called *endangered species*. Our teachers said we needed to protect these endangered species. They had us complete worksheets, word searches, crossword puzzles, and science projects on how to help endangered species.

But they never demanded we puzzle over the more important question: If all of these animals—many of whose ancestors had survived the cataclysms of the ice ages and many of whom had used their bodies and minds for centuries to survive with no human help—were being put in danger, what was putting them in danger? This is an important question.

The answer is simple: it was the *endangering species*.

It is you. It is me. It is us. Nobody likes to talk about this. And we can't redeem anything until we do. It is something with which we must contend.

What makes us an endangering species? So many answers.

House God knows one of them. You're probably inside while reading this. Look around at the walls of the building you are in. There's an answer.

It is our buildings.

We bring the incinerating flash of the megaton nuclear bombs we've forged across the planet. The bang. But the whimper of our destruction rises from the buildings we erect every year. House God knows this.

Of all the energy generated in America every year, buildings use 42 percent of it. We throw 72 percent of all electricity generated into buildings. In these buildings, Americans now use 125 percent more water than they did fifty years ago. Most people on Earth exist on three gallons of water per day, or fewer. Americans use that amount in one flush of the toilet.

Let's just say, for the sake of argument, that each one of these buildings is a fresh parasite on the sacred Earth, *Nahasdzáán*. And in between these buildings, we enter the spaceships of our automobiles and fly more than sixty miles an hour behind glass and steel on air-cushioned hoops of petrochemicals born of the deaths of worlds.

To generate the energy and electricity to run the air-conditioner units and the lighting and the water pumps, we mostly burn oil, natural gas, and coal that will cover us in the death shroud of carbon dioxide that will slowly shave away the ice caps of the planet until large swaths of land are covered in salt water, never to be farmed or cultivated again.

We are breaking down the world—the earth and sky—that allowed us to emerge.

This is the great threat of climate breakdown that no one talks about. The food. Every degree Celsius rise in temperature reduces crop yields by nearly 20 percent. With a six-degree rise predicted by 2075, harvests will shrink and food prices will rise to the point where people will starve, and then they will kill each other so their children won't starve. All because we want the luxury of drinking a hot cup of coffee in an air-conditioned room on a warm summer day in a building that burns oil and other fossil fuels.

Our buildings are killing our world.

We are in for a fearing time, where the spirits of misguided men at their slide rules will haunt us from the sky. I prefer to confront them with the essence of House God. To meet them with Strength and Wisdom and Good Health and Integrity. These are only the thoughts. You have to stand in the right building. The buildings so many people live in are not made for meeting the gods. And by this, I mean the forces in us that make us people we are proud to be.

I have only one solace: we build the buildings. That means we can change what happens. And there are people who know how to help turn things away from the bang and the whimper, to move toward survival. This move toward survival will also be called *sustainability*—the ability to do something with dignity *forever*. It will never stop. Sustainable builders know how to do this.

You will meet nine of these sustainable builders in this book. They are from northern New Mexico, from Taos, Mora, and Rio Arriba counties. They use the force of the sun, of gravity, of the skyward growth of trees, of the compressing of earth by water molecules and machine press, of the compacting of earth into tires by sledgehammer and the calories of the human body, of the arranging of strands of straw into bales, of the compression of earth into bags.

These people are hard to find. You are not supposed to find them. This book is about how I found them. It is a book about doing something meaningful. This means it is also a book about pain, and the kinds of things that grow out of deep pain. One of these things is called compassion.

This book is also about how that compassion pushes people into quests. Some might call them fool's quests. But this is mine. I grew up in the Ganado valley in *Diné Bikéyáh*—Navajo country. I know that my relatives there will be facing a more difficult world that will demand more of their money and hardship as gasoline and natural gas become scarcer and as prices rise and the climate continues to break down. This offers many problems. The solutions go beyond buying a trailer or a Weather King shed, as many families have done. I don't know if House God can wait in the doorway of a Weather King.

The proper house, the proper *hoghan*, can soften these problems and make life less desperate. A question formed in my mind: How can the people in Navajo country have the most comfortable, affordable, replicable, easily maintained, sustainable homes that also gather rainwater and make it easier to live with solar electricity?

The iron wood stove sits in the corner. In the winter, it feeds. It gnaws with flame the trees born of the mountains that make the *łeezh* (soil) that promises the growth of food, the staff of life everlasting. Cut down enough piñon trees and the slopes go back to desert sand dunes in less than a decade. I have seen this.

So this house will help the mountains. That makes it an act of service. Not just to people, but to the *diyin diné*. The Great Ones. To let House God know that we are capable of participating in Strength, Wisdom, Good Health, and Integrity. That we are people to be proud of, to whom the gods will listen. We need to live in better buildings. And maybe we need to live in these buildings so that we can live with ourselves.

To answer this question, I moved to the far eastern edge of Navajo country, to *Tóóh Ba'áád* (Female River—Río Grande) at Taos, New Mexico, where builders live. I went out into the country to examine the methods and to try to answer this question.

But this book is not a how-to book about sustainable building. It is a book about *why*.

Why does a person want to jump off the grid and live this way? And what does it do to their mind and spirit when they make that jump? And what can they give to us? What do they have to say to House God? What is House God saying through them?

Maybe these builders are not jumping off. Maybe they're jumping *in*.

Maybe they are building something.

They are.

They are building to the sun so that we can live on Earth. Forever.

THE RAIN DOG

This all started with Earthships and dogs. So let's start with them.

Earthships are houses that try to mimic the physics of the cells of our bodies to capture energy and distribute it through the structure. They call it "biomimicry."

On average, a million new homes go up in America every year, according to the National Association of Home Builders. There is no major builder in America—no Toll Brothers or Horton or Lennar—that seems concerned with biomimicry. Most of these American buildings— like the hotel that hosted my senior prom—chug oil and electricity made from burning coal or splitting uranium atoms. Most of them ensure that places like Black Mesa and Church Rock get mined and destroyed again and again and again.

Earthships emerged from the imagination of visionary architect Michael Reynolds, who works out of Taos, New Mexico. The Earthships create a counterforce to the typical American home. For the past four decades, Reynolds has been designing and building these Earthship homes. They seem a cross between a space station from *Star Wars* and a Hobbit hole from the Shire. The Earthships collect water on their metal roofs and store it in underground tanks behind the structures. Small solar-powered pumps and the force of gravity circulate the water through the building. The water runs to sinks for drinking, through the shower or washing machine, and then through an indoor plant feeder, where you can grow your own food. The water then runs to a graywater tank that is used to flush the toilet, and finally into a black water cell outside the building that feeds landscaping plants.

The Earthship buildings heat themselves using an array of glass windows facing to the south. In the winter, photons from the sun flash through the glass and leap along the back walls of the building. These walls are not built from two-by-four boards with wallboard screwed onto the face. They are built from old rubber tires filled with dirt pounded in with sledgehammers. Each tire swallows three wheelbarrows of dirt and weighs more than three hundred pounds. The wall spans in a rainbow shape, which means it can take the impact of a dump truck driving into it and still keep its form. The tires become steel-belted, insulated, rammed-earth bricks. And they store the heat of the photons running through the glass. At night, all the stored heat spills out of the tire walls through the process of convection. This creates a stable temperature without any fuel-guzzling air conditioning or expensive oil-chugging furnace.

Most people who live in these homes pay few utility bills, aside from the propane to cook food and heat water. Many of these homes have banana trees growing in the planters of the greenhouses while snow falls through zero-degree air outside. Let me restate that there is no heater. Earthships now cost about as much as a "normal" American home.

These buildings made me believe that human beings could be better relatives to what many people call the Earth Mother. The *Diné*—Navajo—call her *Nahasdzáán*. That's what I call her.

So I went to Taos to learn from Reynolds and his crew. I worked as an intern for a summer. Then it was time to leave. Everyone went back to Illinois, Wisconsin, Tennessee, Sweden, and Brisbane, Australia. I wanted to stay in Taos. They say the Taos Mountain stands as a guardian mother. In Taos, they say the mountain either sucks you in or spits you out. The mountain decided to keep me. I found a job as a teacher at the local high school. I settled in. But I was alone.

I knew by the time I was twenty-five years old that I could not live like a person I admired unless I had a dog. I grew up with dogs. We had five in our pack on any given week. Sometimes eleven dogs at a time. Some were wandering Rez dogs that we fed. Some were adopted from the dog pound in Gallup. Some we bought from breeders. Some had mange. Some killed chickens. Some hunted rabbits. Some fought bears. Some pissed themselves if you clapped your hands too loud around them. All were my best family. And they have all died.

I have cried harder for a Rez dog I fed for a week who I found frozen to death in a ditch than I have cried for the death of my own grandparents. I have had forty-two dogs up until now. That's about a dog for every year of my life. And I have loved them all.

So when I moved to Taos, I looked for a dog. It wasn't hard. Taos is a dog town.

You find the Stray Hearts Animal Shelter on the southwestern part of town on St. Francis Street. Inside the shelter, you'll find at least one picture of that sainted Italian man from Assisi who had once said that people ought to imitate animals because they lived with absolute obedience to the force of creation set forward by God.

But even St. Francis was tested when he met the wolf of Gubbio. They say a fierce wolf had been killing sheep and goats outside the village. The people of Gubbio went out to hunt and kill the wolf. The wolf instead hunted them and developed a taste for man-flesh. The villagers would not leave the town for fear of death. St. Francis decided to walk out with a group of hunters and find the den of this man-killer and properly meet him. When Francis reached the rocky cavern in the forest, the wolf rushed Francis before the hunters could so much as nock an arrow to the bow. But the spindly holy man only made the sign of the cross and the wolf paused, cocked its head, and trotted up to Francis's feet. Francis laid his hand on the wolf's head.

Francis spoke: "Brother Wolf, you have killed beasts of these men. But you have also slain men. You ought to be hanged like a robber. But I will restore peace and no man or dog will hunt you again. Instead, you will be fed every day by the men of this land. You will no longer be hungry, for it is hunger that has brought you to this killing. If they feed you, you must never attack any animal or man. Will you make this promise?"

The hunters watched the wolf place his paw in St. Francis's hand.

It is a better world when such promises can be struck between wolves and men.

No such promise was made in New Mexico. The wolves have all

fallen to the rifle, the poison bait, the trap. They howl no more in Taos. But Jason, a friend of mine who pounded Earthship tires with me, has been volunteering here at Stray Hearts for four months. Jason is a veteran who fired his M-4 rifle at Al-Qaeda in the streets of Baghdad and tried not to shoot the regular citizens who lived in the city of eight million people. It would be like fighting a war in Los Angeles, where the enemy doesn't wear uniforms.*

When Jason finished his contract, he had enough of war and moved back to Ohio, looking for a purpose. Then he read this quote from Michael Reynolds on the Earthship website: "If all the soldiers all over the world put down their weapons and started building sustainable housing for the people, life would finally begin on this planet."

Jason heard something. I would say it was the voice of Calling God. Of House God. Jason shipped out for the Earthships in Taos, New Mexico, on orders that did not come from the military.

One day, a half-drunk man pulled up to Stray Hearts with two stray dogs he found sleeping in his horse trailer. He told Jason he wanted to give them to the shelter.

Jason put a flashlight on the dogs in the back of the trailer.

"Ah, sir," he said. "Those are coyotes. I think you can probably just turn them loose on the mesa. They'll be fine."

Most biologists agree that a coyote is a kind of small wolf.

I walk into the squat brick building and fill out forms on a clipboard so I can look at dogs to adopt. The woman at the desk wears glasses with bright-pink frames. She looks distracted. "Rough day?" I ask. She explains that a man dropped a cardboard box of puppies at the door in the middle of the night.

"Every day is a rough day here," she says. "One of our staff will be right with you to help you look for a dog today."

A rusty blonde named Donna wearing a set of scrubs walks out of the metal door leading to the cages. We shake hands and she leads me to

---

* The population of the city of Baghdad is actually the size of Los Angeles and Chicago *combined.*

some cages along the wall with several cute Labrador mutts and soft-eyed shepherds. They are all excited to see me. Their tails wag at middle-height, a sign of calm energy.

"These are our current cuties," she says. "I'm sure you could find a forever friend here. You could pick one today. These guys will probably be adopted soon."

I'm sure they will be. That's not why I came here.

"So, what dogs are you going to kill this year?" I ask.

Donna seems a little shaken.

"I mean, which are you going to 'put to sleep,' you know, because they're probably not going to be adopted?"

"Well, we have three," she says.

"Can I look at them, please?"

She takes me.

Stray Hearts keeps most of their dogs in four outdoor, heavy-plastic Quonset huts. Inside each hut, two rows of ten chain-link kennels run on either side of a concrete walkway. Donna leads me into the first hut. She shows me a tall wolfhound–pit bull mix named Titan. He looks like he wants to *kill me* through the fence.

We see a second dog, a beautiful gray mastiff–pit bull mix. But it turns out she has a taste for eviscerating cats. And my landlord, Molly, owns a cat. No dice.

We walk to the last Quonset hut. All the dogs erupt into barking. All the dogs except one. She is a black-and-white Staffordshire bull terrier–border collie mix and the smallest dog in the loud hut. She quietly stares at the ground and shakes. She has a three-inch cut on the top of her head that has bloodied the white badger-stripe between her black eye patches.

She has been given the name "Rosie." Life doesn't seem so rosy for her.

She is also the only dog with a piece of plywood wired to the top of her kennel.

"Why does she have that over her cage?" I ask.

"Oh. Because she'll jump out." Donna explains she's jumped out twice. Two days ago, she jumped up and scaled the fence and leaped to the ground and bolted to escape. She ran into a shelter volunteer walking an aggressive dog on a leash. The two dogs got into a fight that left the scar on Rosie's head. The other dog didn't look so good, either.

Stray Hearts has two large, fenced-in dog parks to let people interact with their potential "forever friend."

Donna brings her out to meet me there. Rosie trots away from me and won't let me come within ten feet. She walks the edge of the fence, probably testing it for weaknesses. My friend, Jason, walks up to see how she's doing.

"She seems a bit aloof," I say.

"Yeah, she was that way with me. But I've taken her out on walks and hikes. She can socialize."

"How did she end up here?"

"Some guy found her starving out near Tres Piedras." He nods north and west to the forested steppes leading to the mountains on the Jicarilla Apache Reservation. "They found her near some dead puppies she'd been raising out in the middle of nowhere. She was hunting out there and nursing them. But something attacked and killed them. Could have been coyotes or other dogs. None of them made it."

Rosie sniffs the dry brown grass against the fence on the other side of the yard.

This dog owes me nothing.

I come back three days later with a plastic baggie filled with bacon in my pocket. Rosie finds me more interesting. But when the bacon is gone, I am invisible. She trots the edges of the fence, looking for weak spots in the chain link.

Dogs usually display "alpha behaviors" with high-energy and a strongly inquisitive sense of purpose. They tend to lift their tails high during any confrontations.

Rosie never drops her tail while she paces the perimeter.

Jason asks if I still want to adopt her. She has been in fights. She has been a killer of beasts. So no one's really interested in her. They'll keep her here another three months. Then she'll be put down. I worked for a veterinarian for two years. I've helped put dogs to sleep who were suffering.

Watching those dogs injected with a chemical that looks like pink Pepto-Bismol was one of the reasons I never became a veterinarian.

Rosie does not chase the tennis ball. She trots along the northern edge of the fence. She sniffs the wind coming from that place where she perhaps remembers leaving her puppies.

Rosie is not suffering. She wants out.

Three days later, I return. Molly, my landlord, has visited the shelter and decided that Rosie is friendly. They walk her past a cage full of cats. Rosie is not interested. Molly gives me the okay to adopt her. But I'm not sure.

I ask to see Rosie in the dog park again. She takes the bacon, then trots to the edges of the park with her tail held high. I call her back. She comes to me. Then trots away. I call her back before she can reach the fence. She returns and drops her tail. She turns to her back and submits. Black spots cover her pink belly and chest. Her white throat is soft as cloud.

"Hey girl," I whisper.

She rolls to her feet. The light changes. A long braid of gray cloud stretches and cold raindrops smack the sand. I extend my hand to her. She pauses, cocks her head, and trots up to my feet.

I lay my hand on her head.

"Okay, let's go," I say.

I turn to leave through the gate. And there it is. A full rainbow spans in every color across the town. It is my first Taos rainbow.

I pet Rosie's head. "I'm going to call you Rainey," I say. "The Rain Dog."

They will not let me adopt her without having her spayed. While working at the veterinarian clinic, I helped spay at least fifty dogs. Their organs that cook new life in the womb come out into stainless steel pans like bloodied pasta. She has stitches when I pick her up. There will be no more puppies to nurse for Rainey. And none to defend.

I take her back to the adobe cabin I'm renting from Molly on the mesa above the grassy valley of Arroyo Hondo.

When I'd moved to Taos and hunted the local newspaper for rentals, I'd found what was described as a "green living" adobe cabin. The adobe cabin is formed of walls thicker than my torso. Like an Earthship, its solar room faces southwest and takes heat into the greenhouse and bathroom. A SunMar composting toilet mixes sawdust or peat moss below in a drum and allows you to compost your own poop and use it as fertilizer after a few months. The wood stove heats the cabin, which is no bigger than the garage of some of the $450,000 homes built just a few hundred yards down the road. The beautiful *viga* and *latilla* ceiling had been shaped and cut with a chainsaw by Molly's late husband, who had built the first roads out to the mesa and lived in a cabin he'd reassembled with pine logs given to him at Taos Pueblo.

The first night, I roll out my sleeping pad. Rainey and I lay on the wood-block floor. We are not cold.

The next day while I am teaching in the halls of Taos High School, Molly shows Rainey the stone labyrinth she built—aligned perfectly with the four directions on the northern edge of the property. She tours the dog through the woodshop, the chicken coop, and past the outhouse.

Molly had come to the Southwest while studying the architecture of the Anasazi at Chaco Canyon for her master's degree in architecture from Boston Architectural College. She'd fallen in love with the Southwest for the same reasons I had. She had seen *atiin diyinii*, those rainbow paths, and she had followed them.

Now she would help me take care of Rainey.

She takes Rainey into the yard behind the cabin and lets her walk over the pine needles beneath the piñon trees. The dog sniffs the fence and pees or poops while Molly sits in a chair in the shade and reads a chapter out of her book. Sometimes she reads to Rainey.

Rainey eats and puts on muscle. After the sun burns into the rolling slopes near Tres Piedras, Rainey rests on a thick pile of blankets in a cardboard box while I grade essays at the small kitchen table. Her paws twitch and flicker in long runs through her dreamworld of memory. Her eyes roll and convulse. She growls and whines. She fights something only she can know.

On Halloween night, I light the first fire of the year. Rainey's teats have swelled. I worry she has an infection from her spay surgery. She lies on her side and I press finger to nipple and milk seeps out. Her uterus is in a biohazard bag in a dumpster behind the animal shelter.

But her force of life demands she nurse something. Her body knows some deep memory of her puppies and will not be denied. She sleeps with me on the floor under my Pendleton blanket and twitches.

By the beginning of the next week, her teats have shrunk. The Rain Dog will follow me out to the driveway and hunt mice in the woodpile while I split kindling. She chases the tennis ball I throw for her down the dirt road. We walk the arroyo to where the Río Hondo and the Río Grande meet in the Río Grande Gorge.

These are good days. I have come into the country with a new people. I am going to search through this new place, this new culture, that allows people to learn the ancient ideas and modern techniques that allow them to build to the sun. And the Rain Dog will keep me moving. The Rain Dog licks my hands and face as though I secrete bacon grease. I feel there are good days ahead. I am happy for the Rain Dog.

But I also know that I come from an endangering species that thought it proper to lock a dog like her in a cage until they could quietly execute her.

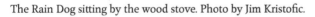

The Rain Dog sitting by the wood stove. Photo by Jim Kristofic.

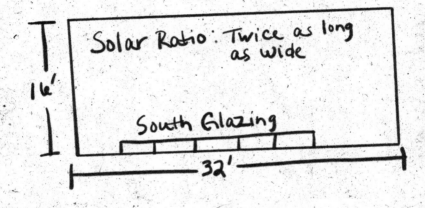

KEEPING CHINGÓN IN LOS HUEROS

The officers who wear the uniforms have turned their backs on material wealth in an era when the nation has turned its back on everything except money. They find in the deserts and grass and mountains the only Americans who actually share their values, men dedicated to an idea of combat and valor. And so they join together in a mutual death dance where they jointly destroy the last sanctuary for human beings who do not worship Mammon. This joint suicide is never discussed. Instead the talk is of settlements, pioneers, civilization, missions, Christianity, farms, railroads, factories, cities rising on the plain, golden fields of grain, purple mountain majesties, and that fruited plain. Everything the warriors on both sides have fled.

—CHARLES BOWDEN, TRINITY

The aspens lose their gold and the pines shine dark green as autumn moves toward winter. I have split the last spruce and aspen, and I tarp my wood pile next to the gravel driveway. Frost spans the glass of the greenhouse when I walk Rainey in the morning. The adobe walls of the cabin take in the light of the winter sun. I press my hand to the smooth plastered wall and feel its heat after the sun has set.

The homes in the valleys of Taos begin to show their mists of woodsmoke in the mornings. It has drifted in blue shadows as I drive Route 518 across to the eastern side of the Sangre de Cristos Mountains to Mora County. Mora is a place where pretensions fall away. Rich people live in large plastered houses. Poor people stoke their wood stoves and vent smoke from the small chimneys of their trailers. Nobody is what they are not. At the edges of the fields, mountains rise beautiful as myth. You might expect a mountain lion or black bear to poke its head from any edge of the pine or aspen, and if you saw that you might become the kind of person you can tell stories about.

You will see road signs raised by the local people. Cows and sheep painted in black and white graze next to large red letters that read, "RANCHING NOT FRACKING." Mora County has become the place where Jeffersonian democracy collides with the shadows of corporations who have taken the reins of the Washington stud.

The corporations have the money, the lawyers, the federal cabinet positions, and the drill heads to bore through ancient aquifers to reach the gases trapped between pastry layers of shale rock. With their concrete casings they can force gallon upon gallon, ton upon ton, of pressurized benzene, toluene, paint thinner, and diesel fuel into that shale rock and send the gasses fizzing skyward. With the shale fractured (or *fracked*), these petrochemicals drift into the voids and find where water flows. From there, it's a matter of time before it finds peoples' wells. This is all underground and complex. Many things in Mora are complex. Men in Mora cheat on their wives. They drink too much. They beat their children. But no man in Mora would tolerate another man walking into their trailer and dumping even a teaspoon of paint thinner into their child's bathtub. This is simple.

The corporations have their systems. The people in Mora have their land. They have their Jeffersonian democracy of local laws and county commissioners. And they have nowhere to go.

The Americans around Mora need ways to cook food, run the lights at night, power the hospitals, and drive the industry. It's not that the fangs of civilization are ready to chew Mora up. It's that this is really part of a greater system. And some Americans really don't mind if a mountain valley like Mora (population 4,500) is crushed on the anvil. Some don't ask the question of what place might be next.

Other Americans think this system might be failing. Some Americans think we can cook the food, run the lights and hospital rooms, and build new industries with the power from the sun and wind.

I drive through all this as I travel to Ocate to meet Willy Groffman and learn about how to build to the sun.

I drive past the *Pelón,* a volcanic mound blond with autumn grass where buffalo once dotted the horizon by the tens of thousands. This was Comanche country, and they made it their own. There is a story that Spanish soldiers wrote of a band of Apaches who made camp in this country and used it to stage raids into what is now northern New Mexico. Then, one summer, those Apaches never showed up. They were gone. The Comanche put them all under the earth and ended that people.

Let us hope that Mora is not a place where people come to die. Let us hope it is a place where House God still walks in the morning.

I drive down past Willy's turnoff. Blue sky opens to the blond horizon of sloping plains and autumn grass. The East stretches forever into what will become Texas.

I call for directions when I get lost and Willy redirects me. I drive past Duran's Outfitters, where two elk salute each other with locked antlers from a custom iron gate, past the Montoya Ranch. I drive up the dirt road, pass the white car with red stripes. Wave. Two fingers. The *Norté* wave. *Eyee-bro.* Drive past the fields of sandstone weathered by showers of rain descending from the eight-thousand-foot rimrock ahead.

A wild turkey flies out, and his striped tail fans across the road. Western flickers tap their orange-fire wings into the air and drop to the scrub oaks. These rolling plains of grass once fed the buffalo herds that Kiowa and Comanche hunters drove into the black basalt canyons snaking back into the ponderosa pines. They hunted the buffalo and took their robes over the mountains to trade for maize and beans at Taos Pueblo.

Drive past the adobe house with pitches and valleys in its roof. Drive through cattle guards. Past the white church and the abandoned adobe houses giving themselves back to the ground.

This village once survived on sheep, with the skilled, self-reliant ranchers keeping their flocks roaming over the grass. They sold their wool to one of the several wool mills in Mora. Those mills are now gone. The wool fabric was replaced with synthetics. The train came into northern New Mexico, and the automobile brought with it the money-based economy that we now call The Economy. The barter-based, land-grant system with its network of families and kinship trading was asked to die, but it has done so only slowly.

The village below Willy was a place where many French trappers had decided to settle and take up the life of sheep and cattle ranchers. Their children were often born with blond hair. The village became a place where you found these blondies, these *hueros* in abundance. And so it became Los Hueros. The houses in Los Hueros still fight gravity. The roofs still take the snow load. The cattle still roam and graze, but the sheep are scarce. Those sheep scored the ground of grass back before the witchcraft of nuclear war emerged from the cauldron of Los Alamos on the other side of the mountains.

But Los Hueros will stay small. It is a place that cannot exist with money.

Drive past the blue-roofed house with cement stucco scratch-coated on the outside. Pass by and drive through the willows. Drive the Prius uphill through curving rocky road choked with boulders. Small turnouts have been cleverly dug to flow the water off the road. This is a four-wheel-drive road. I steer the Prius and hover its tires between foot-deep ruts. Ponderosa pines die brown into the air from drought.

A high-speed internet box lies torn and smashed alongside the road where a bear got curious and ripped it apart.

Go around the curve and see the window shining in the late-morning light. Willy Groffman walks out to meet me near the greenhouse. He adjusts his Santa Fe Indian Market T-shirt with red and turquoise kachina dancers. His white goatee is fringed with gray hair. His tan skin stretches tight over his thin, muscular neck.

He has a shifting, mercurial face. Sometimes you'll think you're looking at a Roman general emerged from a wax death mask, talking the truth from the fields of Elysium while the intelligence shines out from the brown rims of his green eyes. Other times his grin will pull back his tight, wrinkled face and you'll hear his thick *Norté* accent and swear you're talking to an old *cabrón* whose roots go back into the land. Other times he'll doff his Carhartt baseball cap, tilt his face, and wink a dopey smile that reminds you that you're also talking to a wise-ass Jewish kid who grew up on the south side of Chicago and then did the best he could to get the hell out.

Along the way, he taught himself to juggle and practiced until he became a semiprofessional.

After enough time talking with him, you realize Wilbur Groffman—Willy G—is all these things.

He points to the large greenhouse facing south. Its massive east and north walls reveal the adobe mud and cordwood. Adobe mud-building is one of the oldest methods humans have used to create their shelters. That clever compression of sand, clay, and water mixed with some kind of fiber, whether straw, grass, or small sticks, has been keeping the rain off babies and nursing women and focused craftsmen for over three thousand years. In England, this method is called *cob*, and the shaping of the mud wall is called *cobbing*. The houses where William Shakespeare and Isaac Newton grew up were cob houses. Paul Revere's house in Boston—which still stands—was built with the same method. In northern Europe, many people build houses by adding logs from their wood pile. Take a log as long as your arm. Lay it in the mud like you're laying a brick in mortar as you build up the wall. The ends of the logs expose to the outside and give the wall a beauty that resembles the matrix of a honeycomb.

In Willy's greenhouse wall, the logs come from the pine forests around his home, and they don't rot in the mud because their ends poke out and dispel any moisture into the air. The wall is fourteen inches thick. The wooden logs set into the brown mud seem like something that shouldn't work. But they do. They have for over a thousand years.

The greenhouse is a post-and-beam construction, with the cordwood and adobe filling the voids. He and his wife, Steffie, and his friend Jody Armijo built it on the slope in a hundred days.

"Come on into my church," Willy says. "This is where I come to worship the sun. I come in here to get religion. I don't follow any religion. But this here is where I get the truth. The real truth. This is where I get inspired. I build to the sun."

We walk into the twenty-by-forty-foot greenhouse. The twelve-foot ceiling at the east end and the twenty-foot ceiling at the west end rise to catch the sun's energy under the polycarbonate panels. The panels prevent heat loss and keep rain out. The plastic is also lightweight and easily replaced after hailstorms.

Willy keeps large water barrels along the south wall to catch the energy of the photons flashing through the windows. Their heat energy is stored in the water inside the barrels. This is called *solar gain*. Materials like water and concrete gain heat and release it slowly. Materials like wood and stone do not.

Willy has also painted the inside of the wall in white plaster to bounce the photons into the room and spread them among the plants. Two workbenches covered in tools sit beside a patch of dirt where tomato plants staked to oak staves grow seven feet tall. Green tomatoes bulge on the limbs. A large metal firebox extends in the middle of the greenhouse with its center bowed inward to receive a large tank.

"This firebox is nice and long. Big mouth," Willy says. "You can put a six-foot log that you cut from a standing dead tree straight into there."

The still is for making alcohol.

"You can distill anything, really. You can make fuel and alcohol with anything that has a starch or a sugar. Corn companies are trying to get people to do it out of stockfeed. But that's one of the worst things you can do it with. The alcohol yield is just really very low. Why not do it with weeds? Whatever you can walk out and weed whack should also be able to run your car. You know, there used to be distilleries all over this country. The original Model-T that Ford built would run on anything. You could make that alcohol down at the distillery. John D. Rockefeller, he was the one who gave money to the women who ran the Prohibition Movement. And they had their reasons, since they didn't want their husbands going out and getting drunk and coming back and beating them up.

"But he was giving them money because that way he could shut down the distilleries. He wanted to sell everyone this gasoline that he had. People didn't like it. It stank. But once the government closed the distilleries, gas was all there was, man. And people were trapped. People weren't free. I want people to be free. This would close one of the last loops. That's what this greenhouse is for. What if? What if every community, instead of building a community center, built a community greenhouse? They all worked it. Everyone used it. And they could heat it with the lumber they had around, feed it into the still. And the still could make their alcohol. Their fuel. And fuel is freedom. But the plants would be good for people, too."

House God, Calling God, would stand in the doorway of this place.

We walk to a set of long, steel water tanks. They will hold tilapia or some kind of fish to work aquaculture in the greenhouse. He can use the fish poop to fertilize the tomato plants. His tomatoes will be growing strong through December. Last spring he grew and sold over a hundred hanging baskets of flowers and gave away dozens of tomato plants.

"Great turnover. Little communities could have little projects like that, you know. It wouldn't be hard. People just have to want to do it. But it doesn't seem like people want to do it, you know?"

Willy spots a place where plastic has blown out during a storm. "All that blew out from where I replaced it last. I'll fix that."

He takes a piece of plastic, tears it, and stuffs it into the three-inch gap.

"There. That'll be enough to stop the bleeding until we can find a permanent solution."

Willy reaches into a nearby planter and hands me a sprig of mint. "Crush it. Smell it."

Willy pulls back his hand from where he stuffed the plastic. I point to where his hand is bleeding.

He stares at the cut and sucks the blood away.

"I leave a little blood on every job. Today you came along the Sangre de Cristos. Here is the Sangre de Willy!"

He laughs and sucks the blood from his leathery hand.

I **walk to** the Prius and let Rainey out of the car. She gets into a staring match with Willy's female shepherd, Pinky. Pinky's an adopted stray from the Española pound. Low growls. Both dogs' tails are up. Not good. But then Willy's Boston terrier, Maxwell, comes romping into the mix. Rainey plays with him like he's her puppy. All is well. Willy and I let them romp and rip.

We walk up to his place. "You caught me in the middle of my chores. Let's go out back."

We walk along his eastern deck. His photovoltaic array faces south on an aluminum rack. The five forty-watt panels that he'd bought for four hundred dollars each are wired back inside to the house. He has a simple inverter the size of a shoebox that fits neatly beside his charge controller. His breaker box and batteries are below the floor. They off-gas their hydrogen into the crawl space below.

"It's a simple system. Simple. It's enough for me," Willy says. "My wife, Steffie? She's used to city things. Wi-Fi. Internet. The television. She'll have the television on a couple hours a night. She uses way more juice than me. And I'll get after her for it, you know? She'll say, 'Just leave me alone. This is my vegetation time. Then I'm good.' But I still get after her. She calls me the Juice Nazi. Me! A Jew from the South side of Chicago. I'm the Juice Nazi! Ha!"

We walk back into his garden of six raised beds covered with shade cloth and plastic, full of lush, green lettuce and mint. He gives me more mint to crush.

"And here's my apple tree. Too weird. *Too* weird, man. Those branches still have green leaves on them. Green leaves. And when is this? November. Alyo, bro! *Muy mal.* Something's happening with this change of climate, of weather patterns. You know we're in a real drought here, bro. People say it's a twenty-year drought. But it could really be a sixty-year drought. Or a hundred-year drought. We don't know the full cycles of rain and how the seasons are supposed to behave. We just don't have the scale of time. Either way, we need to be ready."

We walk to his compost heap in the center of a small circle of stakes, fenced in with chicken wire.

Rainey and Maxwell romp between the pines while Willy rolls a smoke.

I point to a ring of plaster figures holding hands around a small tree in one of Willy's side gardens near his toolshed. The figures are shaped from polyester resin molded over a wire armature skeleton. The skin cracks and rolls over the figure like intense gray flames. More figures stand around the garden. A tall man stands sentinel next to a willow. A group of musicians—trumpet, drum, violin—flank a small patch of flowers died back for the autumn. A curved torpedo-shaped bird lifts a tapering gray wing smooth as glass.

"My dad did these," Willy said. "He was an artist. The guy could draw like a motherfucker. Anything. Pencil. Oil. Canvas. And he was a sculptor. He worked at a factory that refurbished mannequins. He used to take me to work with him all the time. So, at four years old, my first job was lugging around parts of models of naked women. Not that it warped me. I think."

Willy smiles and his eyes light up. He enjoys the pause in his fast conversation style. When that smile stretches, you can't tell if he's sixty-five or sixteen or six. Wise adult, shit-eating teenager, and hellion child emerge magically at once. He juggles all three.

We walk through the garden and up to the shed. Willy brings out a framed copy of a map of the area. The lines for Colfax county intersect with the lines for Mora county. The nearby village of Ocate sits up against a rocky mesa spiked with piñon pines at the base of the grasslands that drain to the Mississippi through the Canadian River through Texas. But just twenty miles from here, the rivers drain to the Río Grande.

So much land between those rivers has been hacked and divided.

"But that was the story of the West, bro," Willy says. "That's what the West has really been. One big drainage ground. One big extraction of minerals, mining, beef, and timber to ship back to the government of the United States back in the East. You go *back* East. You go *out* West. But the people here in New Mexico, these Hispanos, were here for a long time, bro.

"They followed up the Río Grande, farming and settling. They didn't come up here over the mountains until the 1840s, bro." He waved a finger. "Too dangerous up here, bro. Jicarilla Apache and Kiowa and Comanche hunted all over here. This was all buffalo-hunting grounds. But even the Pueblo would come over here and hunt and trade during the year. Right over the mountain, no? But the Apache, they were tough here. And once the Spanish lost control over the horse, it was over for them with the Comanche, bro. So those Hispanos had to really fight their way up here. They set up their rancherias. They dug their acequias. They dug in. And then they were just up here. And these mountain people speak a different Spanish from the people they left behind in Mexico. They came up here to herd sheep. They lived out here that way for forty years. It was all barter. Everyone get along with your neighbors. Then the war with Mexico came. Then the railroads came in. The railroads changed everything. Everything. The companies came in to claim the land. The government attacked the land grants. They broke them up. They busted them. They extracted. And then all the money came in with them.

"That money economy brought those canned goods out from the factories. And people gave up the land. The kids moved away for the wages. Mora County used to have fifteen thousand people. It was vibrant. Now it has five thousand. The kids left. The grandkids left. The sheep are gone. Some are here. But they still have their old ways. And we have those old ways. I know they're there because I've studied the history. See, I *read*. But some say I want to turn back the clock. To take things back to the way they used to be. But I say no. I don't study history so I can turn anything back. I want to explain how we got here. What I want to do is to *combine* the old ways and the new ways.

"You can do things now they couldn't do then. We have glass now. Glazing lets us heat with the sun. They couldn't do that back then, no? They only had sheets of mica to cover their windows. The Puebloan people had windows, but they were mostly little and didn't allow for much light or airflow. That's why those little kiva fireplaces vented all that smoke. Those people just breathed that stuff in. That's why they died so young, no? So we need to not think of those old things as perfect. We have new technologies now that will help us live better. Be happier. We can fucking do it, no?"

Willy places the map back into the shed and shuts the door.

We walk past the garden with its small rail fence. I point to one of the polyester resin statues. A large bird, the size of a raven. Willy says it was his dad's. "It's fallen over and the armature's broken. My twin brother was up here a few years ago and saw it like that. He said, 'Why don't you restore it?' I said, 'Well why don't *you*, fucker?' But, no, I'm going to leave it there. It's a reminder. Of the passing of time. We only get one life. And one life is not enough. I know some of my friends are over there. My parents are over there. They talk to me sometimes in my dreams. I can't understand what they're saying, but they're there. That art of my dad's. It's there to remind me of it. To live the day well."

As we walk up to his trapper's cabin, Willy explains how he grew up near Hyde Park in Chicago, how he played in the rough surf of Lake Michigan. His twin brother hovered over him as an artist, a prodigy who took classes at the Chicago Art Institute before he was in fourth grade. Willy can't draw for shit. He can only draw buildings. And Chicago is a country for buildings.

Willy's progressive-thinking parents pushed him toward a cultured life. But Willy ditched his piano lessons to hit the streets of the city.

"I would just rip. Raise hell. Wander. Get in some trouble. Make a little of my own, no? But then I would get down to the downtown. And then I'd see those buildings. Chicago's got some dirty sides, right? Dirty air. Dirty water. Dirty politics. Dirty streets. But those buildings were just beautiful. They really inspired me. And then, you know, that was the city that really embraced Frank Lloyd Wright. And I loved his stuff. Six of his houses were right there in my neighborhood in Hyde Park. It's weird, no? It's like all my life I've been following the path of the atom. You know, they split the atom there under that squash court under the field at the University of Chicago. Then I come out here to the land where they test the first blast at Alamogordo. Strange, no?"

Coming up in the South side of Chicago left simple options. Steel mills there. Stockyards there. Which one you want? Willy said no to both and was gone after his eighteenth birthday.

His uncle had partnered with a Norwegian carpenter who owned a day camp in the forests of upstate New York. They put Willy on the crew. For a year he chainsawed, swung a sledgehammer, and cut with an axe. He loved it. After a year they noticed his intelligence. They gave him a tool belt and told him he was going to learn.

"And that's when I really started to understand carpentry," Willy says. "And the carpenter's square. All cuts can be made from the carpenter's square. And that family of Norwegians were excellent carpenters."

Willy would spend almost a decade setting massive oak beams, laying the foundations for the homes of the Great Gatsbys of the world in five-acre estates in the hills of the Hudson River.

We walk southwest of Willy's cabin to his trapper's cabin, where he first lived when he moved to the rimrock. He had looked around in the Southwest for a year, working in Albuquerque and Santa Fe before he decided on this property. He and his wife at the time camped all over the forty acres before deciding on where to build. When summer turned to autumn they harvested some trees. He showed her how to strip the log with a drawknife. They worked ten- to fourteen-hour days and got the cabin under roof in six weeks.

Willy didn't put in a foundation. He just stacked sandstone rocks. Willy stacked the logs so they extend out toward the west, with a beautiful ascending face toward the sun.

The wife faded into her own labyrinth of Jungian psychology and trance meditation. Willy built some bunk beds, and they ran a retreat. But the wife got further and further away from him.

"But that was her crowd. New Age types. And I just couldn't stand being around them. They were just a little too flaky. They just worried too much about themselves. It's like, 'Bro, does it all really have to be this complex? Does it all have to be so complicated? Just focus. Get to work. And everything is *chingón*, no?"

Willy adjusts his white Carhartt hat. *Chingón*. Mexican Spanish for, "That's great." But it more accurately means, "Fuckin' Great."

We walk back to Willy's cabin. The building sits on a foundation of stone and concrete. When they first built the structure, they used the bottom space as a woodshop, where he carved specialty doors and sold them to those rich bastards in Santa Fe and up in Colorado. They used the second floor as a studio for his ex-wife.

"She was multitalented," he says. "She could work with anything. Drawing. Painting. People. She became a hell of a carpenter, too. I trained her."

We walk into the kitchen from the front door. Inside, a tile floor extends into the kitchen, where a counter faces the sun. The tile sparkles in pink, red, turquoise, and orange on the walls and counter tops.

He and his wife, Steffi, had ordered the tile together. A refrigerator rests back from the wall.

A set of stone steps descends from the kitchen into Willy's greenhouse. It is built slightly below the main house so that its heat will rise up and warm the building. Potted flowers, aloe, and parsley rest against the gray stone. A long raised bed of soil runs near the wall, filled with *estiércol de oveja* (sheep manure) from the local pens of Los Hueros. He sprays the cilantro, tomato plants, fig trees, and ivy until they glisten as though jeweled.

His shower fills the west corner of the greenhouse. The white showerhead is fed by gravity from a small hot-water heater. A pipe runs in from a three-thousand-gallon cistern buried outside. The force of gravity fills the tank from a spring that comes out of the rimrock, pushing the water down a pipe into the manifold of pipes spreading like capillaries against the wall of polycarbonate of the greenhouse. From there, the energy of the sun sets the water in motion and produces heat. As long as the thermal element is below the tank, the water will move heat through convection up the pipes. This is called thermocycling. Willy uses the same technology on his iron cookstove. A pair of copper pipes run upstairs into a pressure tank that then runs into a Bosch on-demand hot-water heater. This runs to the shower.

"That's how people got their hot water," he says. "The old ways. Now we have the new ways. They can work together. They're going to have to work it out."

In the farthest eastern room, *latillas* of logs cut from less than fifty yards away herringbone in the ceiling in a dance of brown knots and blonde bars.

At the center of room sits Willy's masterpiece of rock: a solid chimney of cobbles rising up around his cast-iron wood stove. He knows that fireplaces distribute only 15 percent of their heat. In the traditional design, the fireplace's cobbles go up through the roof. Then the cold air strikes them and they transfer that cold down into the house. Cold sinks. Heat rises. Some people build them with the cobbles facing the outside. House God shakes his head at them.

So Willy put the stone cobbles at the center of the room. He ran the pipe through the roof, super-insulated it, and only a small pipe sticks up outside.

"So now this stone fireplace is my heat sink," Willy says. "It's *mass*. And mass stores temperature. Like a battery. Fucking *chingón*, no?"

The sun streams across the floor. We step outside to the front porch. Willy rolls a smoke.

"See, you can feel the chill here in the east on the deck. But we go to the front, to the south, you'll feel that sun."

We walk out along the deck. Rainey and Maxwell are tussling. I take off my Ganado Hornets sweatshirt in the heat. I tie the sweatshirt around my waist. Willy sees my T-shirt. Geronimo stands with a cadre of four Apaches. They are combat veterans of the wars with the Americans in southern Arizona. Above them it reads: "Department of Homeland Security." Below it reads: "Fighting Terrorism Since 1492."

"I have that same shirt," Willy says. "In fact, I have several variations of that shirt. There he is. Old Geronimo. He knew how to deal with those bastards. I feel for Geronimo. He thought everybody should be free. I think everybody should be free. It's like that old spiritual that the abolitionists used to sing: 'If one of us is chained, we're all chained.' If you say we're through, 99 percent won't do. If we're not free, what are we? Living under corporate bullshit. Living in the kind of houses they say we should live in? I drive down the road and 99 percent of what I see is awful. Horribly built shit. It's just garbage. Now I don't gripe about it. I don't let it tear me up. I stay in the positive. I stay free. 'Cause those bastards can trap your body with their crap. But they can also trap your mind. So you gotta stay free. I don't let them get me down."

He sweeps his hand across the forest. "I'm up here in the rimrock. I take my water from a spring that comes out of the rock up there. I drain at least four gallons a minute out of it. I store it in a three-thousand-gallon cistern. I got my own water. I got my own power from the sun. I got my own food from the garden. I'm my own company. I'm away from all that bullshit out there. I'm not part of that military industrial complex out there hunting the world for resources and cheap labor. Shoving other people around. I don't need them. I don't need their friends. I don't need McDonalds telling me how to eat. I don't need Monsanto telling me how to grow. These bastards are a little too good at killing people for me to take them seriously. They covered parts of Vietnam with Agent Orange. Destruction and death for the plants and the people for generations. But they learned their lesson. Now? No more draft. It's all volunteer army now. Now they pick up kids with no hope and no other options, lie to them about all this money they're going to get to go to college. Then they get to college and can barely read. And they graduate and still can't find a job! When Vietnam came around for me, I told them, 'Fuck your war! And *fuck you*! You guys don't want me in your army. I'm gonna misbehave. I'm going to get too rowdy for you.'"

The government tried to find Willy in order to enlist his help to setting fire to the jungles of Southeast Asia, that the rubber, tin, and oil of the region might pour forth for the United States and its allies. They could not find him. He had moved out of Chicago after high school. Tried a year of college. He was up in New York working for the Norwegians, being paid in cash, under the table. No address. No phone. No pay stubs. They sent a letter to his mom.

"I was lucky to have progressive-minded parents," he says. "They knew the war was bullshit. And they didn't want me going to it. So I went in and I acted like myself with no filter. They soon realized I was a maniac. And I went back to New York and got the fuck back to work."

Willy grins. "I had my freedom. Everybody needs to be free. That's when we'll all be free. 'We will not truly be free until the last politician is strangled with the entrails of the last priest.' That's Voltaire. I don't see any politicians up here. You get some religion, though."

He points down the slope to the East where the ascending horizon of blond grass hosts one adobe-and-plaster building with a gray metal roof. From this distance it is the size of my thumbnail. Willy says it's six miles away.

"That's a morada. One of the last in northern New Mexico. It was run by the *penetentes*. The brothers. You know, the flagellators who would whip themselves? The brothers used to live down there. They were servants of the people, especially here in Los Hueros. Because priests never came up here. They weren't looking out for people. But the brothers? They made sure everyone was taken care of. That everybody was fed."

Willy helps take care of the building. He helps his neighbors. He helped restore the white church in the valley.

"I helped because I know it's important to them. It's one of their traditions. It's part of their heritage. They have their religion. And the brothers used to come out in the morning on their festival day. Twelve of them. They had their whips and their robes. And they would walk through the valley. And you'd hear their chants all the way up here. These *beautiful* chants. And they would process through the valley. Now there's only one of them left. Only one. So they don't do the chants anymore. I guess they can't. But they never came up here and tried to convert me. No Mormons, either. I had one Jehovah's Witness try to get up here. I just had to tell him, 'Look . . . I don't give a shit. You've got your religion. Great. But I don't want to hear it.' I'm out here in the world, in Nature."

Willy walks back to his cooler and takes out another icy bottle of St. Pauli Girl beer.

"This world is my religion. Nature's my religion. I mean look at *this*."

He sweeps one of his mitts across the blond plain below. "It's all good. It's all sacred. Every part of it. I know where the sun rises on a day-by-day. I know that when we get to the equinox, the sun is going to rise directly on the Pelón there. The world will be perfectly aligned. Night and day. And then it will shift away again. The world's always shifting and always changing. It's a constant. What can you do? You can juggle, right? Up here, you learn to juggle or you *die!*"

In the juggle, Willy gets along with his neighbors. All except the *bruja*. Willy's *bruja*. His witch.

"She's this crazy, skinny lady from Canada, bro. She came in here with all this money. She owns all this property down in the valley."

After buying seventy acres of property, she tried to cut Willy off from the road he built up the rimrock.

"I built that road when there was nobody here, bro. Just me pounding down rocks with a sledgehammer. I left a lot of time and sweat on that road. And blood. Don't forget blood, too, bro. I leave a little blood on every job I do, no? So this *bruja* wanted my road. But I wasn't giving that up. Sometimes when the bully comes around, you gotta stand up and you gotta fight back."

The *bruja* hired the most expensive lawyer in Santa Fe. She spent more than a hundred thousand dollars in legal fees to take away access to the road. Willy called upon his neighbors. He spent his good will.

The local church. The Acequia Association. He sat everyone down and said, "Listen, I'm not asking for you to pay with me. I just want you to know what I been going through. And I'm fighting a *bruja*."

"So they supported me. And once she knew that everyone was against her, she gave up. And now we reached a settlement. After five years, bro. I was out here Thursday night, howling at the full moon, bro. I am free of the *bruja*! And it's good to be free."

Willy walks to the edge of the deck and unzips his fly. "You know you're a free man when you can piss off your own deck in the middle of the day."

He zips up and grabs another St. Pauli Girl from the cooler. Rainey and Maxwell get into another round of mud wrestling.

I notice Maxwell is much younger than the gray-faced Boston terrier I saw in one of Willy's pictures. I ask about the other older dog. Willy says that coyotes got him and ate him.

"You see a lot of animals up here," he says. He rolls a smoke. "We've got our flock of turkeys that migrate up here. We've got our coyotes. Coyote everywhere, bro. Hard to keep chickens up here. I've always got to watch out for that little frog, Maxwell. Can't let him get eaten.

"We get bears up here, too. Take a look at that apple tree back there. You can see where one of them broke the limbs going after those apples. I use rubber bullets to scare them off."

Willy says that one night he walked out on the deck and a mountain lion was looking up at him from the steel stock tank near his garden.

Willy puts his smoke between his lips.

"You see, people come up here with this dream in their minds. They think they can pursue their own type of freedom. And that's great. Some of them just have trouble starting it."

Willy tells me the story of his buddy, Tony, who was a professional nature photographer for magazines. Tony came to Willy looking for land and Willy showed him around until they found a beautiful spot on a ridge. He wanted to build there.

Tony showed Willy a huge binder full of photographs he'd collected of his dream home. He'd spent twenty-five years thinking of his dream home and building up this vision. Willy sat him down. They did some drawings. That's what Willy does now. The drawings. He was once 185 pounds of solid muscle. Now he weighs about 145 pounds. He is a skinny old man. Still, they got to work on Tony's place. Tony wanted to learn. Willy showed him the hatchet. The axe. The chainsaw. The spokeshave. The drawknife. They finished the house.

"Two months later," Willy snaps his fingers. "Divorce. His wife moves out. Tony has to sell the place. And he's gone. That's what I'm telling you, bro. People come here with their dreams. But their dreams die. Pretty quickly. You've got to be ready for this place, bro. Because it's ready for you. You'll see tomorrow, bro. You'll see all about it with the buildings. A lot of dreams die. Unless you learn how to juggle."

The sun is dropping to the West, falling behind us on the other side of the rimrock.

Willy grabs another St. Pauli Girl. He pops the cap with his lighter. He rolls a smoke. The sun drops. The blue and purple line appears like a dark serpent god stretching from the blond horizon beyond the volcanic rock and pine of Ocate Peak to the ridges of the plains where you can still walk the wagon ruts of the Santa Fe trail, beyond to Fort Union, the heart of the supply chain for the United States army into the West, built up by Col. Edwin Vose Sumner in 1851, just two months before he built Fort Defiance in what the New Mexicans called *Cañoncito Bonito* and what the *Diné* called *Tsehootso'í* (The Meadows Among the Rocks), and twelve years before Sumner's name was appropriated by one of his former brevet majors, James Carleton, as a name for a place where the army tried to bend the *Diné* into agricultural servitude. Thousands died. The *Diné* starved. They could not build *hoghans*. There was no doorway. *Haashch'ééhoghan* (House God) had no place to dwell. He could not wait outside for the waking person to give them Strength, Wisdom, Good Health, and Integrity. And without their proper houses, the people forgot House God and they forgot his essence.

Some began practicing human sacrifice as a way to free themselves of the army's control. But the army held them. The men could sometimes escape on swift horses. But the soldiers held the women and children. And so they held the tribe. The army called the place Fort Sumner. The *Diné* called it by the Spanish name, *Fuerte* (fort). But that name became *Hweeldi*. A Place of Suffering. I look at the bruised sky. Sometimes it's hard to know if you're looking into a sunrise or a sunset. The future or the past.

"Here it is," says Willy. "Magic hour."

We go inside. We feed the dogs. We share a pot of Willy's excellent green chilé stew.

I feed Rainey. She eats quickly, hungry from her play with Maxwell. Pinkie stalks to her side. Rainey growls. Pinkie growls.

She snaps at Rainey and bites her just below her eye.

I call Rainey off. Rainey curls up on the couch. I can see that she's shaking when Pinkie stares at her and growls. Rainey comes to my side. She is shaking. I can feel her muscles tensing.

"She's vibing on her," Willy says.

Pinky is shaking, too.

I go to wash my own dish after two bowls. I give it to Willy. The man knows what he's doing with his stew.

I turn and have to chase Rainey away from Pinky's bowl.

"Come on," Willy says. "Let's go outside." We head to the doorway. All the dogs bolt for the entrance. Rainey and Pinky collide.

There. You've read this sentence. That's how long it took for Rainey to drive Pinky out through the door onto the deck and clench her fangs into the soft muscle around her shoulder.

There is no railing on the deck. The drop is at least fifteen feet.

Willy yells at the dogs. He kicks blindly for where Rainey is clenched, where that bull terrier blood is at work. I don't yell. I know I have to get her off. Now you've read this sentence. That's how long it takes me to shoot through the doorway and grab through the dark, find Rainey's thick leather collar, and yank her back before the fight circles to the edge of the deck. I pull her to me and lift her off the ground. She stays clenched. I walk backward. Willy yells for me to get her off. I put my knuckles up against Rainey's throat and push them into her carotid artery. In jiu-jitsu, they call it a blood choke. I've had people do it to me in training and it nearly knocked me out. I always woke with a headache that lasted the rest of the day.

Before I'd driven west to live in Taos county, I'd taught in the suburbs of Bucks county, Pennsylvania. I was working at least sixty hours a week just grading and creating assignments for the Honors English classes at an upscale high school. I was writing several books and editing for writers and publishers on the side. But I made it to jiu-jitsu training at least twice a week for three hours a night. Some might call that juggling.

I clench the choke. Rainey gets heavy and goes limp. She lets go of Pinky. I take my knuckles off her throat and carry her to the front of Willy's cabin. Our breath smokes in the air while I calm her down. She breathes through the choke and shakes her head. I know the feeling.

Willy walks around the house. I hope Pinky is okay and that Willy isn't in the mood to bitch-slap me and shoot my dog.

Maxwell dances around us, nipping playfully at Rainey like it's all a game. Rainey doesn't react. Maybe Maxwell is right.

"How's Pinky doing?" I ask, now feeling the pressure of my heart pushing the night chill.

"She's okay," says Willy. "How's she?"

"She's conscious." I touch Rainey's ear and it bleeds from where Pinky's fang ripped it open. "I'm so sorry, man. I should have . . ."

And before I can continue, Willy's at my side, that gentle touch on my forearm, his gray stubble shining like prickled silver. "Hey, Jim, no worries, man. We did the best we could. We were watching closely to be sure it didn't break out. But they got in that doorway. Things got tight. But you reacted. You did the right thing. I've seen plenty of fights break out. I've seen *so* many fights. This one isn't the end of the world. It's cool, man. It's cool."

I take Rainey down to Willy's greenhouse and set up her crate for the night. She'll be warmed by the sunlight that heated the cordwood and adobe wall all day.

We go back up to the house and tell stories of Kiowa raiders, Comanche buffalo hunts, the Santa Fe ring, and the Catrón family who took most of that land grant and also helped defend Willy against the *bruja*.

That night I drift away while sitting up and talking with Willy. The fire in the wood stove crackles. I pull my Pendleton blanket over my body. It's the chief-style blanket from my time as a ranger at Hubbell Trading Post, striped red, white, and blue. Some might call these the colors of freedom.

The next morning, Willy and I sip black coffee after I take Rainey on a patrol through the ponderosas.

As we muster to see Willy's other buildings, Maxwell perks up. An engine hums up the hill and a tan Toyota Tacoma pickup parks near my Prius.

A short, muscular man shifts out of the cab. His curly black hair spills to his shoulders in a wild mullet cut. It's Jodie Armijo.

"Hey, bro!" he yells to Willy. "How's everything hanging around here? You drunk enough yet to go to church?"

"Only if you're preaching!" Willy calls back.

"Don't listen to all this guy's craziness," Jodie says to me.

We shake hands. His ropy arms balance out at his sides, like he's just finished carrying something very heavy. He laughs gleefully through the few teeth left in his mouth. I knew Jodie and knew that he'd spent a lot of bad nights selling drugs in Denver. He'd been to prison. He got in more fights. He sold more drugs. He went back to prison. To pass the time he started drawing ornate, multicolored crosses. He works on Willy's crew now. And he works hard. The harder the better. He likes using the heaviest sledgehammer to pound and break rocks. On the inside of his left forearm, a tattoo of a shed elk antler is carved with the name *Armijo* in the middle.

Jodie came back to this valley where he used to hunt those elk. To hunt them again. To work. To stay out of trouble. He leaves us after drinking a beer and says he'll be back.

We hop in Willy's white Toyota Tundra. We bump down the other road, the one he would have used permanently if he'd lost the court fight with the *bruja*.

He indicates the young, black-barked ponderosa pines and the elder trees that take on the special orange color. Willy calls them "the pumpkins." He knows the trees are living through the brutality of a twenty-year drought. But it might be a hundred-year drought. Americans have only been in the Southwest for 150 years. For all they know, it could be a two hundred-year drought. Only the Anasazi understand the cycles of rain.

Less rain and snow falls. But the temperature is rising. Just a few degrees of heat, and the trees lose more water. They can't make the sap they need to move their food between the roots and the needles. But they also can't make the sap they need to push out the borer beetles who fly in to eat them.

"That pumpkin there," Willy says, spinning the wheel to avoid a rut in the road. "It's ready to go. So I'll take him down with a chainsaw. Strip the bark with a drawknife. Or I'll use him to make a cordwood wall."

We drive over a rough, steep part of the road where the Verizon workers ran fiber-optic cable for internet. Willy points to the pale-green fiber-optic connection box at the junction of the road.

"The modern world found its way up here, bro," Willy says. "So did climate change. Look at those trees. But what can you do? You can't control it. You can't stop it. You just have to adapt to it. You have to juggle and stay ahead of the pace."

A connection box next to it looks like it's been run over by a truck. "That's the box for the copper wire they ran up here. A bear got it."

We park in front of a cabin he'd designed and built for one of his friends who was a painter. He offers to have me come out and work on fixing it up. It's a cabin with a Dutch gambrel roof. It has since been occupied by wood rats. Their droppings litter the floor. The front logs fade with rain and UV damage. A loft runs out over the room suspended by a large "V" of vigas running up to the *latillas* in the roof.

Willy isn't worried about UV rot outside. He wants to remove the window and run a polycarbonate greenhouse out the front with a graywater recycling system.

"It'll be beautiful. You can grow tomatoes down here. Swiss chard. Fucking *chingalito*, no?"

We take the road through the ponderosas to another longer wooden structure. It's built of Oriented Strand Board (OSB) knocked up quickly. The doors and windows have been covered for the winter. It's going to be a library and radio-station office for his friend. Willy loves music. His nickname while he was working construction was "Tunes." He listens to jazz, salsa, Mexican pop, just about everything. He listens currently to a lot of Flaco. They usually call him "Flaco" in Los Hueros. Willy can't wait to get the radio station off the ground. He loves radio. It's the one thing for which he'll spare his solar juice with abandon.

We drive farther down the bumpy dirt road, following the path of the fiber-optic cable snaking down into the woods, its silent glass body thumping beats of light under the soil.

We drive down to the cabin that Willy built for the wayward son of a hedge-fund manager. It stands in the traditional L-shape of many homes in northern New Mexico. The L-shape gives you that *portal* facing the east. The glass brings in the sun during the day. And then the right angle blocks the devastating late afternoon light from the west.

We pull up to the building and it's truly beautiful. A tall building. Propanel roof. Valleys and pitches in the *latillas* of the roof. Curved limbs of aspen wind between the posts so that the building has the character of a great hall of an elven lord. Willy walks me through the space.

The cordwood and adobe wall rises to the west.

"The wall looks beautiful from the outside," he says, "but I'm going to have to tear this all out. Jodie was probably in here working while he was drinking. Just look at that."

I step in against the wall. The cordwood angles in a small cresting wave. Imagine a tilting brick wall.

"He didn't even come close to staying plumb. And I gave him my four-foot level. Yes. He was probably drinking again." Willy sighs like a disappointed uncle. "If I'd caught it earlier, I probably could have knocked them back in. But now I'll just have to tear it all out."

I ask when the owner is planning to move in.

Willy says the owner is dead. He was obsessive about keeping his small camper free from pests. Every corner was packed with rat poison and moth balls. Willy thinks he poisoned himself to death.

"But, hey. That's what happens when you have a lot of money and not a lot of sense. And the dreams come and go. The dreamers leave."

He explains how he likes to get started early. He would often have his crews show up before dawn, work in head lamps, and be done for the day by one o'clock. This way, you finish with the work before people start getting tired in the afternoon sun and they start making mistakes.

After the work on the L-shaped house was finished for the day, Willy, Victor (his crew boss), and Jodie Armijo took out their rifles for target shooting. They were on Willy's property with a safe backstop. The *bruja* heard the shooting and ran down to this area and got in Jodie's face, yelling at him.

"No sense to it," Willy says. "We were interfering with her little dream of peace and serenity, I guess. We were screwing up her 'Nature.' So she came out and yelled. And yelled. She called the state police on us. And this guy came out. And you could tell he was just like, 'Look, I have to show up here and check on this.' In the end, they stopped coming when she would call them. They were just, like, 'Lady, get along with your neighbors!'"

Willy points south to a rocky ridge swerving back toward the rimrock. Trees in brown and gray shadows of their former selves run along the edge of the canyon back into a cleft of gray rock and pine.

"That whole trust of land she owns running back into that canyon? That place is like a national park. It's beautiful. Just beautiful. And I doubt she ever even goes back there. That *bruja*. You can see that standing dead there. I don't know what it is. Something about that canyon gives off a bad energy. It's just a creepy vibe. Like something bad happened in there a long time ago. But that's the *bruja's* land. So that probably explains it. The fucking *bruja*!

"No more dealing with the *bruja*. I was a nice guy. I conceded and made compromises. Things stay civil that way. I like to get along with my neighbors. I live to be a good guy to them. And she's not a totally bad person, you know. She's tough. And she's smart. And she's been really involved with this anti-fracking effort. You've seen the billboards, right?"

I nod that I have.

We drive out along the dirt road, past the *bruja's* place.

"You see, all these people out here. They think they want this secluded life. They start building. Everything goes fine then. They're participating. They're literally living their dream. And some people do stay. A friend of mine is from Italy. They came out here one time. They saw the place. It just blew them away. Then they went back to Italy. A year later he called me and said, 'Willy! We want to come back and build that house!' So they did. He'd never picked up a chainsaw before. Never touched a drawknife. But he wanted to *learn*. He made lots of mistakes. But he *learned*. He and the kids and the wife moved into a small cabin. It was simple. But they could add to it later if they wanted to. That was the point. And they still live there. They still love it there. It's their attitude. And I think that's what makes a *big* difference. It's the *attitude*."

We drive down into the willows and past the left-hand turnoff leading to a large greenhouse building that Willy built for a landowner. He wanted a greenhouse, forty feet by sixty feet.

"It was beautiful, bro," he says. "When I built it, it was the largest greenhouse in northern New Mexico. Then he never grew anything in it. It's just sitting there now. It gets warm when the sun is up. It stays warm when the sun goes down. It's doing its job. But nobody's working with it."

The Tundra gets us back to Willy's place against the rimrock.

Man, that felt like a full day," Willy says. "Feels like two o'clock or something."

I check the clock. It's barely 10:30 a.m. We've been moving since 5:30 a.m. Willy grabs a St. Pauli Girl and rolls a smoke.

Pinky is bleeding again from her shoulder from her fight with Rainey. Willy mixes a solution of hydrogen peroxide and iodine. Pinky hides in the bedroom.

I suggest that I could hold Pinky while Willy applies the solution.

"Oh no," he says. "She'll snap at you. She won't let me put a collar on her. She'll even snap at Steffie. And she loves Steffie."

I'm impressed that Willy has allowed his dog this measure of freedom. But then I'm not.

Willy walks calmly into his greenhouse. Fig trees still glisten from their earlier watering. Watercress and nasturtium grow along the edge of his shower. He gets a spray bottle from the edge of the greenhouse. He fills it with the solution so he can spray the wound while she's not looking.

"That'll work. Don't worry about it. I've seen plenty of dog fights. Broken up plenty of fights."

He tells of how a local mastiff mutt nearly killed his Boston terrier, Jake. He tells of another beloved Boston terrier, Bando, who would follow him as he rode down the hill on his dirt bike. One day, Willy looked behind and Bando was gone. He drove back and found Bando lying still in the little arroyo there. He may have chased a rabbit and gotten kicked or put his weight down the wrong way. He broke his back. Willy had to take him to the vet and have him put down. The doc took an X-ray after it was over and saw that Bando had a broken back before Willy had adopted him. Something jarred it loose.

"So you never know, bro. Dogs teach us all the time. All the time, bro. They teach us how to live. They also teach us about death. About how to handle loss."

Willy says dogs teach us other things. About fighting. About how they demand territory from each other. They demand dominance over each other.

"When are we going to look at that and learn? When are we going to put aside our want to fight? To push each other around? I mean, we're *social* creatures. We need to help each other out. We need to be here for each other. We have all these people showing up, telling us how to live. How to think. How to act. But I'm not interested in their answers. What interests me are the questions. And when you come at things with the right *questions*. Ah, man. Then all these amazing things really start moving. But it doesn't answer the things we need to know to survive into the future that people we don't even know have set up in front of us. They've got all these answers. But I'm interested in the questions. The *questions.*"

The afternoon is coming, the *lunché*. It is time to travel back to Taos. I retrieve Rainey from her crate and load the Prius. I notice a section of rocks in the stone wall on the east side of the greenhouse overlooking the plain. Willy laid the stone in a way that uncannily resembles a human fist flipping someone the middle finger. I ask him about it.

"Oh, yeah, me and Jody put that in there! The fucking Texans are trying to get all that land over near the *Pelón*. They want that gas and oil out of the ground, man. But we're up here building to the sun. So we say *Fuck You!* to them, you know?"

I leave Willy with a loaf of blue cornbread from my small oven. Willy and I bump fists. He says I'll be back. He will probably not be wrong.

I drive down through the trees off the rimrock. The Pelón shines in the late afternoon. I pet Rainey in the back seat. Her ear has opened up and the blood is on my fingers. She licks it away. The washboard road shakes the Prius. I wonder whether the trip has been worth it. I wonder whether any trips will be worth it, to visit these builders like Willy G, keeping it *chingón* in their part of the world, these magicians who build to the sun, so that I can find a way to honor *Haas-hch'ééhoghan*. House God.

The debate lasts as long as it takes the *dólii'* (bluebird) to fly down to the fence post along the road. We eye each other through the window.

To the *Diné*, the bluebird is not just a bird to sit on your shoulder to tell you that everything is zip-a-dee-doo-dah and satisfactual. The *Diné* people have known the bluebird since the emergence through Ni'hodootl'izh (Second World). They call him *ayash dootl'izh*. He is singer in the dawn. The first voice under the stars. The messenger from *Tsoodzil* (Blue Bead Mountain or San Mateo Mountain), where the bluebirds laid their eggs after the *diyin diné* drove the flint knife through the center of the mountain to ground it to this Glittering World, to recall our minds to *nahatá* (Planning). When you walk out to greet the dawn, the bluebird's song will find you from the piñon trees. It speaks for the gods. For House God. Strength. Wisdom. Good Health. Integrity.

The world you want to live in is coming, he sings. Wake, rise up, think, and plan to walk as House God walks, to be counted by the Sun as one of his children.

He waits, perhaps to take your white corn up to the sky where the Great Ones can receive it.

I wave and the bluebird hops from the fence. It flies in front of the Prius for the length of ten of Willy's cordwood-adobe greenhouses as I rumble to the East. Are these trips worth it? The *dólii'* flits to the south, the way I am driving. Message received.

The Prius handles the dirt road through mountains past Ocate Canyon. We stop and Rainey climbs boulders and pisses in the aspen groves now gone to standing ghosts for the winter. The herd of elk walks out from the trees into the meadow in the final golden hour of the day.

We hit the paved road about ten miles outside Angel Fire, New Mexico. This is the ski-resort town where many Texans have purchased condos so they can ascend the slopes and fly down the mountains on their fiberglass blades. The elk graze nearby. The calves have grown tall to survive the winter. The Mercedes sedans rest in the garages of the resort condos. The polished SUVs wait in the driveways at the end of the wide suburban streets.

It is a Chicago suburb crammed into a valley of the Sangre de Cristos. Willy G would recognize it. He built many of these buildings, and those jobs paid for his solar system, his groceries, his St. Pauli Girl beer, and his timbers for his log cabins standing in the shadows of the ponderosa pines under the rimrock.

He said he was ashamed of himself.

I stop for coffee at the local gas station. The Prius doesn't need a refill. Skiers come and go. They are sleek and well-financed. They have few worries. But perhaps, back in their Dallas or Houston suburbs, they are doing their own kind of juggling to reach these mountains.

The coffee is good. As I drive the switchbacks up the mountains, the setting sun hammers the peaks above the valley with scarlet and gold light. The Spanish thought it glowed like the Sangre de Cristos—the Blood of Christ. The Anglos said the light was like an Angel's Fire on the mountains. I think it looks like something else.

Perhaps it is that final reminder, that song of magnificence that reminds us of the splendor of the energy we've felt all day, that last light, like that first bluebird at dawn, that juggles between the darkness and the light, that travels in a path as invisible and strange as prophecy, but somehow finds the patterns needed to keep everything *chingón*. There, House God is calling.

Cordwood set in adobe in Los Hueros. Photo by Jim Kristofic.

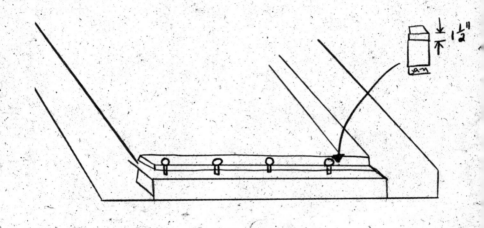

BEYOND THE BRIDGE

The winter turns toward darker skies. The cold settles and spreads out. The wood stove in the adobe cabin begins to gnaw spruce and piñon logs down to red coals. I take out the ashes after it feeds. Any shower I take in the greenhouse makes plumes of mist in the air. As an experiment, I fill a plastic five-gallon planter with the sawdust that has absorbed and composted my defecations from the autumn. I water it. Two tomato plants grow from it. Their pale yellow blossoms yield small orange tomatoes. I reason that they have grown from the seeds I have ingested while eating salsa or tacos. They have passed through my gut, slept in the drying pile of fecal decomposition, and found a new life in the shower-misted greenhouse.

They say the coldest place in the lower forty-eight states is the San Luis Valley, just a hundred miles north. It fills with the cold air drainage that spills out of the Arctic, and the nights drop well below -40 degrees. Much of this cold air reaches the Taos valley and the nights drop to well below -20 degrees. The sunsets shine on the snowy mountains. Then the nights steal the warmth from your blood.

Yet the tomatoes can live here. House God says so.

On a late winter afternoon, I drive out from the adobe cabin to meet Mark Myers by the Río Grande Gorge Bridge.

The bridge spans east and west above the black snake of the Río Grande Gorge that slithers across the Taos Plateau like a smaller version of the Grand Canyon, carving through layers of ancient sand dunes and dark basalt left over from centuries of volcanic eruptions from the six now-extinct volcano *cerros* doming to the tall sky. Out here, among the gray sagebrush, pale-blonde chamisa, and the dark rock, the shimmering strand of steel bridge seems laid down by some alien civilization and then forgotten.

Begun the year John F. Kennedy left Camelot for Arlington Cemetery, the 1,280-foot bridge was completed before Kennedy's successor had set the torch to the jungles of southwest Asia. Prior to the bridge's construction, people on the west side of the gorge had to travel to the small junction bridge at Pilar, then to Taos. The round trip cost you four hours of your life, if the roads were dry. The Gorge Bridge makes where Mark lives genuinely habitable. After a $2.4 million renovation, the more than thirty-three thousand people living in Taos County who cross it at least once a week never notice that the bridge is always moving.

The gorge was formed by the flow of the Río Grande, like the Grand Canyon. But some say its first splitting came when a volcano standing to the stratosphere, over what is now the Jemez Mountains or *Dziljzíín* (Black Mountain), blew its top toward the stars and annihilated the landscape. Some say the crust of the earth lifted with its mountains when the continental plates collided to form the ripples that would become the Southern Rocky Mountains. As the mountains pulled to the sky, they tore the thinning skin of the earth and volcanic magma escaped like blood from a wound. It boiled over and created pockets in the earth sometimes four miles deep. It would take the lifetimes of 253,164 modern Americans to walk back in time to see this happening. If we saw it, we'd think the earth was killing itself. We might ask it to consider suicide prevention counseling.

Five million years ago, about the time our ancestors took to walking on their hind legs, the waters of the modern Río Grande found the folds of the wound and washed it and peeled back the layers of dried black lava. It flows today with that slow current that *Diné* people call *Tóóh Ba'áád* (Female River).

But the ground still moves. They say the bridge at the east side of the gorge rises a few centimeters a year.

The land no longer seems suicidal. Tourists come now to snap photos of the Taos Mountain and the spanned steel bridge. And some of those erect humans come here to jump and kill themselves.

Since I have lived in Taos, at least five people have jumped from the bridge to their deaths in Río Grande more than five hundred feet below.

Some people are living in Taos when they jump. Many people drive in from Albuquerque, Santa Fe, San Antonio, and Phoenix. Cities.

One guy drove down to Taos from Minnesota. He didn't tell his wife or his kids. Just rented a car the day before, drove through the night, parked the car along the bridge in the gray light of dawn, and leaped off when he saw the sun breaking over the mountains. It was his birthday.

People in Taos are torn with every suicide. The Taos Search and Rescue then risk their safety hiking down into the gorge to retrieve the body. A group of people in town pushed to install call boxes every fifty feet on the bridge that would link people to a suicide prevention line at the push of a thumb-sized red button. These were eventually put in place at a $3,500 expense.

But people still jump. People in Taos talk about installing an eight-foot-high chain link fence to prevent people from getting over the edge. Some of them know what the Center for Disease Control knows: that in America, you are more likely to kill yourself than be killed by another person. As of 2015, for every three homicides in America, there are five suicides. Among teenagers, it's even higher.

This—of course—says nothing about Americans as a people or anything about the American affair they have decided to call "civilization." Perhaps those people who come to the bridge have had too much civilization. Perhaps they have lost that thing that their ancestors once called "Hope."

Whatever they are missing, the people leave their cities and come out here to leap into the empty dark where bighorn sheep, golden eagles, rattlesnakes, coyotes, mountain lions, peregrine falcons, tarantulas, and trout do their damnedest to survive in the gorge below.

There is no record of any of these animals ever jumping from the Gorge Bridge.

Mark pulls up in a blue Toyota 4Runner that looks like it's been through a sandblaster. The rear bumper sticker reads, "Go Solar."

He steps slowly out of the Toyota and zips his Carhartt jacket against the cold breeze. His thin, sun-tanned neck and sharp face bear the signs of many rough days working outside. The blue-collar wizard has wandered in from the wastes. His long, gray beard trails to his collarbone but cannot hide his clever smile.

Snow reflects from the ground with an almost supernatural light. Small dots of rainbow gleam from the crystals between sagebrush and chamisa.

It's a beautiful day. Mark smiles.

Shaking Mark's hand is like grabbing the trunk of a sagebrush. His rough fingers end in thumbnails pinched sideways from carpentry accidents and carrying hard loads.

He drives us out toward Two Peaks. The Spanish called it *Cerro de las Taoses*. It's a bowled country of sagebrush, chamisa, and rocks. The wind has swept it free of trees. The sheep and the ranchers stripped it clear of grass during the mid-twentieth century.

We drive out to Mark's turnoff. I talk of Willy and his rimrock, how people come into that country, how if they were dreamers, their dreams died.

"Oh yeah," Mark said. "We have a lot of that out here. You'll see Earthships that got started, then someone ran out of patience. Or they ran out of money. People started some adobes out here. Or they started a foundation and couldn't stand the winters. We call them 'Mesa Monuments.' There are a lot of them out here."

Mark's flinty voice is patient through rasps. He recently collapsed a lung, an old injury awakened from when he had fallen off a ladder a few years before.

We turn down a dirt road that reminds me of roads in Cornfields or Klagetoh back on the Rez. Only there are no junipers here. It is as flat and undefined as the seafloor.

Mark says the community was all a con-artist scheme from the beginning. A pair of brothers had inherited all of the acreage as sheep-grazing land. But they didn't want to herd sheep and they didn't really know what to do with it. So they divided it up into twenty one-acre parcels. They just measured them from one end to the other and then broke them again into quarter-acre parcels. They didn't bother to measure where those quarter-acre parcels actually were. Then they sent a guy to one of the World's Fairs and set up a booth with a free raffle.

"If you entered a ticket, you could win a quarter-acre of pristine New Mexico wilderness at the base of the Sangre de Cristo mountains!" Mark laughs.

People entered the raffle. The brothers sent every one of them a letter congratulating them that they'd won. And for only a fifty-dollar surveying fee and a fifty-dollar title fee, they could own this piece of pristine wilderness! People reasoned that a hundred dollars was not too much money. But the brothers never surveyed the land. And the titling fee was only five dollars. They pocketed the money on the little quarter-acre plots.

When the people came out to see the quarter-acre plot, they saw no infrastructure. There were no roads. Until the government built the bridge over the gorge, the only way up here was to take the dirt road over the small bridge near Pilar.

"So people drove up here and saw the land and knew they'd been swindled," Mark said. "But, remember that the raffle they'd staged was at the *world's* fair. Some people bought this land through the mail and never bothered to come to see it. They just knew that they owned this little piece of wilderness. That was enough for them."

The dreams. Here, they are scattered upon the earth.

Mark says he's run into several people from Germany and France and Holland who show up and say their uncle or grandfather had won this little piece of wilderness in a raffle a few decades ago.

The people who did come out to settle their land didn't know where to find their plot. Eventually, people just figured it out. They settled on the land and made a life.

Mark drives past a parked school bus painted in bright reds, blues, and greens. It's marked with a sign that reads, "General Store."

We pass a junkyard littered with the rusty corpses of Volkswagens, Chevys, Toyotas, and several small buses.

We turn left past a crowded yard of old engines, rusted-out Toyota pickups, and shredded plastic flaps from the ribs of greenhouses patched together with duct tape. Goats nibble at lettuce. A pony nods his head inside a stall built from wood pallets and chicken wire and whatever the hell else people have cobbled together from the dumpsters of the Walmart and grocery stores of Taos.

We pass a small plywood shack with a sliding front window like an admissions box outside a rodeo. A sign outside reads, "Free Box." A cardboard box spills clothes from the front door. Mark says people usually just consign something to the box and take some clothing in return for free.

His gray work shirt and vest look like they might have come from that box.

We pass a few adobe places, some converted buses, some houses shaped like small gambrel-roofed toolsheds. These are "Weather Kings," the prefabricated storage sheds of 2×4s nail-gunned together under a metal Pro-Panel roof. They have proven sturdy and have handled the wide temperature fluctuations of the Colorado Plateau. Some Navajo families use them as homes.

We drive past a set of these larger Weather King homes. A small work shed and a small chicken coop sit clean and sparse inside a chain link fence. It looks like nobody lives there.

Mark nods to the fence and says the guy who lives there used to be a computer technician for the National Security Agency. Then he retired with the money he had and now he lives out here, free and clear.

"Most of the people who live out here want that freedom," he says. "They want the freedom to live how they want to live. To not hurt anyone. To be left alone. They want to live away from the system."

Mark had spent most of his life living away from the system. Growing up in a working-class family near Niagara Falls, New York, Mark had learned to plane wood and frame walls before he left high school. He loved the clarity of geometry. He thrived within the dark topographical lines of xylem and phloem falling and rising through the wood that he cut and sanded into roofs and flooring.

Then he read *The Good Life* by Scott and Helen Nearing, who moved into a stone house in the mountains of Vermont just as the New York bankers speculated the American affair through a rye field and over a cliff.

Mark had slouched through a semester of an engineering degree at a state college, but the confining theoretical atmosphere choked him. He loved the lines of wood and stone. He respected the confines of the carpenter's square and the Pythagorean rectangle. But he didn't respect the confines of thought. He dreamed of those carpentry jobs out there on the horizon. He began to entertain the notion that the world was not in his textbooks or in equations. It was *out there*.

He dropped out of school and bought a utility truck that had been manufactured before the United States had any idea about detonating small suns over Japanese airspace and raking fire over the rice fields of Vietnam. Mark got the engine tuned up and designed the truck into a small apartment on wheels. He read a book that summer written by an Oxford professor about a wizard leading a young man from the fireplace in his cozy, middle-class hole into the wilds where all that glittered was not gold and not all who wandered were lost.

Mark named his remodeled utility truck "Frodo."

He wandered from forest-service utility jobs to building cabins and playgrounds at children's camps. He helped homeowners build green-houses and remodel their garages. Then he kept moving. He didn't think of stopping until he was working with a forest-clearing crew in Georgia. He was throwing a Frisbee to his German shepherd, Samson. Mark stepped too close to a frozen waterfall at the edge of a wide, frost-haunted meadow. He felt a lurching sensation and Samson tilted out of focus.

After he woke up in the emergency room, one of the nurses explained that he'd slipped and fallen down the waterfall and broke his back. He would be able to walk again. Probably.

And he did. When he recovered, Mark had to sell Frodo to keep wandering. He ended up in Colorado, working music festivals and small carpentry jobs. He traveled up to Oregon and worked the night shift in a bakery. He met a woman, married her, and began tapping payments into a piece of land to start homesteading. Then the marriage with the woman fell through. And no American man keeps his land after a good divorce.

So Mark came here. He looks into the sagebrush. A jackrabbit ghosts between the pale-green branches and is gone with the flap of a black tail.

Mark smiles. "Not all who wander are lost."

Mark's wanderings brought him to Taos in 2001, where he interned for Earthship Biotecture, where he wired solar panels and built interior walls from cement-infused adobe mud and recycled apple-juice jars. He traveled north to complete an associate's degree in renewable energy from San Juan College in Farmington, New Mexico, in 2004. He decided Taos, New Mexico, was the place to use his knowledge. So he found some land near Two Peaks and moved to Taos in a 1970s bus refurbished as a home. The land spread before him in sagebrush splendor under the warm sun.

Then the winter came. Mark hadn't thought about that. Most people who visit northern New Mexico or *Diné Bikéyáh* (Navajo country) don't think about it, either. The visitors will marvel at how green and lush the grass grows between the white aspens. But wherever you see green grass in northern New Mexico in the summer, you will see it covered in snow during most of the brutal winter.

And it is brutal. The wind throws in cold air from the north that can freeze water in a bowl on a kitchen table at night in a poorly insulated house. People have frozen to death on their mattresses in the community in Two Peaks. Mark almost did. He didn't know anyone. He didn't have a chainsaw. He hadn't spent his summer getting firewood.

He often had to take wooden pallets from behind Walmart and cut them up with a handsaw to heat his bus through the night.

We pull up to the fence around Mark's adobe casita. A black sign at the gate reads, "Capitalist-Fascist-Free Zone."

We walk past the 1,700-gallon tank Mark built from poured concrete to catch rainwater off the sloped roof of the adobe house. A pipe runs in from the base through a small filter and dispenses water in his kitchen from a Depression-era hand pump mounted to the counter next to the sink.

Mark's casita stands out on his road. Mark's buildings rise from an elite vision while the others seem built by committee. One art cooperative built a geodesic porch onto a swerving adobe hut. An octagonal strawbale has collapsed beneath the skeleton of its roof-that-never-was. They are unlivable cautionary tales. Mesa Monuments.

Mark's house rises from the sagebrush with a kind of adobe dignity. Its metal roof gables out into large overhangs to protect the two-hundred-square-foot casita from snow and rain gnawing away its plaster. Mark did all the finish work in rough-sawn lumber from the local sawmill.

On the north side of the house runs the garden shaded by a canopy of rough-sawn lumber fitted through with old plastic conduit bowed into ribs for a shade-cloth canopy to keep the peppers, pumpkins, beans, tomatoes, and herbs from being cooked by the summer winds that spare only sagebrush and grama grass. In the summers, hummingbirds fight over the hollyhocks and sunflowers. Dragonflies drink from the rain buckets.

He mounted solar panels on the roof. His refrigerator runs off a simple inverter and charge controller mounted on the western end of the house. A loft bed hangs above from large utility ropes.

Much of this grew from Mark's mind. He doesn't draw up plans. He will look at a section of the house. The roof. The foundation. He will stand and think. Then he will move on to the next section and zone out into the part of his mind where the drafting table is always busy.

Mark calls this "grokking." He takes this concept of "grok" from the Martian language spoken by Valentine Smith, the main character in Robert Heinlein's *Stranger in a Strange Land*. In the novel, Smith was born human but raised by Martians on Mars and then returns back to Earth in 1961. When you *grok* something, you understand it intimately, in the way one's body intimately understands water that it has drunk.

But Mark understands that his mind is not enough. He knows he couldn't have built any of this without his partner, DeLynn. When she met Mark, he was living in the unfinished shell of the adobe casita. The floor was dirt. Grimy tools and a table saw sat in the corner where the couch sits against the wall that DeLynn plastered in bright adobe.

To make it out in Two Peaks, you need skills. But you also need a partner. Mark shines with his good luck that he met her. DeLynn looks back at him across a room with her green eyes. She turns a wisp of her red curly hair. They share the place.

They had a Native American ceremony for their partnership on the property in August many years ago. Drumming reached the sky. Earlier in the day it rained. Then it hailed. Lightning scorched the far peaks. A double rainbow emerged from the storm. The person who officiated their wedding said they'd done more than eighty of them. That day was the one that felt the most real. Their vows ended with the promise that—whatever issue they would face—they would always move toward healing.

Mark built a house. But DeLynn helped him build a home.

It is always painful for me to come out to Two Peaks. A man from Two Peaks suffered seizures and other demons that roam easy out here in the wind. He took a handgun to his head and dropped his corpse to the sagebrush in the night. His girlfriend found him. She was brilliant. She did her university work at Cornell. She built machines that are a generation beyond scanning electron microscopes while earning a PhD from Cornell University. But she gave up the academic life to come out to Taos and work as a solar technician for Earthship Biotecture at poverty wages.

And she was a dark-eyed Portuguese beauty. If you saw her on the beach, you wouldn't be able to hide that you were looking at her. She taught science for special education students at the high school. I joked with her in the halls that she was the most overqualified teacher in northern New Mexico. But that didn't stop her from taking a handgun and putting her dead body on the ground before the end of a weekend after she found her boyfriend had killed himself. She had worried about what would happen to her dog if she died. So she shot her dog first.

If she hadn't used the handgun, she could have used the bridge.

Outside Mark's window, DeLynn has nailed sagebrush to the eaves so that hummingbirds can perch in between the flying and feeding that leads to their building of the circle, the nest, that will fly more hummingbirds from eggs to this thing we call the future. Those *dahiitíhii*, that deliver the messages of the *diyin diné* (the Great Ones), who are the speakers for House God. These are the things that build the nest: Strength. Wisdom. Good Health. Integrity.

Beyond, the Mesa Monuments rise from the sagebrush.

The weathering adobes and failed roofs and the voice of House God speak the secret: Pick the right partners.

This is all to say that we have an idea that if a man has enough grit, gumption, pluck, and luck, he can come out to the wastes and build a paradise. That is a false quest in the making. It takes a partnership. If he meets the right woman, that man and that woman are unstoppable.

Outside the casita stands Mark's innovation here beneath Two Peaks. The Powerhouse. On first glance, the wooden utility shed looks like a Scandinavian-designed outhouse with a pitched roof. It's actually Mark's power source in the Capitalist-Fascist-Free Zone. The concept emerged from all the problems Mark faced while installing solar panels across Taos county.

"I am so fortunate that I got into solar power. I've installed hundreds of panels," Mark says. "I don't even really know how it works. It's the closest thing I've ever seen to magic."

That magic started in 1939 when Russell Ohl noticed how certain crystals reacted to each other, especially if they contained certain types of metal. Scientists had known for decades that certain metals create electrical currents when they are placed next to each other. Albert Einstein had won his Nobel prize in 1905 for his discovery of the *photoelectric effect*, how a strange, near-light-speed caravan of electrons races across a skin of metal when it is struck by photons from the sun. Eventually, two scientists at Bell Laboratories, Calvin Fuller and Gerald Pearson, noticed how two pieces of silicon embedded with different metals would work much more efficiently. Thus began the quest to capture this caravan of electrons into an electric current inside a cluster of metal encased in crystalized silicon.

Solar looked promising. But the first photovoltaic cells could only capture less than 3 percent of the sun's energy. Eventually, scientists like Fuller and Pearson learned that two metals—Boron (atomic number 5) and Phosphorous (atomic number 15)—are especially great dance partners at moving an electric current. It's all high school science: when you grow phosphorous into a silicon crystal, the bond between the phosphorous and the silicon leaves behind an extra electron in the silicon. This creates negative-charged silicon. On the other side of the solar cell, you grow boron into the silicon crystal, and the bond between the boron and the silicon leaves space for one extra electron in the outer shell of the silicon atom. This creates positive-charged silicon.

When you place these two cells together and photons from the sun strike the cells, the electrons rush from the positive to the negative like wind in a hurricane. Except the wind would be moving at the speed of light. This creates an electrical field. These cells are soldered into each other to become a "module." You package the module into a frame. There you have it. A solar panel.

Solar panels were really only useful to power devices far away from power lines. Like in space. Some of the first satellites ran off solar power. It was almost too expensive to bring back to Earth. In 1972, solar panels cost over seventy-four dollars per watt.* Today, solar designers and engineers and factories in China have dropped the price to less than seventy *cents* per watt. That's 99 percent cheaper.

Utility companies are now catching on. A 2014 analysis of government data reports that high electricity-delivery costs make coal-fired power unable to compete with solar. The worldwide use of solar cells has expanded by over 50 percent. The solar systems of the world can now match the output of at least one hundred nuclear reactors.

If you want to know why people like Mark Myers are so passionate about solar power, you need only look up into the invisible miracle of our atmosphere. In that thin band between sky and earth, we create the conditions that help us grow food. When we practice the ceremony of mining and burning, we reawaken the energy of long-ago forests and animals that gladly ate our ancestors. We call this darker world into this world that the Navajo people still call the Glittering World.

That darker world puts these reawakened spirits into the sky so that the heat of the sun begins to smother the plants upon which we depend for food. Ice melts and fills the seas. Salt is loosed upon the earth, and fields cultivated for centuries become places that promise starvation.

This is the real horror waiting behind loosing these dark forces into the sky. The numbers are simple: every one-degree Celsius rise in temperature reduces crop yields by nearly 20 percent. With a six-degree rise predicted by 2075, harvests will shrink and food prices will rise to unprecedented levels. That means more than paying ten dollars for a

---

* The "watt" is named for James Watt, the inventor of the steam engine that drove the Industrial Revolution in the late eighteenth century. The watt is the capacity of electricity to do work. It is calculated by multiplying a current's volts (force) by its amps (pressure).

box of Pop-Tarts. It might mean regional and even global wars, especially in Asia, where most of the rice paddies on the Mekong Delta could be infiltrated with salt water and become unusable. People have been growing rice on that delta for over three hundred years.

Solar power keeps many of those dark forces in the forgotten worlds where they belong. Most people understand this to be a good idea. Anything else is a slow-motion suicide.

"The good news is that most people who can afford it *want* solar power," Mark says. "Even the people who can't afford it want it. The bad news is that most people want solar power the wrong way."

Most paying customers want to add solar panels to their home. But their conventional homes were never designed with solar panels in mind.

"You will have to penetrate their roof with some kind of fastener," Mark says. "And that leads to a possible leak."

There is also the issue of batteries. The typical 12-volt batteries that solar electricians wire in series have to be placed in the house with large vents to allow the toxic hydrogenous gases to escape, lest they gather in corners and closets and slowly kill their masters.

Mark's solution to the problem is to build the powerhouse in easy walking distance from the home. You sink the batteries in an insulated concrete foundation. Above, in the shed so closely resembling an outhouse, Mark mounts to the wall the charge controller—the brain that regulates that caravan of electrons running between the solar panels and the batteries. Next to this, he mounts the inverter—that device that converts the direct current used in all cellphones and laptops into a doppelgänger for the sine-wave of alternating current common in almost all household appliances. Then you dig a trench from the powerhouse to the breaker box in the house. You now have solar power without off-gassing your batteries into the living room or driving a new screw through the roof.

He considers it a less insane way to find the energy of the sun rather than splitting the atom and indulging in the dark ceremonies to the death gods of plutonium in Los Alamos in the Jemez mountains less than a hundred miles away. It is a way to be part of life. Not death. It is a way to talk to House God.

Mark uses the powerhouse to run the electricity to his larger building he's framed out with rough-sawn lumber and plywood. Instead of insulating the insides, he's nailed wooden pallets between his studs. Then he filled the pallets with adobe mud. He sealed them with plastic and bonded them to the frame with metal lath. This way, the mud creates mass that holds the temperature near his wood stove.

He and I sit while he kindles a fire with hatchet-split white fir and some cardboard egg cartons. The sun is down.

He asks me what I've been wanting to ask him: how he can help me start a solar-energy club at Taos High School.

I tell him I want to teach students how to build a solar cellphone charger. There is a reason I want to take my students' cellphones off the grid.

The electricity used by the more than two hundred million iPhones bought over the next year will be more than the electricity powering all the homes in Taos County. For the next five years. This number only includes iPhones, not the other brands of cellphones. This burns more than three hundred thousand tons of coal per year.

The three million supercomputing facilities that help run cellphones and laptops burn up unknown tons of energy. No regulatory body of the government understands exactly how much coal and natural gas these facilities really burn.

Mark walks over to his desk in front of the south window. He comes back with a solar cellphone charger he's already built. It's perfect for what I need.

We sit down and start sketching some ideas. Mark thinks about the size of the box, where the pilot holes will go, where to set the hinges, how big the batteries will need to be.

He stops and rubs his beard. "We should keep doing this," he says. "I'm really excited, but I need to think it over. I've got to take time to grock it."

It's all part of Mark's carpenter philosophy: Go slow. Measure twice, cut once. Don't screw things up. You can't recut a board to make it longer.

"You know, there are a lot of people who have been trying to solve the problem of people getting off fossil fuels."

He goes into a monologue about Stanford R. Ovshinsky—the Ohio inventor with over four hundred patents who innovated the nickel-hydride battery that runs my Prius, the flexible thin-film solar panels that can be mounted to skyscrapers in Albuquerque, and the rewriteable CDs I play in my car. He also developed hydrogen fuel cells to run cars over the highways and leave only the emissions of water. Ovshinsky never went to college.

We talk about men like Rudolph Diesel, who wanted to put fuel into the hands of the farmers with a heavy-torque engine that could do serious work by burning any vegetable oil. Both men used their spirits to end fossil-fuel use among humans. To make us less of an endangering species. To make it so that we could be modern and still talk to House God.

"Once you get doing the research, you find out what happened," Mark says. "The tools are already on the shelf. We can't do anything about what we've already done. But we can change the course of the next ten years."

Mark uses an analogy to World War II for the problem of political will. "We could do the same thing for climate change if we understood that fossil fuels are a threat to our sovereign nation. And they are. The planet is our sovereign nation. This is what the new warrior needs to look like."

Mark zips up his Carhartt jacket and asks if I'm ready to head back to the Gorge Bridge visitor center. I nod and follow him to the door.

We bounce down the dirt road in his 4Runner. We talk about the banned TEDx talk by Graham Hancock—who explained that mankind's emergence as deeply symbolic thinkers, who can become people like Rudolph Diesel and Stan Ovshinsky, was invoked by our interactions with "visionary plants" like psychedelic mushrooms and DMT-laced cocktails like ayahuasca. We talk about the best explanations of the Roswell alien landing. We talk about Willy Groffman and how he's juggling things over in Mora county.

We pull into the parking lot. Mark is reluctant to break the connection between us. We are both comfortably lonely men enjoying our conversation. I worry about whether a night security guard will swing by and think Mark and I have come for a little romantic interlude.

It is hard to break the connection with such a man. Here is a man living in a community that was a lie from the beginning. The land is bound and surveyed, but it is not. Not really. There is order, but it is a farce. There are borders, but they are fantasies. There are neighbors, but they steal from you when you are not home. You want paradise? You want a Garden of Eden within which to work? Go inside your self. You'll find it there. You want a perfect world? Don't wait for it. No one does anything that way out here. You build with what you can find, rough-sawn or no.

In the end, it is simple: you choose to be part of life. Or death. If you don't want to build to the sun, it is an easy six-mile drive to the bridge. Go and stand on the spanned steel. Look into the river below. Lean forward. Or lean back. Gravity accepts either answer.

Before you do anything else, see the sun making the river shine bright as any photovoltaic panel. The river is many things, but it is mostly built of water. So are you. The river flows on. Do what you must.

I unbuckle my seat belt. "Thank you, Mark, for giving me your valuable time, man."

"Oh, don't worry about that," Mark says. "We're both in the business of empowering people. So there's no need to thank me."

I turn to open the door when the gray shadow trots between the orange parking lights. It is *mą'íí*—the Coyote—and he is making his rounds through his territory. He walks to the 4Runner, sniffs the door handle, and the little wolf trots on through the night with the casual pace of any wandering stray dog. We have been visited.

"Wow," Mark says. "I've never seen that before."

Here are the drawings for the solar cellphone charger that Mark and I built by the end of the spring.

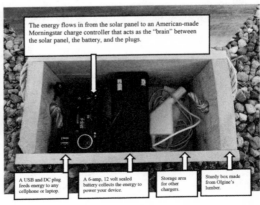

The energy flows in from the solar panel to an American-made Morningstar charge controller that acts as the "brain" between the solar panel, the battery, and the plugs.

A USB and DC plug feeds energy to any cellphone or laptop.

A 6-amp, 12 volt sealed battery collects the energy to power your device.

Storage area for other chargers.

Sturdy box made from Olgine's lumber.

There you have it. Now your cellphone is off-grid. Build it. We're connected now, you and Mark and I. Go and plug in your phone whenever the power goes out. Do this in remembrance of us.

And when you feel that pull of gravity at the edge of any cliff, lean back toward the solid ground. If you need us to tell you why, find us beyond the bridge. If you can wait until the morning, walk confidently through your door. House God waits there, calling for you.

The Powerhouse in the Capitalist-Fascist-Free Zone. Photo by Jim Kristofic.

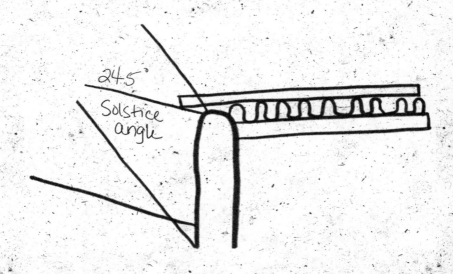

24.5°

Solstice
angle

SOLSTICE OF CRUELTY

The winter solstice comes. The air absorbs the winter breath of the Rocky Mountains running in the East. Outside my door, a spear of crested wheatgrass has become completely encased in ice, as though frozen in glass.

In Navajo country, there is the *hoghan*. In the old ways, the *hoghan* was not a house; it was the area where you lived. There was a shelter where you slept. That shelter helped you survive the winter. A fire burned at its center, as a fire burns at the center of the earth. At the door of the *hoghan*—or at any house—lives *Haashch'ééhoghan*. Calling God. House God.

You cannot build in the winter. You have to build something else. You do ceremonies. You have gatherings. You build your humanity. You build the things that live inside the buildings and give them their purpose. You talk to *Haashch'ééhoghan*. House God.

So when Ken and Molly invite me to the New Buffalo commune in the valley of Arroyo Hondo for a winter solstice "re-awakening," I accept.

The fields of tall grass I walked in the green summer have gone to brown sleep. The *dilch'ooshíí* (juncos) fly in their lion colors of brown, gray, and white between the sagebrush flecked with snow. The Río Hondo talks with cold voice over smooth rocks toward the Río Grande. And each person invited to the New Buffalo Solstice Re-Awakening is bringing a covered dish.

Birds carved from fence pickets line the driveway to New Buffalo. Ken parks in the frozen grass next to the gazebo and prayer garden.

New Buffalo was one of several "hippie communes" started in Taos County in the 1960s, and it has hosted the likes of Tim Leary (the Harvard psychologist who led the charge of the 1960s counterculture into the temple of psychedelic drugs) and Dennis Hopper (the hard-living actor and filmmaker who navigated "Easy Rider" in and out of the western United States). Few of my high school students with the last names Vigil, Martinez, Maestas, Medina, Romero, or Mondragon know who these men are.

I walk to the kitchen, shake hands with men in their mid-sixties, many of them young in smile and old in tooth. They wear dream-catcher earrings. Their ponytails smell of patchouli and their breath smells of marijuana. They wear turtlenecks, leather hats, and slimming pants. Their handshakes are warm. I set my "superfood salad" of kale, shaved carrots, blueberries, edamame, and cashews next to their pans of oriental soy balls, tabouleh, and butter-free blueberry cobbler. All the food is vegan. Once the food is set, we walk outside for the drumming. Some of the women walk with canes.

Four of the aged hippies gather in a circle with their drums pointed to the east, south, west, and north. Molly takes her position to the west and holds up her round drum tied with dark leather strapping. A sea turtle painted in blue and green, whose shell is the Earth, spans the center of the drum skin.

She pounds the drum to the Pacific, where *Asdzą́ą́ Ligai* (White Shell Woman) made her walk to the house *Jóhonaa'éí* (the Sun) built for her. She asks for guidance and wisdom during these hard times. But this is the solstice, when the sun has stretched out to its farthest arc on its azimuth. It will soon soar back toward Earth and the light will fuel the spring and summer. So they all pray. Peace for Palestine. No more chemtrails in the sky. No more war in Afghanistan. Leonard Peltier needs to be pardoned. That the peacemakers should invade politics. That the whales might sing and float in respite from the many cruelties of the world.

Tonight will be the longest night of the year.

The Anasazi once farmed and hunted this Hondo valley. I have found their petroglyphs and campsites in my first autumn hikes in Arroyo Hondo. I wonder what the Anasazi might make of the suede-fringed vests, polka-dotted ascots, and green felt berets on these hippies' elderly bodies.

We walk into the main gathering room of New Buffalo. It is a round room, like a kiva raised out of the earth, a giant *hoghan* with a skylight fifteen feet off the carpeted floor. The hippies pour coffee in the kitchen and steep herbal tea. I sit with an older Hispanic man with a gray mane rolling down his slim shoulders named Reuben. His family is from Arroyo Hondo, going all the way back to the first invasions by the Americans in 1845.

The rest of the hippies shuffle in. They take large pillows from the edge of the room and lounge on them in a circle. The conversation rises to the skylight. The older hippies seem happy to rest. They make ironic glances at each other and wave and smile at faces they haven't seen in perhaps a month.

Many were part of the diaspora to Taos County as the Vietnam War set fire to their family orthodoxies and plans for the American dream. They all smile to know the American dream is doomed. And they seem to grin at the irony that their graying, liver-spotted bodies are also doomed. They are still the young rebels who cursed the old. Now they have become old.

The wood stove pops in the corner.

"This place, Taos," Rueben says. "It will test you. It's an easy, hard place to live. There aren't many jobs. Not a lot of money. But a lot of *beauty*. You have to really want to live here."

Reuben has found a way to make it work. He's a craftsman who builds guitars in his workshop and sells them on the internet. He sculpts guitar picks and pendants out of tortoise shell.

He asks where I'm from. I tell him I grew up in *Diné Bikéyáh*— Navajo country.

"Oh, then you'll fit right in here," Reuben chuckles. "You already know about living in hard places."

The hippies slow their chatter and begin to close the circle. Someone has dimmed the lights. Everyone relaxes back into their tweed jackets and hemp sweaters.

"Are we drumming now?" Reuben asks a tall man wearing a sweater that looks like it came from the wardrobe department of *The Cosby Show*. The tall man is John Albright, the current owner and manager of New Buffalo. He smiles and nods. People take drums out of neoprene and leather cases. John takes down a wide, flat drum for me. He apologizes that he has no drumstick. It's fine, I say, I can strike with my hand.

"That's very good of you," says the old hippie woman sitting next to me. She speaks in a thick German accent. Her thin, wrinkled face holds blue eyes that still feel the borders she broke in her adolescence.

John says we're going to drum for five minutes to "open our vibrations." Right. So we do.

The beat echoing off the domed walls of the round room makes a kind of beauty, a sound of the human heart generated into the open air to tell the universe it is alive. I'd heard that beat during those summer powwows on the Rez.

Then the hippies' arms get tired and the drum beat slows and stops. Good. No more drumming with the geriatrics.

"Very good," John says. "Now we'll turn it over to you."

He points to me. What? Wait. He's actually pointing to the woman sitting next to me with the German accent.

"Thank you," she says. "And thank you all for being here on the winter solstice, a time when the light comes back to us. Today, we will be taking our shamanic journey."

Say what?

I thought Molly and Ken invited me to this place so we could sit around, maybe gossip about who made the best pot brownies, and sing some songs about how much we hate the millionaires running the government.

"So, I can see that many of you have your pillows and are comfortable. If anyone needs to go to the bathroom, they are to the left just as you leave the round room."

She sounds like a flight attendant for a moment: Yes, folks, we don't want any accidents on the carpet during our shamanic journey.

The hippies shift their bodies and lay aside their drums. I try not to make eye contact with the woman. I'm afraid she'll ask me to help her with something.

She turns to me. "Can you help me with something?"

"Of course," I say. Of course.

She lifts a tote bag of sticks and a tote bag of yarn. She asks if I can pass around the bag so that each person can take a stick.

As the sticks go around, she says, "We are going to participate in a shamanic journey today for the solstice. I will drum for us and lead us out of our bodies. You will journey into the dark. There, you will meet your spirit animal or your spirit guide. They will take hold of you and show you what you need to know. Then you will return to your body. Some of you will feel like you might need some extra time to come back into your body. If you need that, then lie down and I will come and call you back."

There it is. I'm in a room of hippies with hip replacements and now I'm going to meet a spirit animal.

"The new year is coming," she says. "The snake sheds its skin. The moon sheds its shadow. And the sun is moving back to earth. So today, I want you to think about the things you want to make new. Often, this means we must leave something behind. We must give something up. You have these sticks from the northern European tradition to help you. So I want you to focus on something you have inside you that you want to get rid of. It could be an addiction you have. It could be an emotion you have toward another person. We will go on the journey and your spiritual animal will put that thing you must be rid of into that stick. Then we will throw the stick into the wood stove. And it will be gone."

She describes this with the same certainty I would use to describe how to make a pot of coffee.

This from a woman in a purple alpaca-wool vest, wearing a hat that makes her look like she should be selling tarts at a Renaissance Faire. I've sat through Catholic masses and Jewish worship services. I can do the same with this shamanic journey. Polite but distant. Just keep the head down and it will be over soon.

The old German woman picks up her drum. She clears her throat.

"Every morning, I wake in my cabin and I walk out to greet the dawn and I say a prayer. I was a small girl in Hamburg during the Second World War. The Americans flew over and bombed the city. The bombs made fires that tore through the streets. The heat made great winds. I saw women and children running in the streets who were lifted by those winds into burning buildings. They never came out. More than forty thousand people died in those fires. I came to America. I found a way to have a good life. But I will always remember those fires in Hamburg. And so I say a prayer every morning. That there will be no more war."

Now I am listening. This woman deserves things. And I know what I need to get rid of.

She drums.

I close my eyes and look into the dark distance behind my eyelids, where only the mind's eye can see. There is nothing. There is only the drum. I imagine her small, birdlike muscles driving the beat forward, taking these aged renegades into a world where their bodies can't fail them, where the snake eats its tail. The drum becomes the heart and the heart becomes the drum.

These events are past and always here. I know what I want to put into the stick and burn away. Cruelty. And I will tell you why.

I am a park ranger at Hubbell Trading Post National Historic Site in my hometown of Ganado, Arizona, in the summer of 2012. My best friend died of pancreatic cancer that spring. He leaves behind a wife and two young sons. I am in Ganado to lead visitors through adobe cabins and stone barns built at the turn of the twentieth century so I can distract myself from feeling like a clay pot cracked and leaking water, to dull my questions of why the forces of this good earth might find it satisfying to put my good friend into the grave and break the hearts of his children.

One hot July day, the director of maintenance, Clifford Dougai, calls me over and asks me to help him with a "situation" at the front gate of the park. We walk fast. We pass tall green cottonwoods hissing like rain. I have seen bobcats leaping for rabbits in the saltbush lining the edge of those cottonwoods. Grasshoppers fly through the grass and bulrush lines the banks of the stream. Clouds part in white strands in the blue sky. We had hoped it would rain that morning. Now Clifford and I hope the cops show up.

A neighbor has complained about some screaming and yelling.

Someone calls the cops. But the nearest Navajo police officer is thirty minutes away. The Apache county sheriff is twenty minutes away. Our National Park service cop, Kyle Allen, an Army veteran who had fought for the interservice karate team, might be more than two hours away at Navajo National Monument. Clifford and I are it.

We take it in. A battered green Saturn sedan parks in the shade of a cottonwood. A *Diné* woman in torn sweatpants and a dirty purple T-shirt leans against the barbed-wire fence down in the wash next to the parked car. Her hair is salted with dry cottonwood leaves, like she's been rolling on the ground. A *Diné* man with a shaved head and tufts of a mustache rocks back and forth in the front seat, pressing his hand to his swollen eye. His woman had elbowed him during their fight before we showed up.

Two young boys sit quietly in the back seat. They watch intently, the way all kids watch when their parents are drunk and fighting.

"Hey," Clifford says to the man in the front seat. "Where are you guys coming from?"

"Hey, brother," the man says. "White Cone. White Cone, brother. Just heading back home. My, uh, my woman and I got in a fight. We'll be fine. We're going to drive out of here in a second."

"Ah, that's probably not a good idea," Clifford says. "Maybe you should just go lay down under those trees? Sober up. Then be on your way."

I nod. Clifford is being sensible and pragmatic. Almost everyone on the Rez has relatives who are *ghlaanii* (drunks). So has Clifford. So have I. It is all simple.

Clifford and I know that if these people continue to make a scene, the cops will show up, they'll be arrested on federal property, and they'll be processed at the court in Flagstaff, more than a hundred miles from White Cone. It will cost the family hundreds of dollars in court fees and gas money, and their green Saturn sedan doesn't look like it can handle many more highway miles. Then come the payday loans. The kids will go to the state or to grandma. They might not make it through the school year; they'll be held back a year, then be uprooted again. It's going to be a big hassle. The man in the front seat knows it.

The man gets out of the car. Three cans of Poco Loko scatter under his feet. Two of the cans are empty. The rest of the four-pack is in the back with the kids. Poco Loko is sold in sixteen-ounce cans that contain 8 percent alcohol. The rest is stewed with the gaurana and taurine typical of energy drinks. The drink has been banned by several state liquor-control boards after dozens of college students ended up in emergency rooms with alcohol poisoning after partying with Poco Loko, or "Little Crazy." At some college campuses, students call it "blackout in a can." The Poco Loko on the floor of the Saturn sedan is green-apple flavored.

"Okay, bro, let me get the kids out," he says.

The woman storms up the hill. She will have none.

"What the *fuck* are you doing!?" she bellows. "Don't be fucking coming after my *kids!*"

Clifford and I are the men in the gray and green uniforms. We wear the Department of the Interior badges. This helps. But not much. Within seconds, she is shoving Clifford and me. We are keeping our hands out to catch most of her punches. I shove her hard enough so she stumbles back over the dry, brown cottonwood leaves lining the barbed-wire fence.

The man in the car uses this as a chance to grab the kids. "Hey, come follow Daddy," he says. "We're going to get away from Mommy right now, okay?"

The kids don't hesitate. This probably isn't their first rodeo. They walk over to the other side of the fence while the mother sits and leans like she's been hit with a tranquilizer dart and is fighting the effects. She punches the barbed-wire fence. Her hands bleed. I hear the voice of my mother—a ten-year veteran of the ER just down the road at Sage Memorial Hospital: *Watch out for that blood. Who knows what she's carrying?*

Clifford has followed the man and the two boys into the wash, into the cottonwood trees where owls have built a nest to raise two chicks the summer before. Nobody had to call the cops on those owls.

The mother regains her balance and sits on a cottonwood log. She burps loud and wet. She picks up a handful of dry cottonwood leaves and wipes her mouth.

I stand by the Saturn, hoping my presence is enough to keep things peaceful. I've already taken the keys out of the ignition and put them in my pocket. I call to Clifford. I don't hear anything back. It's just me, the drunk mother, and the buffalo etched into my National Park Service badge.

"What the *fuck* are you looking at, mother*fucker*?" she asks.

I tap dirt from my brown leather shoe. "Not much, I guess."

"You're just some pussy man, just like those pieces of *shit* walking in the ditch. Yeah! You heard me down there! You better not come back up here! I'll break a bottle off in your ass!"

Two teenage girls cruise their pink and green bicycles over the bridge spanning the wash. One of them waves and rings her little bell on the handlebars. I wave back.

"What the fuck are you waving at?"

"Just the neighbors," I say.

I see movement in the wash below and Clifford comes walking out from under the cottonwood trees. Our other ranger, Sandra, a retired kindergarten teacher from Texas, follows behind with the boys in front of her. I'm glad Sandra is here and I know she may be able to calm the situation.

A hand rises at the edge of my vision. The mother is back, pushing at me, trying to strike my head with her bloody hands. I tuck and dodge. Then she's really after me. Within a second, she is screaming and striking. I could say that she is thrashing like a she-bear. But she-bears do not thrash and scream. The *shash* (bear) is a sacred mountain animal. They don't try to get a Little Crazy. They do not endanger their children. They die for them.

The boys are watching from the edge of the wash. I know because I am watching them. She is not.

I step in close. I have fought guys in octagon cages and trained in jiu-jitsu for two years. I just do what I've learned in the gym and lay the woman into the earth. Dust puffs from where her back strikes the ground. Dry leaves fly out of her hair. The boys are crying as they walk up the hill. I back away from the mother. I don't think I need to hold her down. She shakes her head and blinks. She wheezes, trying to get her wind back.

Heavy tires roll down the road. It's Kyle, our Park Service cop. He steps quickly out of the vehicle and he's pissed. I can tell he's probably seen our scuffle. Now the woman is afraid in her eyes. She knows the role she has to play. She barely moves when Kyle steps up and cranks her wrist into her back. He handcuffs her in the dirt and throws her into the back of his truck. The ambulance comes just after the Apache County sheriff. They arrest the man while he talks up how crazy his woman is and how he was just trying to keep his children safe.

The woman leans out of the Park Service vehicle and throws up on the road. She tells Kyle I assaulted her. Kyle shoves her back into her seat and slams the door.

The ambulance brings the kids to Sage Memorial Hospital, where my brother and sister were born. I follow in my Honda Civic, fill out some paperwork for the social worker, and leave the boys with some bags of granola from the trading post.

I try not to think of the mother. But I do. Are these the people I am here to help? Am I trying to learn to build a house for a family like *this*?

These people are *Diné*. They're supposed to be Tough Noodles. Not drunk child abusers. They survived the murders of the Mexican slavers and the American cavalry. Coyote taught them how to make love. They are supposed to offer prayers to the dawn, not throw Poco Loko cans into the wash. They are supposed to be Five-Fingered-Earth-Surface-People. They are not supposed to be members of the endangering species. They are supposed to know *Haashch'ééhoghan*, House God.

A *Diné* mentor I once knew speaks into my ear: *We Navajos are the hardest, meanest, toughest people on the planet. But we don't know it anymore.*

Put these people all in the cop wagon. Douse it in gasoline. Drive it to a cliff. Light a match. Roll the burning vehicle off the edge and get on with your life.

These are thoughts I have. I would sooner orphan these boys than help their mother. Who is worse?

That is cruelty. And I carry it like a stick that won't leave my fist. I bring that stick to every argument now, with my ex-wife, with my friends, with my coworkers, with my neighbors. To anyone I see fit.

Back to the drumming.

There is only the darkness of the mind's eye. But the darkness is moving. It *shimmers*. It takes on qualities of shadows. It drifts and I am looking at black hairs. They cover the back of a neck. The neck turns and I gaze into the face of a black wolf. The eyes of the wolf are yellow. The wolf's breath caresses my face. It is wet. I remember how North America is the only continent where one finds black wolves because they once bred with dogs.

I might as well be gazing into the eyes of the wolf of Gubbio. The wolf turns and I follow it. I pass through threads of air and the wolf runs into the mountains. He stalks a rabbit through the ferns. He tears the animal's throat and shakes it until it goes limp. He carries the rabbit back to his den in the rocks. His pups run out to greet him. He drops the rabbit and licks his children with his bloody tongue. They lick his black muzzle and white fangs and tear at the rabbit and practice killing. I am with him for days.

He runs down grouse and brings them to be shredded into the bellies of his pups. He mounts his mate from behind and they send steam into the night air from their lovemaking. The pups play with bones and the wolf licks them clean.

The wolf turns to me. The eyes speak and the voice is yellow as *tádídíín*, the sacred corn pollen: *Now you have seen. You have seen me hunt. You have seen me kill. You have seen me tear flesh and drink blood. And not one of my kin bears a scar that has come from my fang.*

He lifts his chin as though I should place my head under his paw to receive something. He turns and his black hairs fill my vision until they are only the distant darkness. I gasp long and deep, as though I have been holding my breath. I shake and sob. My sweaty fists clench the stick. I've have been somewhere my body is not and will never be.

Where are you between two drumbeats? Between two heartbeats? Where are you between two thoughts? I know I have been there. Without my permission.

The old German woman slows her drumming until she stops. She helps some of them up from the ground who are "not back" yet. They smile and gaze into her blue eyes like she is some lost mother pulling them from death's cradle.

The hippies limp to the wood stove in the corner. I throw my stick into the fire and my cruelty goes with it.

The fires in the steel box gnaw the stick to ash. The fires are all there. In Hamburg. The fires of global burning that will sear our agricultural climate, wrapping us in the death shroud of an atmosphere that will melt our glaciers, invoke demonic hurricanes, and torture the soil with heat and schizophrenic rains that will either drown or desiccate us. This Glittering World will become a place where we can no longer plant the *naadą́ą́' bi'woo'* (corn seed) or gather the *tádídíín* (corn pollen) from the *'azóól'* (corn tassel). We will make no prayers. Who will bother to hear them? What do you build to help that?

Maybe you build a new kind of prayer. Maybe you build to the sun.

And maybe you build this prayer not because people deserve it. Or because it will somehow stop them from beating their wives or wounding their children. Perhaps you build it to save yourself from your own cruelty, so that in your own solstice, you too may drift from darkness toward light, where the sun is ready to warm us.

It all happens in the building. In the kiva. In the *hoghan*. There we use the winter to build the things that keep us alive. Perhaps it is about making a place to talk deeply to ourselves. Perhaps it is about talking to the gods. To House God.

The hippies braid friendship bracelets out of red, yellow, blue, and green yarn to mark their celebration of the solstice and the leaving of old things. I do not know where mine is.

But I do know that if you need my cruelty, walk down into Arroyo Hondo, New Mexico. Go into the gathering room of New Buffalo, find that wood stove, open and feel the ashes. Try weaving them back into a stick. When you do, come find me, and you will meet a cruel man. A willing member of the endangering species.

Crested wheat coated in ice in the winter sunrise. Photo by Jim Kristofic.

THAT DAMN COMMUNIST SUN

The snow shines on Taos Mountain under the new year sun when I walk to Paul O'Connor's place off Coyote Loop. I had seen him in the light of the bonfires of Taos Pueblo on Christmas Eve a few days before. The flames spiraled more than thirty feet into the night. The traditions of Christian conquerors mingled with the Native songs. Whirlwinds of smoke spun from the flames like spirits. Sparks shot into the cold air. Someone yelled out, "It's snowing fire!"

Then I turned and saw Paul. His intelligent blue eyes stood out beneath his winter hat. We shook hands. The three-story adobe building of Taos Pueblo glimmered like a vision in the orange and red flames. It has stood for at least fifteen human lifetimes with no foundation, shaped year after year with mud, straw, and sand by the hands of the people. So we talk of sustainable building. What the hell else are we going to talk about?

Paul is a photographer. He's probably best known for his award-winning book, *Taos Portraits*, featuring the mustached cowboy artist Bill Gersh in his tall white hat. Walk into any bookshop in New Mexico and you'll see ol' Bill looking at you with those pale eyes in Paul's black-and-white photograph.

I had seen his photography years before in the Earthship books Mike Reynolds had published in the early 1990s, when I was still learning to wire electrical sockets and to dig a proper posthole.

Paul tells me about his place.

"Out on Coyote Loop, the houses either face south or they face the mountains," he says. "Because people want their damn mountain view. But they're oriented totally the wrong way, away from the sun. If you want a mountain view, go outside and walk your dog."

I walk to his property. The winter sun lights in apricot shades the wood framing of his front glass windows, the can walls along the entryway, the *latilla* coyote fences standing to the sky. The top of one *latilla* post stands in a perfect three-pronged pitchfork. Paul's tan truck is parked out front. I recognize his bumper stickers: The World Cup Coffee Shop. Amigos Bravos—Because Water Matters. Bernie for President.

I step to his east-facing door, standing with a coat of Kelly-green paint. A wooden utility closet next to the door is built from a shipping crate mailed in from France, his wife's homeland. A hand-painted cursive phrase outlines on the door in light-green paint: "No Shoes, Please ☺." I knock using a small bell on a metal lever. Paul answers in his slippers, jeans, and gray V neck T-shirt that reads "Team Sophia." His horn-rim glasses crest his thin gray hair balding back from his scalp.

"Hey, Jim, come on in," he rhymes.

His windows are set in two rows. The shorter windows are single paned and the taller ones are double paned to create that dead-air space that will keep the cold night at bay. Tonight there will be a twenty-nine-degree difference between this thirty-four-degree day and the five-degree night. In his planter against the glass, a fig tree stretches toward the high ceilings that Paul enjoys. Swiss chard grows between planted bulbs and flowers, watered by a hose stretching from a spigot.

Taos—the place—called him before he ever thought of building an Earthship. "My wife and I came out here on our honeymoon. We were here three days and that was it. We drove back to Malibu, packed our crap in three days, and turned around to move back out here."

They rented in Arroyo Hondo. When he moved back, he found an article in the *Taos News* about Mike Reynolds and Reynolds said that if people wanted to learn more, they should just call him.

"It was that simple," Paul says.

So Paul showed up at Mike's door in Cañon and said he wanted to learn. Mike showed him how to pound a tire that day. And once he found out that Paul was a photographer, he wanted his help in creating the books he published. He'd pounded many tires for Mike before he selected his own building site. And he moved slowly.

He and his wife rented down in Arroyo Hondo while they built hand-to-mouth. He drove up into the forest, felled trees, hauled them back in his truck, stripped them with a draw knife, and traded some for larger vigas at Olgine's sawmill just west of town. He left those vigas out for three winters until he could afford enough money for a roof. That is how the vigas took on their gray color of winter deer. They are not the lush orange-blonde of vigas you see in the second homes of Taos.

In those three winters, he went out and worked odd jobs and built. Sometimes he would travel out to California and make big money constructing gated palatial compounds of those imprisoned by wealth and fame within the American affair. Then Paul would travel back.

All the while he would promote Earthships for Michael Reynolds. But when Paul decided to alter the design of the south-facing glass windows, he had no idea of the reaction.

A woman had built an Earthship in Pilar with vertical glass windows. And Paul was "all for it." There is a controversy in creating the south-facing windows of an Earthship. In the winter, photons from the sun flash through the glass and leap along the back walls of the building. This heats the building when it needs it most. Michael Reynolds designed Earthships with sloped glass windows, partly because he admires the geometry of the Egyptian pyramids and partly to capture light that would allow people to grow food in the greenhouse in the summer. But Paul had worked on enough jobsites to know that people had problems with the sloped-glass windows that are the signature of many Earthships.

"The idea of the slope on the glass is that you can grow food in your house year-round," Paul says. "But who needs that? If you really want to grow food year-round, then build a damn greenhouse outside near your property. As soon as you start getting into tomato plants, then you're talking about all kinds of bugs and white flies. Also the buildings get too hot in the summer. I'd go out into the Earthship community in the summer and I'd just laugh. We have this beautiful sky view. Out there in the summer, people would have shade cloth draped over their windows. What is the point of having these windows if you can't see into the sky? Also, the sloped glass and the greenhouse planter is really another system. And when you're talking about systems, you're talking more maintenance and more expense."

A woman from the Earthship staff would bring tours out to Paul's house to show them the Earthship concept while he was building. But when Paul got to glazing his vertical-glass windows, the woman looked at their lack of slope and then told all the students to get back in the van. Then Mike Reynolds came down to the build site and laid into Paul. Paul was then banned from the Earthship community for years.

We walk back into the meditation room on the east side of his house. It spans quiet as a cave. The temperature is constant, buried back into the Earth. The Neanderthal blood in me stirs and sniffs. It knows something about what's happening in this room, decorated with orange and blue throw pillows.

We walk back to the windows, to the light. He has some heat loss at night through the tall windows. And he could put dual-pane windows along the base of his windows, but he's not sure it would be worth it.

"Everything is still very Mom-and-Pop for me here," he says. He still opens his bottom windows with a large nail attached to a small chain. "I like to know I live in a house that *breathes*. I mean, I know I could buy into one of those super-sealed German designs that are just super tight. But then it's like you're sealed in. Like you're living in a Ziploc bag. No thanks."

The structure of the Earthship is built around the concept of the catenary arch, a shape formed by the gravity of the planet. Here it is. Take a long chain in your hands. Give the other end to a friend. Walk away from each other and each stand on top of a large boulder. If the chain is not too tight, it will span and dip into an arching bowl shape. Then take that chain and invert it, so that the dip is humped into the sky. That's the catenary arch. You see it in flashes whenever kids play jump rope on an elementary school playground. You see it in the rainbow.

It's one of the strongest shapes in nature. You see the catenary arch on the top curve of a chicken egg you might buy in your local grocery store. It's easy to crush an egg in your hand. But try placing your palm on the bottom of the egg and your other palm on the top of the catenary arch. Crush that egg into your palms. Good luck.

Earthship builders arrange the tires into catenary arches, then tier them at a slight terrace, so they can handle the weight of the tons of earth compacted behind them.

Mike Reynolds accomplished this by setting the "U"s against each other, like eggs laid in a carton, like so:

Paul laid his in a different arrangement:

Paul signals that he wants to get me outside the Earthship to his *hoghan*. We walk outside to the *hoghan* that Paul has built for his wife's meditations and for use as a guest house.

His *hoghan* began as a sculpture he helped a local artist create for a gallery show in Los Angeles. He used steel to create the effect of the posts rising up into the overlapped beams meant to signify the boundaries of the sky dome joined by rainbows to the sacred mountains of the world. In the gallery in that city—lit with the coal stripped from one of those sacred mountains—the sculpture was elevated on wooden posts so that the patrons of the gallery could walk underneath and look up into the smoke hole at the center of the overlapping beams and pretend they were seeing up into *Yágháhookáá'* (the sky hole).

Paul says the artist told him that Navajo people didn't believe in right angles. That ghosts get caught in them. He's probably right. Drive out to Many Farms, Arizona, to the Navajo Housing Authority (NHA) housing sometime. See if you want to live there.

Paul glazed a single piece of glass in as a skylight so that he could watch its lighting effects as it slowly evaporates moisture into the sky.

The sun heats the plaster. After ten minutes of conversation, I am taking off my Carhartt coat. I ask Paul if Taos might ever see itself become overrun by the sort of people who walked under the *hoghan* in the art gallery, whether Taos could become Aspenized. We talk of how it would not—could not—happen in Taos.

The Anglo sickness of hedge-fund-incubated wealth, halogen-lit parking lots, heated driveways, zip lines, and paintball killing ranges cannot slink down along the Rockies and make it through the San Luis Valley. I like to think there's something in *Sisnaajini* (Mt. Blanca) that will stop it. But really it will not cross the New Mexico border because Taos already has its own sicknesses of payday-loan operations, parking-lot carjackings, heated driveways, and inept state government. It is a tradition of debt peonage and inherited medieval ignorance as old as the Spanish Empire's lancing north more than five hundred years ago. It caused a revolt that started in Taos when the governor whipped and hanged medicine people. One of these medicine people hatched a plan and tied three knots in a set of ropes, sent the ropes out with runners, and told people to untie a knot per day to signal the attack. Within a week, the conquerors fled the conquered until they were watering their cows and sheep along the banks of the Río Grande at El Paso. The conquerors came back, of course; that's what they do. Only this time, they begin to intermarry, and then the children come, and a new people emerge.

And there really is no time for another revolt by the 1840s because new conquerors arrive under a star-spangled flag of states they call "United," though these new conquerors are a mere score of years away from slaughtering each other in great thunderclouds of supersonic lead, the like of which had not yet been seen upon the Earth.

Once the land has sopped up the blood of sons and fathers, and black slaves are told they are free, the new conquerors return, only now they have secreted themselves on an ancient volcano where they practice a witchcraft called atomic physics and invoke flashes of light that devour cities. And they have brought enough sports cars and banks and credit cards and bribes of jobs and Walmarts to fool the conquered into thinking they live in a land of freedom where no one revolts unless they are terrorists.

This is rarely discussed, or that we might need to live in some different way.

"So, no, Aspen is not coming to Taos," Paul says. "You can try to buy land here. But it will be out on some mesa."

Your land will not have flowing water. And you will not run for political office. This is the power of blood and life over money and splitting atoms.

Paul can quickly talk about how certain families in Taos, at Kit Carson Electric Co-Op and certain banks in town, really run everything. Paul prefers that people avoid these forces.

"A mortgage? Why live with a mortgage? Better to build as you have money and savings. People get into mortgages and they've just enslaved themselves for most of their lives. And the problem with sustainable building and building the way you'd like in order to encounter the earth is that a lot of banks don't want to make that investment. They want to be able to resell it. And people want you to look at your home as an investment. I say to hell with that. My home is not an investment. It's my *home*. This is my spiritual center. I will dwell in this place most of my days."

Outside, a string of red, yellow, blue, and white Tibetan prayer flags bob from a wooden frame in front of the vertical glass where Paul often hangs a shade cloth during the summer to create a small porch outside. A large steel stock tank rests in the smooth rocks in front of the house. He fills it with water in the summer and puts a floating solar fountain in the center of the shining metal pool.

"There's something just so comforting about looking out and seeing flowing water," he says. "I get into that thing nearly every day in the summer. It makes the day sacred."

He flicks off a light. Most of his lighting fixtures are built from old tomato and coffee cans.

Paul came out here to create this sacred space. "I knew that when I was living in California there was no way I was going to *ever* be able to build my own house. There are covenants and contracts and engineering stamps. I had a friend of mine who paid over fifty thousand dollars just in permits. These are literally stamps on paper. And if you want to build anything near the beach, just forget it. It's almost normal there that when a new building goes up, the neighbor on one side of the house and the neighbor on the other side will sue the builder. That's just a given. So when I came out here, it was like landing in the Wild West. You could just do what you wanted."

When Paul started his build, he had to go down to Santa Fe to pull his permit. He had a building inspector come out to look at his tire walls going up. He asked Paul where the foundation was. Paul said there was no foundation. The guy didn't say anything. He just walked around the building. Then he said, "Well, call me when you've got the roof on." The only thing he ever pointed out to Paul was a spot where he didn't feel the viga was fully supported by the wood frame Paul mounted to the timber bond beam. He asked Paul to put in a post. Paul knew he didn't need one. But he mounted the cedar post. The guy never came back to look at it. Paul never saw him again. And Paul never bothered to go down to Santa Fe to obtain his Certificate of Occupancy.

I wondered whether Paul had more time to plan and design as he wished.

"Not at all," he says. He advises people not to plan too much. "I say just go ahead and do it. You'll make mistakes along the way, but it's better to get things done."

He describes himself as an "intuitive builder." As he was pacing out the "U"s for his Earthship, he realized they were pretty small for the space he wanted. So he doubled their size and set to pounding them in his tennis shorts and wide straw hat. He knew he'd make up the extra width of the "U"s later. He just kept going as often as he could. He paved the concrete floors as he and his wife began moving in. Now many people come to stay at their place and take part in the yoga seminars his wife runs on their property. They call it the "Auromesa Sanctuary."

Put your shoes back on. Walk with Paul out to his sanctuaries.

A greenhouse, and behind it a studio where his wife paints. Below, a concrete and can wall once held the water Paul used to build his house. Now they store herbs in reused plastic jars. We walk again to the *hoghan*, its layered wooden roof wrapped in shining metal flashing laid down in a fish-scale pattern with tight silicone sealing. It's probably illegal. No matter. This is his sanctuary.

The greenhouse or "solar engine" that Paul built on the front of this *hoghan* keeps the interior space easily above sixty degrees.

Keep walking.

Walk into a steam house, where the people who stay at Auromesa can sit and allow the warm water vapor to fill their lungs. Walk then to a dome built of concrete formed by recycled glass bottles. Inside, the indoor pool sinks in blue tiles into the ground. The surrounding bottle wall set in concrete glows like jewels of green and yellow. The water in the pool is heated by a solar array that runs the water through a solar collector of sun-heated coils inside a glass case. Some days the water temperature rises to 104 degrees. No fuel has been burned to do this.

"It's all from that damn Communist sun," Paul grins, walking back to the house. "Just up there shining for free and giving energy to all of us."

We make our way back into Paul's kitchen. The finish work is all recycled materials. His counters, cabinets, and sink counters are all built from the old Overland Sheepskin Co. sign. The water boils for tea on an old stove range that Paul bought at a restaurant supply store that was going out of business in Albuquerque. We share chocolate and oatmeal cookies while we talk about the Navajo building culture.

It can be difficult to get home-site leases on the Navajo reservation. It can also be very difficult to be allowed to dig even twelve inches below the ground or below the frost line. It's almost impossible to get a well drilled. So many people end up in trailers because they can be financed like a truck and they arrive prepackaged and ready to tap into the grid. I suggest to Paul that whatever would work on the Rez would have to be prefabricated.

People on the Rez now are living in Weather Kings. I am still not sure that House God lives there.

When we go back to Paul's kitchen counter, the chocolate oatmeal cookie left in the sun has melted into the counter. Paul gets a wet cloth to clean up the sticky mess.

There is no heater in his home.

It's twenty degrees outside.

Paul O'Connor's *hoghan* at Auromesa catching the communist sun from the south. Photo by Paul O'Connor.

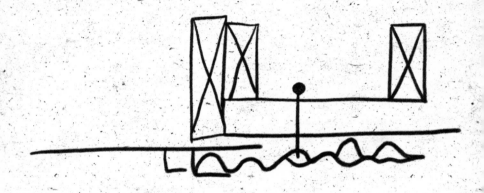

PLAYING FOR TEAM WANG

On the day of the Lord, blood will flow from wood.
The stones of the houses will come alive and kill their owners.

—NIKKO KAZANTZAKIS, *THE LAST TEMPTATION OF CHRIST*

The winter moves through Taos. When I step out of the greenhouse of the adobe cabin in the mornings, *Dził To'woł* (Taos Mountain) and the other mountains seem to gain a thousand feet in height when they are whitened with snow. The earth turns back to the light, the snow melts, flows to water, and follows the acequias—those hand-dug arteries diligently maintained for over 250 years in the Taos Valley.

The winter passes to spring. New pepper plants volunteer from a planter filled from my composting toilet. Moths fly through the dark and pollinate the flowers, and the peppers grow shiny and red.

The woodsmoke disappears from the sky in the morning. The first aspens curl their caterpillar-like flowers in the mountains. The lilacs open in purple and pale violet. The summer spreads its heat, and the corn I plant in my garden spirals its roots into the sand.

It is late May. The crickets have wakened every night. The sun has returned to its summer angle. The magpies hunt grasshoppers in the fields and wing them to the nests they have woven under the porches of the second homes of the wealthy who are slowly colonizing the fields on the plateau that runs to the southern Rockies. This stretch of acequia-watered fields is called Des Montes. Even the birds know it is building season.

I have set down my tool belt at the jobsite in Des Montes, where I will be helping master Earthship builders Dirk Sullivan, Christopher Columbo, and Ted Elsasser add a garage extension to a pumice-crete house.

We pour concrete for the slab foundation. I know to stay back and out of the way until things clear out among the Medina family, who are delivering the material and working the pour.

Ted sees me and we shake hands. His tanned neck and thin athletic build speak to a youth spent stepping over beams and pounding tires. He watches the concrete pour from behind his pair of Penn sunglasses. His green baseball cap has transformed to a faded lime color at his forehead from the deep sweat stain. He is sweating through his tattered black Carhartt jeans and T-shirt with a sea turtle swimming against a SCUBA flag that reads "Bonair." He looks like a guy who might ask you for a cigarette in front of the Taos Walmart.

Once the concrete has spread, Ted hands me a mag trowel—a tool made from magnesium, which has no magnetic charge and will keep the aggregate in the concrete from rising to the top—and asks me to touch up corners and keep the finish clear on the edge of the pour. I'm working alongside Pablo, a mustached local Hispanic man who is a former Marine who still cuts his hair high and tight. He takes puffs from his vaping wand during breaks. One of his cousins asks, "What flavor are you smoking?" Pablo says it's strawberry cheesecake.

Christopher Columbo, a large-boned Italian linebacker of a man with a thick Wyatt Earp mustache and long gray dreadlocks, steps in to joke, "Of course, you've got to say it like this, 'Strawberry *cheese*cake!'" and he flicks his wrist, using this flourish of an over-the-top Hollywood homosexual to playfully mock Pablo's local brand of machismo.

Everyone gets the joke. Christopher is a Navy veteran surrounded by Marine Corps vets who like to jostle him. Some of the Medinas joke about how Christopher's long, gray dreds stick out from the hole he cut in his boonie hat like spider legs coming up out of his head.

Christopher grins, "More like a Portuguese man o' war." Though, I'm sure the joking would be over if they ever decided to find out who actually benched the most weight on the crew. Christopher would win.

Easily. Over his left bicep, he has a tattoo of a wooden pulley that appears to be ripping out and shredding his skin. The inside of his right bicep depicts a mother bending over her small child with the Taos Pueblo behind them.

Pablo playfully mimics Christopher. "No, bro," he says, "you've got to do it with the trowel!" And then Pablo does the wrist flick with the trowel and we are all laughing over the slowly curing concrete.

I'm also working alongside Paul Medina, father to Chico Medina, who is also working on the crew. Paul got out of Taos on a wrestling scholarship to a small college in Nebraska. But he came back to Taos to build. We talk about the honeybees darting back and forth over the warming concrete. Paul says he watched a documentary about Monsanto killing honeybees. We get into a story about a local guy who started raising bees. He installed his hives on a Monday and came to check them on a Thursday. The bees were all dead.

Christopher walks by with a sponge to clean the toe-up board that is waiting near the concrete. "That will make framing a lot easier."

We talk as a crew while we wait for the next cement truck. Ted shows me pictures on his dirty smartphone of the strawbale he's building on the other side of the gorge. He wants to take me out to see it.

The concrete truck arrives with more material. Francis Medina's son, a "rookie," is driving. It's one of the first loads of concrete he's delivered.

"So be nice," Ted says. "We were all rookies at one point."

I help move the chutes with Dirk Sullivan, a trained architect and veteran Earthship builder. His skin is tanned beyond anything his Irish ancestors could have foreseen as we cut the concrete apart with shovels while it spills down the chute. Then we throw concrete into the corners, working with vibration on the shovel. The fellow *peones* work in the middle of the pour in rubber boots. The slab starts drying quickly after the "rookie" leaves.

We work the surfaces with swimming-pool trowels. All we have for floaters to keep our knees off the curing slab are pieces of beadboard insulation. Everyone worries that the little white foam beads are just going to blow around all over the concrete. So Dirk takes duct tape and tapes it over the edges. Very few beads blow anywhere.

"You know if we were doing this for Earthship Biotecture, there'd be at least nine dogs running around the jobsite, tracking across the concrete," Dirk says, laughing. "And the one that would track right across would be Mike Reynolds's dog."

They tell stories of dogs getting hit by cars. Of people aiming for dogs on the roads with their trucks. Perhaps making a game of it.

We eat lunch as the concrete cures. Ted and I talk.

"Building a house is a huge commitment," Ted says. "Most people don't know that going into it. I built my Earthship. I'd work on it every day after I was done building for Earthship Biotecture. It took me forever, man."

While Ted built his Earthship, he lived out in the center of his excavated pit in a tarped tent for a few years. He did this so he would not have a mortgage.

"Sometimes I wonder if it was worth it, whether I should have just got the building loan and banged out the job with a crew of guys," he says. "And I could have been living in my home all along. I mean, I banged all that out when I was in my twenties. But I'm, like, forty-seven years old now and I'd never want to do that again. And besides, Earthships are not the only way to go.

"People think Earthships are somehow cheaper than regular houses. They think they have a smaller carbon footprint. But Earthships have a *huge* carbon footprint. You get thirty people all driving to one jobsite? Where you could really just do a lot more with less? I was down in Texas with this couple. They had a pretty low budget. We're talking a hundred dollars per square foot. So they just couldn't afford an Earthship. I mean, Earthships are a lot of work. Those tires don't just show up to the jobsite by themselves. It's a lot of leg work. You've got to go out and find them and the bottles and cans."

Ted spoke with their pastor at the church—who is also a contractor— and asked what kind of construction people usually do in that part of Texas. The pastor said they mostly frame their buildings in wooden studs. So rather than try to reskill everyone in the area, Ted decided to design a building that uses wooden framing but achieves a fourteen-inch wall packed with as much insulation as they can get.

A magpie screeches from the willows near a small stream at the back of the property. We get back to the job of troweling. Cleaning up the slab. People like my work. That means something.

They have to rework two spots that started cracking.

"It would just be ideal if it was fifty-five degrees and overcast," Ted says. "That way it could just cook slow and cure all the way through."

We start cleaning up the jobsite. Ted is still out on a beadboard, squeezing water from a plastic bottle and shaping with the pool trowel with both hands.

"Sorry," he says. "I get a little anal with my slab and my concrete."

Ted explained that his dad had graduated from West Point and served in the Corps of Engineers. He built up a practice for himself over the years until he became a structural engineer in Manhattan. He was certifying the strength and psi of concrete foundations. Sometimes he didn't agree with the work of the contractors. Sometimes he would get threats. Guys would tell his dad, "If you don't approve our building, they're going to find you in the East River." But his dad never backed down. It was his business, his reputation on the line. He'd tell them, "Look, you've got a thousand people in this building. Their safety is at stake. Do your job right."

The conversation shifts to 9/11 and some of the crew ask Ted about it. Ted's dad knew the architect for the World Trade Center. When the planes hit with the impact, it knocked all the spray-on fireproofing off the steel. Once it was gone, the steel hit its collapse point. The top floors pancaked down. It was not an inside job.

We clean up the slab and I get to talking with Christopher. The conversation quickly turns to his mules.

"Oh, they're amazing, man. They are so intelligent. They know things about the world. And they can teach you things that no human ever could. They're, like, Zen, you know?"

Christopher had gotten the mules from an older couple whose son had died when he was barely forty years old. The older couple couldn't really care for them. So they left the mules out in a four-acre pasture and didn't really do anything with them. They just sort of ate whatever they found on the ground. They ate enough and moved around enough to keep their hooves worn down.

"But those animals are just amazing," Christopher says. "I don't know where I'd be without them in my life, that's for sure."

Christopher learned to do all his own footwork for the mules. That way, a farrier only has to come through once a year and check his work.

Ted walks back to the jobsite and starts rewetting the concrete with a sponge.

"Here he goes again," says Christopher.

We go back to help him. We talk Earthships as we level the slab.

Ted says he still believes in Earthships. But he doesn't believe in the outlaw-renegade mentality that created them. It's no longer needed, he says.

"The way I see it, it's all a game. If you want to change the game, you've got to play inside the game," he says. "You've got to actually participate in guiding the rules from within. Otherwise, when you're done, no one's going to fucking respect you. You'll have no credibility or reputation. Earthships. Strawbale. Adobe. Sustainable building. It's got to fit that game and help change the rules. We're all headed in the same direction. We're all on the same highway. How you travel that highway—whether it's building or writing books—is totally up to the person. We need all kinds of people trying all kinds of things. It's just that people have to figure out how they can travel on that highway. But it's all going to the same place."

The turquoise back feathers of the magpie flash as she flits by and lands flawlessly on the edge of her nest. She feeds the nestling a long piece of meat stripped from a road-killed skunk. She moves as though she could do this forever.

The next day, I drive the slow, swerving road down into the Río Grande Gorge, where the Río Hondo runs down from the cool meadows of the mountains. This is a weekend, but Ted is working. So I am driving to help him.

Canyon wrens flute their dropping calls in the cold air. My Toyota truck rumbles over the John Dunne Bridge that spans *Tóóh Ba'áád* (Female River—Rio Grande). Mallard ducks splat their small orange feet in the grass of the gravel bar where the Hondo meets the Grande. I drive the truck along the switchbacks, up five hundred feet and through 125 million years of history. The layers of sandstone are occasionally cut by hard black basalt. A few thousand years of quiet desert life. Then fiery volcanic oblivion. Then back to the quiet desert where the only thing moving within five miles might be the darting eye of a lizard. Then fiery oblivion. Desert. Fire. Desert. Fire. And now it is desert as I drive up the switchbacks.

When I ascend to the sagebrush fields on the west side of the gorge, I am in *Diné Bikéyáh*, Navajo country. Coyote paths wander out between the black rocks and snakeweed. Anthills rise like micropyramids of a permanent, sustainable civilization. A red-tailed hawk circles in a thermal. Where the dirt road runs north toward Colorado, Ted meets me and waves as he drives past in his biodiesel-driven Dodge Ram.

We drive out to the strawbale he's creating with an owner-builder who bought some property on the edge of the newly established Río Grande del Norte National Monument. We drive more than five miles north, past hexagonal cabins and geodesic McMansions hooked up to solar panels and solar hot-water heaters. They are all enjoying the luxurious solitude of "off-grid" living, along with their refrigerators, plasma TVs, wellheads, and other modern-day conveniences with which the Taos Plateau has had little to no dealings over the past millennia.

Before we reach the build site, the owner's extra-long Airstream trailer gleams under the May sun. After we've parked our trucks, I notice the boards and building materials lay haphazardly near the edges of the lumber piles. It looks as though a strong wind has come by and decided to make it easy to lose everything. Which is probably what has happened.

"I hate a messy jobsite," Ted says. "It just drives me nuts. Things just lay around. Someone is just going to trip and get hurt. This house is about 8 percent done. The foundation and stem wall are built. Sill plates are installed. But the owner thinks he's well on his way. He's only 8 percent done."

This strawbale building rises with post and beams. But rather than the traditional posts, the owner has decided on building "box beams"— hollow columns built by creating a vertical box out of plywood. The strawbales will rest on the concrete stem wall running around the building. Between the box beams Ted has built curb rails—a pair of 2×4s that run parallel like a pair of cross-country skis along the concrete stem wall. The curb rails keep the strawbales off the concrete stem wall so that very little moisture can "wick" up into the dry straw. Between the rails, Ted has already laid down rigid insulation, and he'll cover it with gravel to ward off moisture.

It is hard to keep something dry on concrete. Concrete is essentially a liquid for its entire existence. Like glass, it is always thinning at the top and thickening at the bottom, bowing in quiet worship to the mystic force of gravity. It is always alive with moisture, just what any fungus or microbes in the straw would need to excite them to breed and defecate the tightly compacted bale into a gray, unlivable oblivion.

But the curb rails keep this dangerous romance at bay. They provide the space and breathing room so that any spare moisture can work through the wall and not toxically linger. Strawbale buildings in the snowy Canadian suburbs north of Toronto have had moisture meters in their walls for twenty years. They've always checked out fine. But without the curb rails, fungus eats the wall alive.

Today, we are going to be working on building more box beams. Ted buttons up his light-green and tan Hawaiian shirt, adjusts his sunglasses and soiled baseball cap.

We talk over some details with the owner, Josh, a red-bearded man with a lumberjack physique and a quavering, clipped accountant's voice. He grew up along the East Coast after his parents divorced. He excelled in college and moved out to California to work for Intel. He has a background in engineering, but he's been a product marketer for Intel over the past nine years in the Bay area.

"I'm *so* done with the Bay area," he says, his gray Oakleys gleaming like oil slick against the morning sun. "When you work for Intel, you get paid lots of money, but you don't get to do what you want to do."

We staple-gun tar paper to the exposed box beams so the UV light won't chew and bend them. A silver Jeep bounces down the sagebrush road. The front license plate reads, "#1 Fan" for the Green Bay Packers.

"That's Brian," Ted says.

Brian leans out of the door and I can tell he's seen too many winters. He stretches in his jean shorts and Green Bay Packers hoodie. His two German shepherds, Gracie and Spooky, hop out of the back and go sniffing the jobsite. I am quietly thankful the Rain Dog is not with me. Brian smiles, and crow's-feet etch along his blue Ray Bans. His silver wire earrings and gray ponytail tell me he's probably done mushrooms in the desert. Later, Brian will confirm this.

I shake hands and notice his beat-up baseball cap that reads, "Dangling Rope." I know that is the farthest marina on Lake Powell. I ask him if he's traveled to Page, Arizona. Turns out Brian knows the people who owned the Windy Mesa. I tell him Lyle Parsons used to play there and ask Brian if he knew him.

"Yeah," he says. "He was a really good guitar player."

I look to Taos Mountain. Then I ask where he lives now.

"Oh, I live out in a little place I built near Three Peaks," he says. "Just me and the dogs. And a new mistake every now and then. That's my little joke to myself. I'd been married for fifteen years to a really great lady. Then she died. Cancer. Now I just run into a few mistakes and they don't last too long, man. Thank goodness. Just me, the dogs, and the occasional mistake."

He walks across the jobsite in his Keen sandals. "Oh, I'll tell you, if I could wear these on the jobsite, I would. They're so comfortable. I just don't want to take them off."

Ted walks over to this truck. "I know what you're saying, man. But it only takes that one time, right? One time, I was unloading my acetylene torch from my truck. And usually I could wrangle it out and get it to the edge of the bed and just set it down on the bumper and then let it down. So I'm in a hurry before work and I'm just wearing my sandals. Not even covered ones like you have there, just simple flip-flops. So I'm moving this thing and it weighs a couple hundred pounds, right? And the edge gets caught on the liftgate and I'm yanking and pulling and jerking the thing. I turn to get a better position, and—boom—the thing just falls straight down. It nails the end of my foot and—wham—the edge just slices my big toe. I almost didn't want to look down at it. And you know how blood doesn't flow right away? Well, I could see the big toe and it cut all the way through. It was hanging on by just a little piece of skin. I just hopped to the cab on my good foot and grabbed a rag, like, right away, and just clamped it right away over the stump and drove to the hospital. But that rag was just soaked in, like, two minutes. They were able to reattach it. But it took me about a year to really feel my balance again."

We start setting up for the work. Josh has us look at the drawings. It's an 1,800-square-foot strawbale with south-facing windows to build solar gain. He plans on having two wood stoves to help with the temperature regulation.

We drive up the hill to the red shipping container to get a set of skids we can attach to Josh's Bobcat. We climb into his massive black Ford F-350 pickup. It has a B20 diesel engine, which means it can burn diesel that's 20 percent biofuel. On his rear bumper, black stickers read "Frack the Plutocracy" and "Diesel Inside." We bounce along the dirt road while Josh talks about getting stuck in the wet clay and skidding off the road. He once buried the diesel truck up to the front bumper in mud.

"Yeah, that's the nice thing about a Jeep," Brian says. "You can just put it in four-wheel low and let it crawl. And it will usually get you there."

We return with the skids and a load of three-quarter-inch and one-inch plywood. Josh forgets the insulation needed to sit between the 2×6 curb rails. Before he leaves, Brian notices that some of the posts have moved. Ted and Josh want to check if each individual post is plumb before attaching the beams. Instead, Brian decides to attach a string line to make sure. We tap a nail into the end of one board and screw a 1 1/2-inch block to the face of the post. The string will then tell us whether everything is straight.

After each is walked to the string, Brian argues with Josh about putting up braces on each post. This is a ludicrous debate among experienced builders. One of the good things about building with posts is that they're simple. One of the downsides is that they fall out of plumb and have to be braced with 2×4s anchored into the ground. Josh would rather continue adjusting them with shims, which is also ludicrous.

"He's in a hurry," Brian says. Josh *does* hurry, to be fair. While Ted is jumping in and out of the backhoe (which Ted shouldn't have to be doing because Josh should have had his plumber out to help tell Ted where to dig), Brian and I cut and measure plywood to build the beams.

We build like so: Brian's jig helps us fix the 2×6s in place on a sheet of plywood. We snap a chalk line down the center of the stud and hit it with nails to keep the beam together.

Then we raise the beams up on the posts with the forklift. Josh is still learning, so it takes some time. But he gets the hang of the hydraulic dance of the joystick. Ted would rather people just put up the beams.

Brian then demonstrates how to set the contractor stakes from the braces, how you should twist them as you pound with the hammer to set them deeper in the sand. You want to be careful to keep your leg out of the way. Don't smack your own shin. We plant the stakes, screw them in place, and Josh starts hefting the beams.

"One thing you don't want to do, bro," Brian says and shows me where I left a screw poking out of a stake. "Better to just cut that off there. Don't want any accidents."

Brian and I converse as we work. He once owned and managed the Pilar Café. He worked as a snow maker in the winter and built houses in the summer. He built his own little place out near Three Peaks so he wouldn't have to pull a building permit. He grew up in Colorado, lived near Breckenridge and Boulder for a while, then moved down to Page, Arizona, where he managed the radio station for a couple of years, then he moved to Pilar. I ask him why he chose to move and settle in Taos County.

"Well, all things considered," he says, "it looked like a great place to be poor."

Over lunch, Ted grabs a shim and uses it to eat his salad. Brian does the same with his yogurt. Spooky knows I have meat hiding in my wrap. Josh sits off to the side and eats a perfectly made turkey sandwich off a yellow plastic plate.

We talk about ways to finish the job. Brian and Ted swap stories of crazy builders they'd worked for when they were younger. Then we get back to it. Brian and I work together, talking Edward Abbey and Charles Bowden as we get things done.

Josh thinks we are moving too slow, so instead of mentioning it politely to me, he plays it like he's in his office at Intel back in San Francisco and asks Ted to pull me over to his job. He and I also converse while he works the backhoe. The conversation is important because it slows down the work. And when the work is slow, it gets done right.

We shape the bottom of the septic pit with shovels. I ask Ted about how he ended up getting educated.

"I went to the University of Cincinnati, the same college as Mike Reynolds, actually," he says. "1989 to 1994. It was a co-op program, so you did studies at the university but they also hooked you up with local businesses and got you out into the field."

He helped pay for college by installing garage doors and selling beer at Cincinnati Reds games. Both jobs got him the fresh air outside of the classroom that he desperately needed. We talk about one of Ted's architect friends, who came out to Taos in Ted's truck with him. But they've drifted apart over the years.

"I'd like to make money like my friend, but my problem is that I actually care about people."

His friend will often intentionally raise the cost of a renovation project, for example, in order to raise the amount of money he makes in fees (since his fees move in a percentage of the total cost of the build). The more money you get the public to spend, the more money you make. But there should be a project manager in place to do that, not the architect who stands to gain from inefficiencies.

"My wife says, 'You know, if you really worked at it, you could be one of the most prolific contractors in the county. Why don't you just go for it?' She really thinks it comes down to a confidence problem. And she's probably right, you know? I like to goof around, you know?"

He points to a tattoo on his leg that says, "Team Wang."

Ted got the tattoo while he was building an Earthship overseas in the Asian tropics. The other builders made a joke one night that they were all playing in a band or a group called Team Wang. The name stuck so well that Ted and another builder got it tattooed on their bodies. When their comrades saw the tattoos the next morning, they felt left out. They wanted one, too.

Once we get the pit excavated, we need to change the slope of the ditch running the septic line to the tank. So I throw in dirt while Ted dumps gravel into the bottom. We jump down in and spread it. Ted needs a measure with a level, so he asks me to get a level from Josh. Josh doesn't have one. Brian says, "Ted needs a level? He can use mine. But, hey, man, be careful. This level is my *life*."

I take the level to Ted. "Is that Brian's level?" he asks. "I don't want to use that. It's too valuable. Just go grab mine out of the back of my truck."

I take the level back to Brian and set it down with all the careful ceremony of a samurai sword. "He refused to use it. Out of respect," I say.

Brian laughs. "Hey, all right, man!"

Ted levels and screeds the gravel. "Normally, I wouldn't be out here doing this. I would usually have a plumber to help me," he says. "But it needs to be done, so I might as well."

He digs out the pit as we chat.

"How old are you, Jim?" Ted asks.

"I'm thirty-three," I say. "This is my Jesus year."

Ted nods. "This is the time of your life, man. I'm forty-seven and I'm still spry. But I can feel my strength fading here and there. It's getting harder to hold on to my muscles. But the thirties is a good time, man. I don't trust twenty-year-olds on the jobsite anymore. I just don't. They're just fucking around all the time. That's the thing. When you're in your twenties, you have a great body and all this energy, but you're fucking stupid. When you're in your thirties, your mind and your body are just in perfect sync with each other."

We dig out the tank and it's ready for Josh. Brian takes a snack break.

"Here you go, Spook," Brian says, holding out a peanut butter and cheddar cracker sandwich, the kind you see in any Tom's vending machine. "You'll like it. It's got peanut butter and . . . chemicals?"

That Monday, we have returned to Des Montes. We frame the walls on the concrete slab we'd left to dry over the past few days.

As we mark the jack studs and king studs, Ted remembers his dad: a brilliant designer who built Ted's childhood living room, with a sofa built from foam blocks that wrapped around the room and a bookshelf he made with thin, sleek board and wooden dowels.

"It was just this precision engineering," he says. "I was, like, 'How the hell did he hold that thing together?' We had these beds with custom pullout drawers for storage and this white oak plywood and clear lacquered finish on the front of the veneer. It was this beautiful, minimalist sort of architecture. He was a great designer."

Ted looks down seriously at the sill plate where he's fastening the wall. "He's actually one of the best craftsmen I've ever known to this day. But he was a dick. I mean, you know, he was an international businessman. He knew his shit. And he had high standards. He was a talented dick. But he was still a dick. You know what the first thing was that I ever built? It was a napkin holder. I banged together pieces of 2×4 and bent nails. Nothing was straight. He looked at it and you know what he said? 'You can do better.'"

Ted laughs as he walks to the cut table. "Man, that tore me up. I mean, he was right. But I was five years old."

We build a few framed timber walls. Dirk lays out the bottom plate and the top plate, then drills with a hole saw to catch where the treated lumber touches the anchor bolts in the concrete. We measure the studs, Dirk cuts, and once we have it all screwed together we put up the wall. We mark the location for the windows on the jack studs and brace it all with 2×4s and steel stakes. Then we screw the anchors to the sill plate on the concrete slab.

"Hey, come over here, home chicken," Ted says, and we set up and brace walls most of the day. We also check the walls to make sure they're plumb.

On the first day of June, we return to set the prefabricated timber-framing for the roof, called trusses. Dirk is there to receive them from the deliveryman. He signs for them. Then Ted gets there. Ted checks them over and doesn't like what he sees. He checks the drawings. It doesn't look like the load-bearing pieces of the trusses match the architectural drawings. Ted checks the lengths with his tape measure. He checks the drawings that were delivered with the trusses.

"They said their specs were right," Ted says. "Well, they aren't. That's four thousand dollars' worth of fuckup."

Ted has built many trusses. They used to prefabricate them at

Earthship Biotecture. Four guys worked in a team and banged them out. But they'd only get about nine done per day. It was just too slow of a process, so the company abandoned it.

Ted stoops on his cellphone and talks to the engineers at the company. He comes back to talk to Christopher and Dirk. "The engineer says he'll have a solution within the hour." The solution doesn't come until the next day. We are on job-site time. While Ted and I have to wait, we build a sidewall for the closet. The next day, we reconfigure the trusses.

The next day, while putting studs together, Christopher shoots a sixteen-penny from the nail gun into his inner wrist. The nail penetrates two inches. Christopher pulls out the nail and wraps his puncture wound in gauze and medical tape. We keep working.

Later that day, Dirk and Christopher joke about whether I've brought in a poltergeist situation. They explain that they've both been working construction at least twenty years and they've never had a serious accident. Dirk raises the thick bandage where the ER doctor at Holy Cross Hospital in Taos had to reattach his thumb after he sliced it apart with a circular saw while dimensioning 2×4s two days before I showed up.

"Wonder if we're working on some Indian burial ground?" Christopher jokes.

We work to get the trusses assembled. "I smoked for twenty years and drank all the time," Ted says as he tacks nails into the truss refits. "It's like, when do you finally just decide, 'Why the hell am I fucking up my life like this every day?'"

It is fair to question whether magpies have these thoughts.

We work until Ted calls it good. The next day we lift the trusses into place. The first two we heft up the ladder with Ted in the lead. After that, Christopher suggests we lift with rope. I take the rope and tie a two-half hitch to the end of the truss. We lift as a team. We get the truss into position. Ted and Christopher walk it down to where Ted has a brace set up so the trusses can lean into a stack.

We lift the trusses until they all sit on the roof. We talk of the past. Ted went to college in Cincinnati. His thesis was to design the Volkswagen Museum along the river in Cincinnati.

"The project was supposed to be about transformation," he says. "You know how each VW bug had this exoskeleton sort of shell on the outside and this mechanic interior. So it was going to be this big tube that extended out as a shell, with all the systems of the museum inside. It was supposed to travel from one end of VW's history to the other and it was going to line up with the linearity of the river. You know, you could just go on and on with this stuff. 'Arch-a-babble,' you know?"

At college, Ted learned other things. He learned to love motorcycles. He learned he could fit a case of beer into his backpack. He showed up to college with whatever fit into his backpack and with his bicycle. And he was happy.

We install blocking at the ends of the trusses. This ensures that we have something to nail to when we add the plywood sheeting to the roof.

We break for lunch. Christopher and I talk about his time in the Navy where he worked maintaining nuclear weapons on an aircraft carrier.

"We worked down below the waterline of the ship," he says. There, he maintained all air-to-surface missiles that they armed on F-14 Tomcats. They maintained nuclear depth charges. And then they had the "backpack bombs" that strapped into a steel vessel shaped like an acorn. The Navy SEALs would carry them. They could jump out of a plane, parachute down over the water with the acorn on a rope tether, and then swim to shore. Once there, they'd hump the acorn into the country and arm it. The only guy who had the arming code was the guy carrying the acorn.

"You'd have to leave it, arm it, then get your ass out of there," he says. "That's why those guys had to be so badass."

We sheet the roof with plywood. The nails go through. Ted goes into the past, wandering into where he grew up in West Chester County in New York.

"It was just like this forested garden," he says. "There were open fields and dairy farms and an old steam engine train ran through the place. There were these channels on either side of the tracks that had carp and sunfish in there. It was just beautiful. And now all the money moved in. All the people bought up the property. Now there's big-box stores and parking lots everywhere through that place. And I can't go back now. Ever. It's a place that's only in my memory."

Ted would not want to go back. He learned here how his society treats people who want to use chemicals to seek visions. He broke the law in that place. He is known as a criminal. When he was in high school, he got arrested for dealing acid. His friends and he were buying acid at eighty dollars a sheet and splitting it. One of his friends was taking them and selling them for ten bucks a hit. He got busted, and because Ted was the guy getting the sheets, he was somehow "the ringleader." And the law came.

"They really brought the hammer down," he says.

Ted was not the typical "bad kid." He was captain of the soccer team. He was nearly a straight-A student. He excelled in all the upper-level math and science classes. But that didn't matter.

"I got expelled from the New York School System," he says. "They made me go to mandatory drug counseling. It was this stupid method where they tried to shame you out of addiction. I had to go during the day from eight to five. These people didn't know *what* they were doing. If you missed a day or had a relapse, they'd just yell at you. 'You're *worthless*! You're an *addict*! What are you *doing with your life*!? Why are you even *alive*?' They'd make you wear this long placard that said, 'I'm a drug addict.' And I would be standing there thinking, 'This is *bullshit*.' Now it was probably predicting another ten years of overcoming drug addiction for me."

The only way that Ted could get to his eight-to-five job of being called a loser was with his bicycle.

We go through and cut half-inch plywood to screw up against the studs. The plywood needs to break at least 3/8 of an inch into the stud. The #8 nails need to be separated by six inches at the borders and eight inches in the field. This creates the illusion of a solid wall.

That Wednesday after work, Christopher and I get to talking while the sweat cools our necks.

"You've got to think about houses as *moving* things," he says. "That's what houses are doing. They're doing what that concrete slab is doing. It's expanding when it gets hot and it's contracting when it gets cold. Just like

99

the east side of the house in the mornings. It gets heated up and it expands. The wood expands. The glass expands. The plaster expands. It's going out one way, while the west side is contracting. Then the sun tracks over and then the west side gets heated up. Then it expands while the east side starts shrinking. It's going the other way now. This is happening all the time. There's that *tension*. You understand what I'm saying?"

Christopher pushes a gray dreadlock back from his face. His brown eyes focus, his slanted teeth resemble fangs as he contemplates the photon-powered drumbeats of the Sun's gait that grant to buildings both life and ruin.

"It's like with the Earthships. They're good at dealing with that tension and that travel of the sun. But not always. The front greenhouses on these houses are just money traps. That's what I've been doing for two or three hours after work every day, man. Just replacing all the mullions on the windows. I can't keep up with the maintenance. They once used redwood with a simple silicone seal, but that's just impossible to uninstall and replace. Then you're wrecking your timber and twisting everything apart. What I do now is what a lot of new builders do. I take metal sheaths and lay them over my timber frames."

Christopher takes out a carpenter's pencil and draws it out on his toolbox. The strips of metal sit on top of the mullions—the timber framing that holds the windows in place. The metal is expensive, but it will save the windows over the decades. He chides people for not recognizing the need to control expansion and contraction in houses. And he castigates Mike Reynolds for designing his Earthships with a slight cant to the east to catch the rising sun. But that doesn't compensate for the physics of the sunrise. Christopher had to sit down with an architect friend of his and explain it to him. Every ballooner who flies over the gorge knows that when the sun rises over the mountains in the morning, it's creating all this warm air in the upper atmosphere. And that warm air pushes down the cold air into the pockets and low points of the ground.

Christopher lives in the Earthship Greater World Community. His street lies in an old gravel pit once used by the county that is now lined with eight Earthships. His house sits in the lowest point in the community.

"That means it gets cold as hell down in that pit and it *stays* cold," Christopher says. Christopher has friends who live in five-hundred-thousand-dollar houses on the plains south of town, near the golf course. The houses are built from 2×4 lumber, shaped to look like adobe houses. But they are fakes. Christopher calls these homes "faux adobes."

"During the winter, they've got two wood stoves roarin' in the morning and they still can't get their houses warmer than sixty degrees," he says. "It's because they're in the low spot out there."

He repeats: turning the Earthships slightly to the east does not solve the problem. The sun does not clear the mountains until after seven o'clock in the morning. Once it does, the sun does not warm things until ten o'clock. By then, it's already passed over into the west.

During snowstorms, the angle of the Earthship glass allows snow to linger on the panes. Christopher has to get into his coveralls and walk out with a squeegee to clean it off. The angle of the windows lets water sit and freeze and it creates ice damming. The water and ice weighs down the glass. Then gravity pushes the water down into the timbers. It's got to go somewhere. The water drives into the wood and the wood begins to rot.

"These are natural forces," Christopher says. "You cannot stop them."

He tells of further tragedies of the Earthship glass windows. He helped build an Earthship on the mountain north of Des Montes. They set up their south-facing windows. They put in their butyl tape, a petroleum-based strip of tape that makes the windows airtight to the wooden frames. The Earthship builders thought they could handle the expansion/shrinkage problem by adding in more butyl tape to the windows. The problem was that the ravens started flying down and picking it out of the windows.

"Apparently, ravens love eating butyl tape," Christopher says. "So the ravens ripped out all their vapor protection."

Christopher laughs at the cruel mysteries of this beautiful world.

"Now, the obvious way to deal with the long-term problem is to maintain the greenhouse as best we can and to mitigate the ice damming. Because in that Global Model Earthship, you have that dual layer of glass and timber, it gives you excellent performance. But I don't know about you, but I don't have eighty thousand dollars just sitting around to replace all that glass and timber after a couple years."

He sighs.

"People just don't think about this shit. I didn't either when I first came out here. But I've lived and breathed it and built it for eight years out here and I've seen how it works."

That night, I follow Christopher back to his Earthship to witness his struggle behind the glass. He bought the Earthship sight unseen. It was an act of faith. I wish his faith had been better rewarded. The design mistakes are obvious, even to a novice like me. Steps are mismatched. The water cistern is mounted to the east side of the house, where it receives little sun during the day and sucks the heat out of the building at night. House God would have difficulty greeting you in the door here.

Christopher walks me through the house until we stand next to an addition outside where the previous owner had started another tire wall next to the building.

"You need to ask yourself," he says, "how long is this wall going to take to build? How much of your energy is it going to eat up? Do you want to spend most of your life building and *rebuilding* your house? Don't you want to get up into the mountains? Take that camping trip? Do that backcountry horse ride? That's the question no one asks: What about your *sovereignty*? How much is this house going to ask of your *sovereignty*?"

The next morning, the magpies feed their nestlings under the awning of the front porch near the jobsite. Their nest rises. It makes the circle that spins forever, that holds the horizon, that pulls the sky. Even fire obeys the circle, the sphere, shining from the sun overhead, bright and yellow as the eyes of any wolf that might run through something like dreams.

It gives light even to such a world that has stolen that nuclear fire and hidden it under steel bomb casings. All the while, the nuclear warheads sleep below the waterline. We have bought them. We might call that security. Perhaps even sovereignty.

But that is a lie of power. It falls to the ground and shatters. The magpies do not pick up the pieces. They find new sticks after storms and reweave the circle of their nest. The magpies do not concern themselves with mortgages or electricity or satellite television or what is below the waterline. They are builders. They perhaps know quite a lot of sovereignty. They have bought it. The know the language of House God. That is why they know how to travel up to the sky.

Often we think homes will be the things that grant us sovereignty. That any home will make us kings and queens of a castle. But playing for Team Wang has taught me otherwise. It brings that old thought from the mud in the shores of Walden Pond: Often times when a man finds he will have a house, he will often find his house has him. And when he does not have enough Strength, Wisdom, Good Health, and Integrity, that house becomes a prison.

The magpies chatter from their project. They keep building. Then they fly. Their circle pattern is building to the sun.

Ted, Christopher, Dirk, and I meet outside the garage and strap on our tool belts. Team Wang goes back to work.

Earthships on the southern slopes of
the Sangre de Cristo Mountains. Photo by Jim Kristofic.

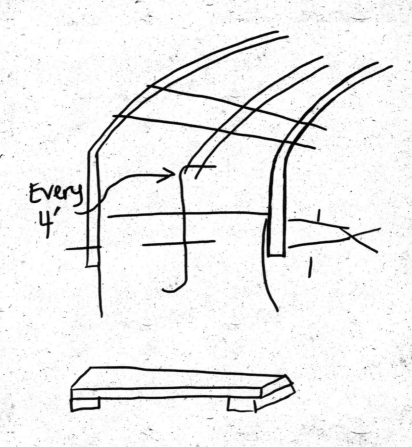

Every
4'

BUILDING ROOTS

The willows bend green and cool against the blue August sky. The cooler winds blow in the mountain meadows where I walk with the Rain Dog. Along my road, the sunflowers bend with the weight of hepatic tanagers chirping and moving down the stalks for seed. The corn in the garden is high with pink tassels and the melons have spread beyond the adobe planters I have built for them. The mornings begin to ask for flannel shirts over the body. Summer's lease that has all too short a date is coming to a close.

I wait, reading Charles Bowden's *Blues for Cannibals* in the driver's seat of the Prius in the dirt parking lot of the Coffee Spot in Taos. Two Labrador mutts trot along in the shade, sniffing at their usual spots. Then they swing their skinny hips in a line to the east, crossing the main paseo, on toward the Taos Pueblo—that model of mud, sand, and straw and that way of life we now call "sustainable." It is a place where House God dwells.

I am reading about mesquite trees. They know about how to sustain. Bowden describes how a copper mining company once found the root of a mesquite tree more than 180 feet below the earth. The tree had sent it down, deep into the soil, to connect to that life force hiding in the quiet dark rivers of the aquifers.

I'm reading this when Mark Goldman steps out of his Toyota Matrix. We meet and shake hands in the parking lot. He doesn't extend his hand far and it is a gentle handshake. Some Anglos might call it "coy." In Navajo country, this would be called "polite," and I take it as such.

His hand—like that of many builders—is tangled with veins and calloused. His nails are the color of worn almonds. He is a lean man, relaxed in his black-and-purple-striped western shirt, jeans, and leather Keen shoes. His trimmed dark-gray mustache, goatee, and balding hair-line create the effect of age, but you can still see Mark's teenage self hiding beneath the hair on his face. His voice has that perfect theater timbre that would sell new cars convincingly. After talking with him for five minutes, you might think he'll next be off to play the role of the sensible father in a family sitcom.

We chat as we step into the Coffee Spot. He offers to buy, which is generous. This doesn't happen often in Taos. Sociologists would describe Taos as an economy of scarcity.

In line, we stand behind a young guy tattooed with a masked Shiva on his back. Creator and destroyer. Shiva's tongue stretches out between fanged teeth. Cut lines in the tattoo tell of more work to be done. The young guy wears a pair of leather cat ears and a turquoise nylon rope around his waist that ends in a furry tail. Mark doesn't seem to notice.

We talk about my upcoming teaching schedule at Taos High School. When we reach the counter, he repeats that it is his treat. He grabs a cupcake frosted and decorated to look like a white fried egg with the yellow yolk at the center. He grabs one for me, too.

"Here you go," he says. "You look like you need it. If I don't feed you, I'll just feel guilty."

We find a table as we talk about how working outside keeps one lean and hungry. That summer I had worked with Team Wang to build a garage addition to a large house in Des Montes, a flat pasturage that runs up toward *Dziltahdal'tai* (Southern Rocky Mountains). The high-elevation plains gurgle with summer water and slow-traveling rain that ponds and meanders through the tall grass, cattails, and willows filling the acequias and streams. The Spanish gradually claimed these grass-lands from the elk and the buffalo. Now retiring Americans who toiled their lives away in the paddocks of the suburbs have arrived in their Subarus and Volvos to claim these lands from the Spanish, who watch from the porches of their trailers and dilapidated adobes much in way the first elk families might have regarded the first herds of cattle.

The man I am working for is a twice-divorced property owner from

Missouri. He broke his body on ladders and in basements of apartment complexes he owned and maintained. Now he drives to the casinos in New Mexico in his Nissan Xterra and likes the fly-fishing.

We sit and Mark asks about my background on the Navajo Reservation, about moving to southern Utah, where my family and I lived in a trailer without electricity for a year, about Californians buying up property in Arizona, about how I think Phoenix is a metastasized Los Angeles.

His son, Ian, has arrived and waves as he walks over. I recognize him from the hallways of Taos High, though I have never taught him in a classroom. We talk about his upcoming journey to American University in Washington, DC, where he'll commune with the ghosts of poets and writers, talking from books into people's heads forever. This is called "the study of literature."

"And this from a kid who grew up on a dirt road in Taos County," Mark says, smiling. I can see his pride and affection for his son.

"So you lived out on the Reservation. The capital there is Window Rock, right?" Mark asks. I nod. "I remember going there back in 1998 to hear what they were deciding to do about their public housing in Kayenta, Lukachukai, Window Rock, and Ganado. And I was sort of depressed about what I was seeing. It was basically against everything I learned and taught myself in architecture school. Everything was just so 'grid,' so cookie-cutter. It was like dropping a section of Ohio suburb in the middle of Indian country. They wanted to hire me to oversee the construction, as a construction manager, to make sure it all got built. I just had to say to them, 'Sorry, guys. I've got this year-old baby boy at home.' And they were, like, 'Oh, is he okay? Is he sick?' And I said, 'No, I just don't want to be away from him too much in his first year. Sorry.'"

Mark rubs his son's shoulder. "So there. You bailed me out of that situation, and you didn't even know it. But, yeah, those plans were terrible. And it was so sad, because you could look around the room and just see that no one was really excited to be doing this. Just bad energy with that suburb plan, like they *knew*."

We talk with Mark's son about how much he'll miss skiing in Taos. He politely shakes my hand and leaves to his job waiting tables at Sabroso's restaurant in Arroyo Seco.

"Okay," Mark says. "Well, be rested. I have to go down to Santa Fe tomorrow morning and I wanted you to come with me."

Mark has that calm tension in his voice, that of the father practicing the act of letting his son go.

"Uh, yeah," Ian hesitates. "I'll go down with you. But I have to go back down there again this week for adult-league soccer. So I'll go with you. Uh. Maybe."

"Well, we're leaving in the morning. Okay?"

He gives Ian some money for his dinner later. He touches his son's hand. "Come on, we'll get a breakfast burrito, head down together, get to my meeting, and get back."

"Well, I'll probably go."

"Well, I'm going to just say you're going. I just want some company on the trip. I don't care if you bring a pillow and a blanket and sleep the whole way down."

Ian laughs to himself and shakes his head. "I'll see you later, Dad." And off he goes under the shade of the tall willows.

"It's so funny to think about the kind of secure life he had with us," Mark says. "He was safe, comfortable, he could drive just fifteen minutes up the Ski Valley to ski. He lived in a house that his parents built. There's not a lot of people who can say that. So strange."

Mark and I pick at the fried-egg cupcakes. We exchange our, "So, what brought you to Taos?" stories.

"My wife had been out here and invited me to come out," Mark says. "I did and I just couldn't leave. I thought, 'Well, this will be a nice year of adventure and then I'll head back to the East Coast.' Twenty years or more later and I'm still here. I became fascinated with all the nuances of this unique place and people. There aren't many places where you have modern buildings less than a mile from a thousand years of architectural history at the Taos Pueblo. And you have a Spanish colonial culture here. Some say it's the remnants of a colonial culture, but once you're here, then it's like, 'No, it's an *active* colonial power still in place.' And then you've got Anglo people who have immigrated in. In Taos there seems to be three Anglo populations. There are the class of working professionals, like you and me. Then there are the trust-fund inheritors and intensely rich beyond what we understand. Then there are the people who are almost ex-patriots within their own country. They're usually living outside of town. You know?"

As Mark speaks, a twentysomething guy walks by wearing dyed red leather armor gauntlets, greaves, and chest plates that chink with brass rings and metal attachments. He looks like he's going to the film set of *Game of Thrones* or to a Renaissance faire. The armor easily hides his dirty sleeveless T-shirt and jeans. Behind us, a tall twenty-year-old Anglo with blond hair shaved into a Mohawk ending in a ponytail talks to himself while nodding to the music soaring through the black wires of his headphones. The tattooed man wearing cat ears and tail has yet to emerge from the coffee shop.

Oh, yes. I know what Mark means about the third type of Anglo.

Mark has much in common with this third type.

He came to Taos and got his introduction to the level of craftsmanship. He saw the three cultures interacting right away. One of his first jobs was building a nine-thousand-square-foot house with huge windows and a huge swimming pool that was probably bigger than the parking lot of the Coffee Spot. The house sat on a hill above the hundred-year-old church in Arroyo Hondo. The house was far bigger than the church.

"I don't know what that's saying," Mark says, "but it's saying something."

Mark wanted to pick up as many building skills as he could. He soon learned that he would never learn it all. He had an open mind to learn when he came here, but he was shy. His shyness came from his background. He did not have the typical "white person, Anglo experience" growing up.

Mark moves my pencil over the tiled table, still warm from the noon heat. His hands shift as he speaks, rehearsing their movements over the drawing table he's worked at most of his adult life.

"I mean, when you learn to walk inside a prison, that's not the normal thing, right?"

Mark was born in Tucson, Arizona, after his mother and father moved to the dry desert to help his mother's asthma. His father was a tall, strong guy. He'd served three tours in the Air Force, starting when he was fourteen years old. When he got out, he lived back in the lower East Side of New York City. He soon became a street-gang member. After moving out to Arizona, he'd graduated to armed robbery. Within two years, he became a federal felon after he robbed a bank.

Mark's mother visited his father in the state prison in Florence, Arizona. She was in the prison when Mark took his first steps. His mother eventually moved him and his sister to southern California.

"We lived in a lot of different spots. When my father was released, we lived in East LA. I was one of the few white kids there in those schools. We then moved to the Crenshaw District, near South Central LA."

Mark was six years old when a California Army National Guard helicopter landed on the lawn of his housing project building during the Watts riots in August 1965, which largely erupted over a lack of affordable housing.

"In the black neighborhood, I was the white kid with the mean hook shot on the basketball courts. Then we moved to a rundown part of LA near the beach, called Dogtown. Everyone there said it was poor. To me, though, at that point, it seemed like a rich neighborhood. I was very lucky to live there. I got to surf every morning before school. I had these friends who were amazing surfers and amazing athletes. They just kept me up, you know? Me being poor was never a thing for them. I kept it hidden, of course, but I think they could tell. I mean, when you're eating dinner at your friends' houses every night, they start to notice. I mean, we just didn't have any food in the house. But it wasn't a bad thing. I was learning to get along with people. And I had support. My stepdad took me when I was eighteen and trained me as a carpenter. He showed me how to pound a nail. He said, 'Now here's a subfloor. Go to it.' And since then I never really wanted to do anything else. So I'm a trained carpenter. Not a lot of architects have those skills."

When high school ended, Mark wanted to go to college, but he didn't have the cash or the confidence to make the final push. He had a friend who was a writer. They worked together at the same restaurant. He took Mark aside during a break and said he had to do something. He had to tell the people at the University of California–Santa Barbara about who he was. About his story. He had to stop pretending. He asked Mark to write them a letter to seek admission, explaining his financial situation.

Mark wouldn't write the letter. So his friend sat down at a typewriter and they typed it together. The university admitted Mark by special action.

The university made the right decision. Mark created the school's first architectural internship, which is still in place. Then he won multiple scholarships to the school my landlord, Molly, had attended: the Boston Architectural College (BAC), one of the oldest architectural schools in the country. The BAC is more than forty years older than the Harvard Architectural College. When Frank Lloyd Wright would visit Boston, he was always invited to Harvard, but he would usually skip to go to the BAC. Wright said the BAC was the place where all the nuts and bolts of real building and design were coming together.

"The Harvard School of Architecture guys were the ones sitting in suits at the lunches, sketching basic designs on a cocktail napkin," Mark says. "But the BAC guys were the ones at the drawing tables, sketching out the plans for the buildings. Slaving behind the scenes."

Mark's mentor, Ned Cherry, had studied under Walter Gropius, one of the German founders of modern architecture, who had to flee Berlin when Hitler took power. The methods were about getting rid of old forms. It was about breaking the old modes of housing. For Mark, who had been confined by those edifices of power and privilege most of his life, breaking those old molds seemed just fine to him.

At the time, those molds really didn't seem to be working.

"After I graduated from the BAC, I was this guy who had just fucking vanished into the wilderness of New Mexico," Mark says. "I came out here to Taos thinking I was a failure. I worked hard and early hours as a builder out here, just skilling up. I didn't go on to the big commissions and big jobs like my colleagues. Instead I built houses of mud and timber. But then the Dream Tree Project happened."

In 1998, Mark was asked to design and build the "Dream Tree Shelter." It was a place where homeless teenagers (most of them abused, neglected, and addicted) could feel safe and live while they finished school. At the time, New Mexico was the second-poorest state in the country, with over a quarter of residents and over 40 percent of children under the age of five living below the poverty line. It was easy to end up as a homeless teenager then. It's easy now.

Mark signed on as the architectural designer and construction supervisor.

"I had never been homeless when I was a teen. I had a support system of friends. I'd had white privilege on my side. I'm sure you've felt it, too. I mean, no matter where you go, you've got that extra incentive with you. You're just expected to be good at things and people will even help you accomplish that. But these kids didn't have that support. It just wasn't there for them. So I thought we could at least give them a decent roof over their head and space for them to live and sort out their lives."

Mark knows it's hard to house people with dignity. When he first came to Taos, he'd have a crew of guys building high-value earth-and-timber homes for a wealthy client. Then the guys would drive home to a rundown, poorly insulated mobile home. So he designed the Dream Tree Project to give kids a solid, well-built space.

"I'm not sure how it makes them feel," he says, "but when you can stand in front of them and share your stories with them, that you've seen the insides of prisons, that you've worked your whole life through school, they seem to respond to that."

So he designed and built the building. The Princeton University Architectural Press wrote about it, how it was the first Housing and Urban Development–funded earthen building in the country. Then Mark got a phone call from the BAC. They wanted to give him an award and make him an honorary member of their distinguished alumni.

Mark laughs wide with his hands up in the air. "And I thought I was out here this whole time as a failure. Looks like someone thought otherwise."

Since then, Mark has gotten more involved in academia. He recently took a position as chairman of the construction department at the Taos campus of the University of New Mexico.

"It's becoming an interesting time for me," he says. "I spent twenty years as such a student of all these excellent builders. And now I'm finding myself in the role of teacher. It's a pretty amazing experience. I mean, a house is the most valuable item that most people will ever own. And in these dusty workshops, I get to teach these kids these valuable skills that will help them create a home. I mean, cars are valuable, too. But most of us can't just go out and build a car. That's got precision components and electronics that most people can't build on their own. But with houses and building, there's still a chance that a person can accrue enough skills to do everything right."

We get into talking over the planned suburbs of the East Coast. The suburban housing that many Americans currently occupy started in Levittown, New York, which has its twin in Levittown, Pennsylvania, just a half-hour drive south of my previous school district. A dear friend lived in Levittown and had to recently pay almost ten thousand dollars to repair a sewer line that went bad because it was built of cardboard tubing, used when the houses were built in order to cut costs.

"It's all part of the curse of specialization," Mark says. "Fewer and fewer builders have *all* the needed skills."

I tell him stories of the bad housing I've seen on the Rez, where people have built *hoghans* on cheap wooden frames with Oriented-Strand-Board (OSB) exposed to the elements that gets ripped apart by wind and sun and frost. The trailer park across from the Walmart in Taos is not much better.

"Well, the story of bad housing in the country is in that trailer park," Mark says. "I was mentioning the Watts riots earlier. Well, two years before, Martin Luther King organized the March on Washington. This is 1963, the really big one. And you've seen the pictures of him, right? During the "I Have a Dream" speech? There's this sea of people out in front of him. Well, if you look out at the placards and handbills they gave to the crowd the day before the March, there are three demands on the list, and the third was affordable housing.* Housing was a big issue. And it still is. When you have people poorly housed, they're often into

* Of the Ten Demands of the March on Washington, the first item asked for was "Comprehensive and effective civil rights legislation from the present Congress—without compromise or filibuster—to guarantee all Americans: Access to all public accommodations, decent housing, adequate and integrated education, the right to vote."

making waves, making trouble. People in power knew this. So when Nixon took office, one of the things he did to solve the housing crisis was to look to mobile homes. Trailers. But they were never meant as a permanent housing solution. It was just something to put out there for the moment. And when they were falling apart, they would just get recycled by the industry. But what happened during the Nixon administration was that Nixon was afraid of the sort of rioting and chaos in the sixties, so he made it policy that HUD would buy and allow loans on trailers, so that these temporary houses now became the new rural public housing. And the effect on rural communities and people has just been devastating to this day. It's institutionalized poverty."

Mark has read that Taos county has one of the highest proportions of people living in trailers. In New Mexico, almost 20 percent of people live in trailers, the second-highest proportion of all the states in the Union. In Taos county, it's higher: 30 percent of its people live in trailers. These people have low income in the first place. If the men have children with multiple women, they are paying the courts child support, economically transporting themselves to twelfth-century Spain where they are peasant serfs. If the family lives together, they are paying four to five hundred dollars per month in rent. They burn through three hundred dollars a month in propane just to keep the thin-walled trailer livable. The windows are not insulated. The floors are not insulated. This is Taos, an easy, hard place to live. The winters are real. The people will burn propane six months out of the year. In these metal-skinned, cheaply built tragedies, integrity is in short supply. These homes rob their renters in the night. They are slowly keeping them in poverty. In these places, it is hard to meet House God in the doorway. It is hard for House God to talk to you.

Mark tells the story of a local businessman who owns the trailer park next to Walmart. He buys rundown mobile homes for maybe three thousand dollars and parks them there. Then he charges five hundred dollars per month in rent, including a security deposit. He makes at least nine thousand dollars per month with this arrangement, just by having the trailers sit there.

Mark had a friend who was a building inspector for Taos County. He resigned when he was told that he could go anywhere in Taos. Yet the trailer park at the center of town, across from Walmart, was off-limits. The businessman who owned the trailer park was the mayor. He was in that office for four years.

Mark shakes his head when he thinks about how immensely profitable trailers have been since Nixon created the legal structures that unleashed them. Warren Buffett—that folksy hero of the billionaire class—and his company, Berkshire-Hathaway, own Clayton Homes, the largest trailer manufacturer in the United States.

"They roll out one per day in their factory down in Albuquerque," Mark says. He's visited that factory. "You hear that steam whistle and the next crew steps in. That's how they operate. They say, 'Hey, we'll put you in this house with a couch and a color TV and we'll finance everything so that you can be poor for the rest of your lives.' Trailers won't be going away. They're just too profitable. Economics demands them."

A cottonwood tree rises next to the steel trash barrel. Its leaves are making that falling-rain sound in the summer breeze. We talk about the counterforces to trailers, the alternatives that can help lift people out of poverty. To help them talk to House God.

"I love the Earthship people," Goldman says. "Just last week I was sitting down with Mike Reynolds and talking with him about this Earthship class that the students are going to be taking at UNM. I'm someone who has a lot of the same values as Mike. I'm just going about it in a different way. Mike was doing some *way* out there stuff when I came out here. Thankfully, it's not considered as 'way out there' now as it was."

Mark differs from Mike because Mark is more like Ted: he wants to work inside the system with hopes of changing it.

"Mike Reynolds says to run the other way from the system. And there's a good point to that. And Earthships are great. But they're very labor intensive. And they're pretty intense in terms of resources like cement. He's got people who want to learn how to build. But they've got little access to resources. We can take that veteran with their GI Bill and get them access to Mike Reynolds through UNM. We can get those young people on their path to higher education and expose them to these ideas. I love Mike. He's about one of the hardest working guys I've ever met. But there's only room on the planet for one Mike Reynolds. The world can only tolerate one of him."

We both laugh in the shadows of the trees, knowing of Mike's beloved brand of egotism.

"But I think that tenacious egotism is what drives him," Goldman says. "It's what makes it possible for him to do what he does. And we need him to keep doing what he does. But it doesn't matter how hard they work, if they're pounding tires out there seven days a week from dawn to dusk for the next hundred years. They're not going to make a dent in the public housing problem. Well, actually they *will* make a dent. But they just can't compete with the economics of the mobile home. The trailer."

And what can we say of an economy that demands the trailer, of this vine that bears this fruit?

The cottonwood leaves golden and then fall. The first snows come. My wood stove pops, gnaws the split spruce and pinon logs to fiery coals. The fire pops and I hear my labor with the chainsaw in the mountains and at the block with my sledgehammer and wedge. The heat fills the thick adobe walls and the house becomes a warm thing. It is an easy place to meet House God in the doorway.

The wood stoves fill the valleys with misty smoke in the mornings. The planet tilts its full 24.5 degrees away from the sun and winter settles and spreads out. Those cottonwood trees are sleeping, dreaming of spring down in their roots on the day we visit the Dream Tree Project. Mark and I meet at the construction shop at Taos High at 3:30 p.m. Mark talks with a fellow builder about how to best finesse clients while I look over the cubes of adobe samples he and his classes have been creating.

The iPhone rings again. Mark checks the number and cancels the call. He tucks away his phone as he says, "You ever get calls advertising how you can make money stuffing envelopes from the comfort of your own home?"

We exchange laughs and walk to his gray five-speed Toyota Matrix that he bought with cash in hand from a dealership in Phoenix. He flew down and bought the vehicle because it was a stick shift.

"I love it," he says. "It's like having a mini SUV. The thing is just a workhorse."

His bumper stickers read "NM for Hillary and Kaine" and "Taoseños for Maggie." The week after the election of Donald Trump, Mark soaped the words "Call Congress 202 315 2122." I called that number while walking past his car. The number was out of order. That is a metaphor.

We step out of our cars in the parking lot of Wired Café, which has one of the best coffee roasts in town. It also has one of the worst dirt parking lots. The culverts at the entrances are torn and shredded, with jagged metal lying in wait to strip tires of their sidewalls.

The wind blows ahead of a snowstorm from the west. The dark-red fruit of Siberian elms whip like prayer beads on the boughs. They have bloomed prematurely during a warm week that descended on Taos. Mark walks out with his hands in the pockets of his New Mexico Trade Builders work jacket. He is layered beneath in a Patagonia hoodie and Patagonia fleece. With this wind, his thin frame needs them.

The mountains stand speckled with the six-inch snowfall from last night. Tomorrow will be the first day of February.

We step through the gravel parking lot. Mark points out where the Dream Tree Project building emerges from the earth on the other side of the street. The two wings of the building spread with metal-detailed windows and hand-spooled wooden corbels running off the flat roofs.

"So this is a very unusual building," Mark says. "As far as I know, it's the first natural building built with government money in New Mexico. And it's a very strange thing to happen here. Usually, when you build tied to HUD money, you've got a set design with set materials, dealing with the bureaucratic way of doing things within the boundaries. Predictable ways of doing it. Concrete block. Vinyl tile. Dropped ceilings."

The deep-red blossoms on the trees toss in the wind. The western sky rolls to a dark blue.

"But this building, I mean, when we were making it, it was like jazz," he says. "It was what we started calling, 'Improvisational Architecture.'"

He had over a hundred volunteers from Rocky Mountain Youth Corps and juvenile detention teens. Prisoners came in on the work crew.

"It was hard to get them to accept me at first," Mark says. "But I told them about my past. How I learned to walk in a prison. How my dad was a bank robber and a career criminal. How I came out of that subculture."

During the build, Mark often needed to look to that subculture, which tends to thrive on improvisation and the taking advantage of opportunity. One day, someone called the crew from Santa Fe to say they'd acquired some high-quality windows from a million-dollar home. The people building the home didn't like the color of the metal frames, so they sent them back. The company sold them to Mark's project at half the price. But this changed the dimensions of the windows. So Mark had to change the plans.

"We had to throw out Plan 5 and go to Plan 6," Mark says. "And that would happen all the time. We would get new materials all the time. Like that right there."

Ahead of us stands a cedar column that seems carved by a film crew to stand in a sacred elven temple in a big-budget fantasy film. Mark and the crew found it behind the build site in a mud puddle and drove it down to the car wash to pressure wash it. On the small pillar supporting the column, an etched stone block reads, "The Dream Tree Project."

We walk to the main entrance. Mark explains to the social worker at the desk who he is. The social worker smiles and goes off to check before inviting us in out of the cold. While we wait, Mark points to the exposed posts and corbels. "All this was painted a hideous green. We came in here with an industrial-size sandblaster and stripped all this out."

The social worker nods. We are clear to tour the property. We walk outside. Some snowflakes fall. The mountains to the East are etched in dark-blue light as though the moon were shining on them.

We walk to the door of the Round Room, and Mark takes off his shoes. Two teens who we may have just nearly caught making out wave and quietly walk to the exit at the far corner of the room. The pair are dressed in fleece pants and sweatshirts. They hardly need them. The warmth is real in the room. It is a larger version of the room that had hosted the shamanic journey at New Buffalo more than a year ago at the winter solstice. And what a room. The circular space is large enough to play a game of half-court basketball. The sixteen-foot walls rise in a circle of more than four thousand compressed earth blocks (CEBs) from a machine that Mark and his crew had on site.

The compressed earth block emerged in South America when an engineer in Columbia named Raul Ramirez designed the CINVA ram earth press.[*] Ramirez built the press from welded plate steel. It sits on two steel skids, each about five feet long. On top sits a steel box that is a foot long and six inches wide and four inches deep. It is all simple. You mix your earth so that the clay and sand are balanced correctly—you want your earth to have at least 15 percent clay. You shovel it into the steel box. You clamp the box shut. You extend a steel lever over the box that also grabs a piston beneath; you press the lever forward and compress the earth. You take the lever the other way, open the box, and an earth block rises from the box looking as straight and uniform as a Lego block. No hydraulics. There is no electrical power. It is all run by leverage.

You place the earth block on a pallet. You let it sit for a month so the sand and clay can become one thing. Then you could take a .357 magnum, shoot it in the center of that block, and the bullet won't go through.

The earth holds it. In the block is where modern engineering merged with the style of building older than the nearly nine-hundred-year-old walls of Casas Grandes.

The Gaviotas community in Columbia, headed by Paulo Lugari, used the CINVA rams to raise dozens of buildings and could usually produce four hundred blocks a day. You can read all about this in Alan Weisman's book, *Gaviotas: A Village to Reinvent the World*. It is worth your time.

Something about the solid nature of the blocks, the connection between clay and sand, about the results of pressure and time, appealed to Mark's nature. He too had been formed by pressure, but that pressure had produced a thing in him called "integrity." Something House God knows. He decided to use the blocks.

Mark and his crew used a hydraulic-powered machine earth press that could churn out eight hundred blocks *an hour*. But this was all part

[*]   CINVA is a Spanish acronym that translates in English as "Inter-American Housing Authority."

of playing jazz with his crew. The Round Room was first planned as a structure built of strawbale, then experimental spray-on cementitious material, then conventional sun-dried adobe, then finally compressed earth blocks.

The windows face the four directions. The fireplace was built by a local expert stonemason, with a custom stainless-steel chimney. As the earth walls reach the roof, they curve delicately inward, meant to imitate the primordially comforting interior space of an egg or a womb.

"It took a lot of careful work to achieve that effect," Mark says. "All this was put together to try and give teenagers a space where they could feel safe. Shit, I wish I'd had this space when I was a teenager. Back then, I didn't have food in the house most of the time. I didn't have a bedroom. But I had the ocean. The waves were my salvation. I could use an inexpensive surfboard and paddle out like a king. I didn't have a bedroom, but I was doing the sport of kings. I wanted people to feel that here. And when we first got here to build on the property, it was just empty. A broken glass and dog-shit-covered backyard."

Mark lies easily on his back, takes out his iPhone, and makes photos by shooting up into the elaborate folding beams of vigas holding up the roof. The massive timbers seem to hang in midair.

"Those vigas were donated by a rich local architect. Who knows where they came from," Mark says. Mark and his crew set those vigas by building a scaffold so that they essentially had a floating floor on which to work. They raised the vigas on hydraulic jacks and shaved and carefully mortared and pinioned them into place. You couldn't slip a piece of paper between them now.

Micaceous plaster glows from the west wall like flecks of abalone. It is a place where the teens might hear the voice of House God talking about Strength, Wisdom, Good Health, and Integrity.

It was much easier for Mark to lay down on the floor when he was helping the Round Room rise up from the dog-shit-covered backyard fifteen years ago. I've been a movement coach while studying Brazilian jiu-jitsu over the past six years: getting up off the floor is a real measure of one's physical mobility. Fifteen years since Mark put in this floor, he can still hop to his feet with the litheness of a practiced surfer.

"This is somewhat confidential," he says. "But when we were building all this, I almost had a nervous breakdown. I had been executing, designing, and planning it all for five years. My wife had to ask me, 'Why are you doing this? You just keep losing money on this thing.' But I knew it was a unique opportunity that wouldn't come again."

Mark explains that the inheritor of the Knight-Ridder news corporation was liquidating all of his real estate and other assets. He owned the building and planned to renovate it. This place was one of the places to get rid of. The property was to be abandoned.

"We'd originally asked for money to help fund the project," Mark says. "In the end, they sold us the property for one dollar. So I had this campus to design and create. Many of my fellow BAC graduates would have killed for that opportunity. And here I'd decided to just cut all ties and vanish out here in the wilds of New Mexico and then this drops in my lap. I couldn't let it go. It was mine."

I ask whether the large square skylight at the center of the Round Room references the *sipapu*—that naval hole from which the people of Taos Pueblo believe we emerged to walk this world. Mark almost grimaces. "No. We wanted this space to be a respectful nod to those traditions. But we didn't want to co-opt anything. We just called it the Round Room and kept it simple as that. More than anything, it was a great architectural space where the two wings of the building could hinge together."

The carved wooden angel playing a guitar perches in the plaster window alcove facing east and gazes down mid-chord as though remembering Mark's trying time and recalling it with what might be called pity. Mark looks up at it with something in his eyes like gratitude.

"I am, like, the most unreligious person you'll ever meet. But when I'm in this space, I just feel spiritual."

House God knows something of the feeling.

We walk to the door and Mark slips on his shoes. It isn't until he stoops to tie them that he realizes they are my shoes. He chuckles and shakes his head free from the memories, the spiritual feelings, crowding in on him.

We walk into the cold wind outside. We run into June Martinez. She is one of my students and I know she lives at the Dream Tree Project. June's body is still thick with baby fat and she talks with a slur born somewhere between Texas and Arkansas. But her dark eyes shine with lived experience that has taught her the lessons of survival. She was born in a trailer on some unmarked dirt road near the Colorado border. She has no social security number. She has no birth certificate. She may have been born out of incest. She may have been sexually abused. She recently turned down a Thanksgiving dinner invitation from a local teacher so she could cook macaroni with her friends in the Dream Tree Project's kitchen on the other end of the Round Room. One of her teachers at the local high school said that June ought to challenge herself more in school.

"Miss," June said, "why would I want to challenge myself at school? My *life* is a challenge."

She comes to school every day. We smile and nod at each other as I walk by on our way to the central courtyard.

Mark notes the boxes of buildings to the south. They also are constructed of CEBs.

"This building over here really grew out of what we did with the Round Room and the kitchen," Mark says. "I had over a hundred laborers here. Three or four solid crew members who ran it all with me. And I know that driving me was always this desire to redeem my family. To make up for the pain that my father inflicted on the world. To show that the Goldmans weren't all bad. I mean," Mark stammers, reaching for the words with his worn fingers.

The cold wind shakes the naked Siberian elms. A fire-chested robin hops between the branches. Mark's fingernails take on the pink coral color of seashells. "It was all this meeting of the right people in the right place. It was truly a labor of love. I like to think of the Round Room as the product of the heart. And the dorms over there are a product of the brain."

Mark designed the blocky dorms, with their right angles and modern lines, with his mentor, Ned Cherry, who'd studied under Gropius, who had run the Bauhaus in Germany prior to Hitler's ascension to power. Art historians almost unanimously agree that modern architecture began on the drawing desks in the Bauhaus under Gropius's teaching. And you can see their energy here in the Dream Tree Project apartments, in the roofs rising and falling and the walls running back and forth at Teutonic right angles.

Once Mark showed what he could do with the heart of the Round Room, where he built what should have been a million-dollar project on a two hundred thousand dollar budget, New Mexico state senator Pete Domenici got him five hundred thousand dollars to complete the dorms.

They started in the late fall and had to bring the building together. So they had to do a "down-up" build. They put down the footings, then raised the walls and decked the roof while also installing plumbing and running electrical at the same time. When it came time to pour the slab for the interior, Mark picked a week of late February where they had perfect sunny weather.

"I ordered the concrete the day before. And that next day the temperature just dropped down to twelve degrees at night. It snowed eight fucking inches. So we had to pour the concrete anyway. I was here all night, in my sleeping bag in my truck, waking up at two in the morning to go inside to make sure these huge heaters were running. Then I'd go at the slab with this industrial-size mechanical float, smoothing it all out. I'd get up every hour and just smooth it again. If I didn't, we could have had cracking. That would have ruined over four thousand dollars' worth of concrete. We would have been in there with picks and jackhammers just getting it all out."

As they were designing and dreaming the building, they found it didn't translate clearly with the building regulators at the time.

"When we drove down to Santa Fe to pick up the money from HUD and we told them that we were building the structure out of natural materials, they looked at us, like, 'Why?' They had no clue about how much money we could save by using local materials. And they didn't understand the damage done by the premanufactured materials they were used to shelling out at a jobsite. We wanted the government money to go to the workers, not to modern material suppliers."

The design for the building often had to conform and shift with the laws.

"I took the building to the county planning department and they weren't going to approve it. They said, 'You've got this zoned as one dwelling, but there are four separate dwellings.' So I had to take it back to the drawing table. I designed four doors that linked all the separate dwellings together. So there was technically now one dwelling linked by several doors. And they approved it."

Mark raises his arms, as though still puzzled by the capricious mystery of it all.

"But we put in cisterns in the back to catch the rainfall and buried three thousand gallons of capacity. I'm sure they don't use it now. But we have it there for them to use if they want."

We walk down the small slope, watching for mud testifying to the approach of spring. Wind shakes a bough of red Siberian elm buds.

I once stood in the Dream Tree Project parking lot next to my Prius after picking up coffee at the Wired Café across the street. A *mą'ii* (coyote) strolled past as casual as any stray dog. Her yellow eyes glinted as she slipped into a nearby backyard, as though to say, "You didn't see nothin'."

I wonder if it was the same coyote Mark Myers and I had seen at the visitor's center at the Gorge Bridge.

"When you take it all together, it was a once-in-a-lifetime project," Mark says, almost staggering back in the face of the memories of the early mornings and late nights. "It was a million-dollar project we built for less than half that. That would be impossible for me today. It all should have been impossible. It all *should not have been*. It really happened because the right people came together with all the right intentions. That's what it was about. All the right intentions."

Nobody knows how deep those intentions have to travel before they find that dark, wet force we call "vitality," that thing that pushes trees skyward, that pushes people to invent ways to compress the strength of earth into bulletproof blocks, that raises people from sleep and brings them to a jobsite to raise a building. That has them up in the dawn, talking to House God and receiving his good essence. The elm and cottonwood trees are always up for the sunrise in Taos County. Should you see one, stand under it and ask that question as you touch the bark.

Perhaps contemplate how deep its roots might be dreaming under your feet. Perhaps contemplate what our own dreams allow us to sustain, from what pressures they achieve integrity.

If you're not sure what it's saying, go talk to Mark Goldman.

The Round Room inside the Dream Tree Project in Taos.
Photo by Mark Goldman.

Solar Radiant Greenhouse

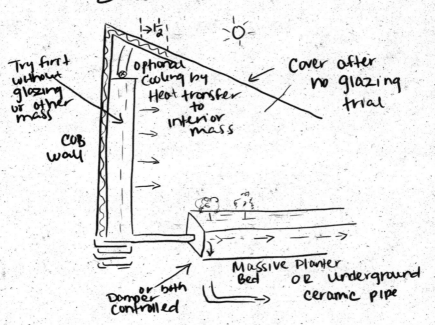

$\rightarrow 1\frac{1}{2}$

Try first without glazing or other mass

COB wall

optional Cooling by Heat transfer to interior mass

Cover after no glazing trial

or both Damper controlled

Massive Planter Bed OR underground ceramic pipe

NO THIRD WORLD IN EL RITO

The winter persists. The Rain Dog stays warm next to the wood stove. The snow falls and bright blue scrub jays screech from the fence behind my kitchen. I watch them through the wide north window. Paul O'Connor sees poor design in building a window to the north. But it is also beautiful. Winter is long in northern New Mexico. The owl hoots at the full moon in February. The voice of House God. The snow subsides during a weekend, and I drive the Prius out to El Rito to see how grass becomes a building.

El Rito is on some maps. It is easy to find. Drive up the Ojo Caliente River, which becomes the Griegos River. Drive through La Madera (Spanish for "The Lumber"). A clean, plastered adobe with a purple door facing the street has just been built by a construction firm from Santa Fe.

Next door stands the La Madera Mercantile building, part of it now barred up and crumbling back to the earth from whence its foundations were laid before George Washington was inaugurated as the first president. A small church vaults a white steeple into the sky. A small dog with a leather collar sleeps in the fallen cottonwood leaves beside a dry acequia. He is sleeping that eternal, rotting sleep of all dogs who have collisions with cars in the middle of the night. As I cruise past, a skinny German shepherd mutt lopes across the road and licks at the cold snout of the dead dog.

In the rearview mirror, the shepherd mutt paws at the fallen dog's leg, as though trying to wake him. What kind of day will this be?

I drive north up the river. The junipers and sagebrush stand along the sandy slopes of the mountains rising above the bosques of cottonwood and willow now gone gray and red for the winter. I go north past hay fields dotted with black Angus cattle and palomino horses and gray-hided donkeys. The road curves and reveals a gang of four magpies perched on an electric line overhead like perfect carved statues of obsidian, turquoise, and white shell. The road climbs. The small ranches and rundown trailers thin out. The junipers start to fill in with a few piñon trees. And then come Willy Groffman's "pumpkins," the orange-hided ponderosas that speak to the posture of House God. Some of the trees began sprouting when the *Diné* acquired the horse; they are at least three hundred years old.

The ponderosas break from between granite outcroppings. The fields widen out. Two trucks pause along the highway to chase three black cattle and a brown calf back down into the fence. The mountains rise in waves of ponderosa ridges and crest with granite. I take the left-hand turn into El Rito. The paved road runs past a one-room post office.

I let the Prius roll down the hill over the river and the *lindero*, the small acequia running at the edge. I roll over the one-lane bridge. A small whitewashed church with an ornately carved wooden door rises next to a polycarbonate greenhouse. Probably one built by Bob Dunsmore, the man I am traveling to see.

An adobe house with purple doors and shutters shines plastered in orange sand. To the right, a large mercantile building falls into the earth. Someone had spray-painted on the sagging wall "HOPE" in blue paint. Then, in red paint, as though at some later date, someone also sprayed "FUCK." FUCK HOPE.

Something in that is the gangster-language of Gravity: raise the building if you wish, but the force of the planet will pull it back down. Form the adobes, but build a roof to protect them from rain, that child of both water and gravity. Once the building is up, you will maintain it. Talk to House God. He will help you. If not? Hope all you want. Fuck you.

Up the street a pressure-treated lumber fence runs with juniper *latillas* in between. A large red metal swing gate sits between rails. Before a neat house hangs a sign showing a loaded and cocked revolver. Below it reads, "Forget the Dog. Beware of Owner!" Colorful wooden chickens, roosters, and potted flowers decorate the house next door. Laundry hangs from the rails of a south-facing porch. A yard sign reads, "¡Obam-anos 2012!" The next house over has a little white sign neatly painted with red letters that reads, "Asshole's Garage." A small red arrow points the way.

I drive to Bob's turnoff indicated along his neatly drawn map on a piece of yellow legal paper. A small dirt road leads along the river and veers left up a small rising hill. Fields dyed blond by winter nights spread south along the river. A flat field of dark earth has been sown with corn and beans that summer. The stalks are still up and cut. I roll up the hill past a red mud-splashed Prius. Bob walks out his west-facing door and waves. He points to a spot against one of the cottonwoods lining his property. I park.

"Howdy," he calls as I get out. He ambles carefully in his leather shoes, ragged jeans, and plaid Dickies shirt as though he's stepping on uneven ground.

He carries a test kit to check the quality of the El Rito's water system.

We shake hands and my long fingers get swallowed by his paws. He stands as tall as my six-foot three-inches and his thick neck could match any roustabout. Bob's a bear of a man. But his smile tells you he's a good bear. He raises his thick arms toward the house.

"Well," he smiles. "What do you think of the land?"

It is just supernaturally beautiful. Valleys lift into the mountains streaked with elk and deer trails. I know the Apache and Navajo would have fought over this hunting ground.

This town was established in 1776, Bob says, chuckling at the irony that while the British rebels that American history textbooks call "patri-ots" and "founding fathers" were fighting it out over things they called "states," the Spanish settlers had already settled here in the sure name of King, Pope, and God.

The people grew wheat and grazed sheep. They built four mills on the river just for making flour. Then Duke City lumber came in after the ponderosas and raped this area with a logging town. About six hundred people lived here at that time. Now there's about one hundred.

Bob's reedy voice rises through his wide nostrils. He speaks reluc-tantly, like an under-confident teenager, though he also speaks Brazilian

Portuguese and Spanish fluently. These are rush judgments, though. Bob likes giving his words time to settle. He goes slow because he's actually *listening*.

Bob was born in Brazil to a pair of hard-bodied, soft-hearted Presbyterian missionaries. His dad would ride the small paths of the Amazon on a donkey in order to preach the Gospel to the people there. He eventually separated from the church when he informed them that the Natives in this ecological Garden of Eden had no need for the myths and stories of a desert herding people who once lived ten thousand miles away and three thousand years ago. Bob grew up in Latin America and didn't move back to the States until he was in his thirties. When he did, the America he moved back to was shooting its young people on college campuses like Kent State, just a half-hour from Bob's campus at Wooster College, and dropping jellied gasoline on poor people in thatched-roofed villages on the other side of the planet. This—according to the president—had something to do with the Great Society.

Since then, Bob had lived in communes in the San Luis Valley, built solar-reliant greenhouses from mud, run greenhouses in Alamosa, rebuilt houses to sell on the market, and worked for the Presbyterian Church in their international programs. With the church, he and Julie were the first husband and wife to receive the same salary, at Bob's insistence.

Eventually Bob became the area director for South America and the Caribbean for Habitat for Humanity. He was overseeing builds and designs in Peru and Chile. Habitat was building nearly a house a day in Peru.

Bob's job with Habitat ended when the executive director of Habitat for Humanity, Millard Fuller, had pressed his First World crotch against a woman's butt in the central office in Atlanta, Georgia. Bob encouraged as many women as possible to testify against Fuller's predatory behavior. Twenty-one women in the Habitat offices in Americus, Georgia, stepped forward and signed an affidavit. It is unlikely that Fuller ever greeted House God at the door of that office building.

Fuller would tell people, "If you say anything, you're fired."

"So people would tolerate it," Bob says. "He'd say the most outlandish things."

Fuller's wife once joked to Bob as they bounced along a jungle trail in a four-wheel drive Jeep that "Millard had such a big heart. He just wanted to hold those Northern liberal women to give them comfort."

When Fuller was finally fired, she was also fired for enabling him.

The staff was happy to see Fuller go. But it didn't last long. Fuller sat down with Jimmy Carter and convinced him that the accusations were part of a political power play to take control of Habitat. Carter believed him and went on CNN to defend Fuller.

"We knew there would be sacrificial lambs," Bob said. "Fuller came back to the Americus offices with moving trucks and workers to move people out. So he got rid of me but good."

Fuller fired thirty people, including the international director, Rev. David Roe, who had served as president of Habitat for thirteen years.

"He was Fuller's best friend. And he fired him," Bob says. "It was a diaspora."

Since that diaspora, Bob has worked in seventeen countries, all the time chasing how to talk to the energy of the sun, how to talk to House God.

He had to travel to other countries. The United States, according to Bob, is not very good at talking to House God. He points down the river, toward La Madera, where the lumber company built the sawmill. They hauled out the logs with wagons but eventually ran a narrow-gauge railroad.

"Then they just took it *all*," Bob says. "Pretty much all the trees you see up there on that slope are second growth. It was a disaster. And the Forest Service didn't want to see it happen again. So that forest you're looking at is one of two 'sustainable yield' forests in the country. The other is in Oregon. But you probably know how the Forest Service has become all about the profit motive."

Willy Groffman's words speak in my head: *That's what the West has really been. One big drainage ground. One big extraction of minerals, mining, beef, and timber to ship back to the government of the United States back in the East.*

I nod. I'd studied the philosophical grappling match between the ghosts of John Muir and Gifford Pinchot that played out across the country. Muir says, "In the woods you will know the voice of God," and Pinchot admonishes us to use the woods for "the greater good" of society. Check to see who is president of the country. You'll understand who is winning the argument.

I relate to Bob the story I'd read in an issue of *High Country News* of families who lived deep in the forests of Oregon, right along the boundaries of Forest Service lands. The families reported Forest Service crews cutting down broad swathes of mature pine. Then they flew helicopters overhead equipped with long manifolds of sprayers that dusted the clear-cut with pesticides meant to kill any plants that would compete with the pines that would regrow on the land. The result was sick kids and possible damage to families on a genetic level.

"Oh my God," he whispers. His large hazel eyes get a faraway look behind his wire-rim glasses. "If I lived there . . . I would just chain myself to the landing skids of those choppers."

A lean, healthy calico cat springs to the top of the fence post. The calico stalks past the six 180-watt solar panels mounted on steel brackets set in concrete slabs.

"This was the most work I had to do here," Bob nods to the slabs. "My friend Santiago came out and wired this place. He's a good guy."

I remember Santiago. I met him the day I first met Bob, at a workshop that Bob led in the previous autumn for his nonprofit group, Heart Mind Alliance. We built a solar air heater from c-channel metal, glass, and silicone-coated insulation for under seven hundred dollars. We mounted it on the side of a local volunteer firefighter's trailer. Santiago wired in the thermal probe and the solar panel to run the fan while the rest of the volunteers enclosed the crawl space of the trailer with insulating foil. When we were done, the solar air heater collected the heat of the sun until the air inside the metal box heated to four hundred degrees, then the thermal probe tripped the fan and blew the hot air under the trailer, turning the floor of the trailer into a radiant heat source. It cut the homeowner's wood burning in half. Santiago moved easily through the crowd with his well-combed, wavy blond hair and white cotton shirt. His daughter—who had inherited that wavy blond hair—drifted behind him in a pink My Little Pony T-shirt.

"Hmm," Bob says. He looks down. "Wonder how that got there."

A dead mouse lies in front of the door. Bob picks it up and tosses it into the grass.

The calico cat watches from the other side of the solar panel. Ah, the little gifts we leave.

"Well, come on in," Bob says. "Comfortable, isn't it?"

When I step into Bob's house, it is so warm that I have to remove my Carhartt jacket. I remove the plaid shirt from over my long-sleeve T-shirt. Nine glass windows salvaged from old patio doors run thirty-five feet from east to west, catching the southern movement of the sun. The winter light speeds through the tempered glass and strikes the dark adobe floor where Bob's chair and couch sit against the north wall. The light strikes the three-foot-high concrete block Trombe wall running six inches from the face of the glass. The space allows Bob to vacuum up the dust, dead hornets, and dried flower petals from the plants growing in ceramic pots along the Trombe wall.

The Trombe wall was coined in the 1960s by the French engineer Félix Trombe. The traditional Trombe wall was a complete concrete slab leaned up on its edge that completely blocked off the light, while Bob's small Trombe wall rises barely higher than my knee and helps mitigate the temperature between the zero-degree winter nights and the warm days when the glass, glue, butyl tape, screws, and wooden framing are expanding and contracting in the swelling and falling of the forty-degree difference between sunrise and noon.

"It's a different concept," Bob says. "The traditional Trombe walls are just an inch from the glass. I just loaded all the glass myself in my pickup truck. It was a careful job. But this is essentially my heating system. So it was worth it."

We walk over the warm floor.

One thing Bob wants people to remember is this: the sun doesn't heat air.

You'll get this information from Bob if you ever invite him to your school. If you have a whiteboard and dry-erase markers in your classroom, Bob will take up blue, green, red, and black markers and sketch out these concepts in three-dimensional drawings precisely spaced, as though he's got them stored in some legal pad in his mind that he can flip open and consult at his leisure. His handwriting will have the careful strokes of a calligrapher.

There you see them, a ring of rocks around the center fire in a tipi. Bob reminds my students that when the Lakota or Comanche would lie around the fire at night they were kept warm not by the flames but by the heated rocks surrounding the fire. The Europeans in their large castles were not as cold and uncomfortable as our post-Enlightenment historians would have us believe. They roasted their great oak forests in large fireplaces that communicated heat into the rocks of the large hearths. The warmth lasted through the night. At the cliff palaces in Mesa Verde, the Anasazi used fires only for cooking. They built their stone houses facing south in alcoves that worked like solar pockets and protected them from chilling winds. The sun struck the stone all day so that they heated their winter nights with their stone buildings.

The sun heats mass. The sun heats *you*. Your arms. Your face. Your neck. Feel that now. Bob will repeat it: the sun doesn't heat air. It heats you.

He points to the floor of his house.

"So this is all adobe," Bob says. He holds up two fingers. "About five inches thick. Four tons of adobe. And below it is a one-inch rigid insulation and vapor barrier. So the floor is not directly rooted to the earth. It accepts the heat from the sun and moves it back into the space of the house."

This working with *Jo'honaa'ei* is the way of House God. He lives here.

The planet Earth is mostly warm. This is because Earth is mostly fire. Swirls of liquid fire. Pick up an apple. Cut it in half. Look at it. If you scaled the Earth to the size of an apple, the white flesh and the core would resemble the inner cores of molten metals forged by the first collisions steered by the gravity of the sun. This became our planet Earth. Back to the apple. Look at the red skin of the apple. That skin is proportionally the same as the thickness of the "crust"—those traveling tectonic plates—that hold the 315 million cubic miles of ocean and all the land on which we live.

The cold vacuum of space cups that fiery planet just like your hand is cupping that apple. There is a point where the cold of space can freeze down into that skin. In most places in the country, they measure that distance at around a foot and a half. In northern New Mexico, we measure that distance at two or three feet. This is called the "frostline."

Many builders will say it's a good idea to get down past the frostline. This is because most of the earth's crust is a constant fifty-eight degrees Fahrenheit, where those swirling fires conduct their heat up through the rock. But builders like Bob beg to differ. He'll get more than fifty-eight degrees of warmth in his adobe floor, where *Jóhonaa'éí*, the Sun, talks to *Haashch'ééhoghan*, House God. If he does, that heat will obey the laws written by the cosmos and chase into the cold rock below. Heat seeks cold and cold seeks heat until all is balance. Thus speaks the universe and the second law of thermodynamics, as scribed by Newton. The fifty-eight-degree ground becomes a cold sink, and the building doesn't stay as warm. Bob stopped this by sheathing the adobe floor beneath with one inch of rigid foam insulation. Now the heat has nowhere to chase but up into the space in which Bob and I stand with our jackets shed. Where House God waits at the door to the East.

The adobe dirt for the floor came from the dig for Bob's foundation.

I'm impressed with Bob's floor. Many builders will say he should have put a radiant floor into the ground. But Bob knows the perils of pipes placed into the earth. He has seen too often where the glycol or water circulating in pipes under the floor became blocked or leaked. Then it's go to the hardware store, rent a jackhammer, and forget about that vacation this year.

The cold winters here demand this kind of heating simplicity. But it is a simplicity that Bob chose. He and his wife lived in the San Luis Valley for nearly twenty years. He loved it there, but he often thought it would be nice to live in a place a *little* warmer. He loved this land when he first saw it. He came out in April that first year and lived in a tent. The next morning, it snowed nearly a foot. Bob came out of the tent and walked the line for the foundation into the snow.

Over the following weeks, Bob laid down a gravel trench foundation with washed, smooth stone. This allows underground water to pass through the edges of the foundation. The smooth stone is then capped with eight inches of screed concrete.

"The nice thing about using the smooth stone is that when you pour it, all those little spaces get filled in immediately, so you're not down in there with rebar trying to get out all the air bubbles you'll get with something like concrete," he says. "And then, when water moves down through the land, you don't have to worry about erosion, about that water impacting the solid concrete and eroding it. Instead, it just sort of *moves* through the stones and goes on its way through the earth."

We sit with our coffee.

Julie walks down from the upstairs of the house. She is Bob's wife and building partner of forty-four years. They raised three children together but the task seems not to have tired them out. Like Bob, she is a twenty-year-old hiding out in an old woman's body. Her silver and gray ponytail runs to the middle of her back. Her smile—wrinkled from practice—pushes up the crow's-feet behind her glasses. She asks where I am from. Where I went to college. I explain I'm here to work on this book about sustainable builders. About why they get out of the American affair and what it does to them. How to best create a house for the Navajo Reservation. How best to house the endangering species. How to talk to House God.

"Well, I'm glad you like the floor," she says. "The only mistake was that we started the floor in the fall. It took *forever* to dry. We would have been better off starting in the summer. But once it dried, we sealed it with pure linseed oil so it wouldn't off-gas any lead toxins."

"It's just wonderful, that adobe," says Bob. "And it's true that I didn't use it to raise the walls. But I put it down to honor that tradition."

We walk to his kitchen. It's a recycled brick floor set on sand. His plumbing runs below the brick. Below is the sand on top of insulation. Bob warms a mug of coffee in a pot of water.

"Here's your coffee," Bob says. "I added real cream to give it that good winter flavor. It also sweetens it without sugar."

Outside, the cold wind pushes aside gray clouds and the sun lights up the valley. In northern New Mexico, February is always making up its mind. That night it will drop twenty degrees as soon as the sun goes down. It will fall to twelve degrees Fahrenheit and Bob will let the cat in.

The coffee is good and warm. We sit in the living room. The walls of the house are strawbale—two hundred bales of barley straw loaded in from the San Luis Valley. Bob and Julie stacked them and plastered them with help from a local artisan.

Some people think building with straw is insane. It will catch fire. It will go moldy. Mice will live in it. It's grass, right? Hay? Don't you feed that stuff to horses?

But straw is wood. It's cellulose. It's small pieces of wood compacted together into a brick-like bale. And it's full of dead-air space. That means *lots* of insulation. Countless animals have survived many a winter sleeping on mats of straw in a barn.

They are also cheaper than bricks. At any yard, bricks will cost about $1.96 per square foot. Strawbales can cost half that.

Strawbale houses are an American innovation used since the early twentieth century. Mennonites living in Nebraska first created the technology, erecting high walls of strawbales and mounting a roof straight onto the bales with no other timber supporting the structure. Many of those first houses are still standing. And they kept those settlers warm during the nightmares of below-zero winter evenings on the prairie.

There are stories of people accidently ramming trucks into strawbale walls and not budging them. Engineers measure heat retention in a surface as an "R" value (for "retention value"). Your fleece jacket has an R-value. Your skin has an R-value. It measures how quickly heat is lost through a surface. A typical timber-framed, batten or rigid foam-insulated wall on a McMansion in a Philadelphia suburb has an R-value of twenty-five. A strawbale wall like Bob's can have an R-value of forty-five or fifty. It also dampens sound from the outside much more effectively.

Most strawbale homes are built like post-and-beam timber houses. You lay the concrete foundation. But then you build up a small concrete wall called a *stem wall.* You then mount to the top of the wall 2×4 boards running parallel to each other, spaced apart like skis. These boards are called *curb rails,* and they keep the bales from touching the concrete. Then you build up the timber skeleton with posts and beams. Once Bob had the skeleton up, strawbale builder Burke Denman led the strawbale workshop. Burke had been building strawbale structures for decades. He wrote the strawbale building codes for the state of New Mexico. He and Bob had lived at the same commune for a couple years. Since then, Burke had owned Santa Fe Stone and the Denman Construction Company. He built the first strawbale *hoghan* on the Navajo Reservation. He helped the grass work with House God. After the workshop, though, Burke never came back to Bob's house. He was too busy running his three-hundred-man crew at his construction company. He developed a tumor in the side of his head. Burke knew it was a tumor caused by his own cellphone. After his funeral, his family buried him just up the road in La Madera.

"He never came back to visit," Bob says. "And now he's buried about nine miles from our house."

Bob's neighbor in La Madera also happens to be one of the foremost micaceous plasterers in the world. He came to Bob's strawbale house, looked to the north wall, and was imagining, *Ah, I see a shade of orange here.*

The walls glimmer with a spectral orange light from the plaster filled with chips of mica. A virgin of Guadalupe (*Tonancín* to the Mesoamerican tribes) hangs from her place against the north wall. To the left of the door, a blue tile holds a glowing, grinning yellow sun radiating ropes of fire. In a small alcove—or *nicho*—above where Bob and I sit with our coffee is a picture of his firstborn son, Aaron Eli. A juniper branch and small pinecone rest in the *nicho* with the picture.

Aaron Eli Dunsmore was homeschooled most of his life by Bob and Julie. He was selected as one of the top high school scholars in the nation and honored by Noam Chomsky and Dr. Robert Bakker at a banquet in Montana. He was accepted to Purdue University in 1993 and studied virtual reality–based surgery techniques. And none of that stopped him from leaving this world when one of his friends fell asleep at the wheel going over sixty miles an hour on a median outside Rawlings, Wyoming.

Aaron had a premonition about his death he shared with Bob just weeks before. The friend who survived the wreck said they'd tried to stop and sleep three times. But each time, they would be woken up and nearly trampled by the cows along the highway.

Aaron Eli gave a speech at his high school graduation just a year before. The title was, "Do Not Be Roadkill on the Highway of Life."

"I talk to him every day," Bob says. "I know he's always been with me. He was with me when I was in the villages in El Salvador and in Bolivia. I knew they had lost sons in these insane conflicts with the United States. And I could say I had lost a son to this same madness. The automobile. This high-speed way we're traveling to where we don't even want to be. And when we take that path, we're all conquered. All we can do is to survive with dignity. All we can do is to put down one brick at a time. So that pain . . . That pain was often my way into the community."

Julie tells Bob she needs the long phone cord. She asks if he could enlarge the hole up in the second story to run the cord down.

"Sure," he says, slowly walking to a small tool case in the turquoise-painted bathroom. He returns with a DeWalt drill and walks upstairs carefully and drills with a 5/8" bit through the wooden floor. Julie pulls the cord through the hole and sets it in the phone. She asks if I can balance the phone on the inverter mounted on an iron-strapped utility rack on the inside of the micaceous wall. I let her know I've got it.

Julie leaves to prepare for a conference call at the community center she helps to run in El Rito.

Bob comes back down with the drill and sets it back in the case. "So," he says, "shall I give you the tour?"

We walk out the east door and Bob motions up to the eaves. "Here, let me show you the roof. This is killer, man."

Bob set the roof at a steep pitch, in the tradition of high-elevation houses in northern New Mexico. But, under its sheathing of chocolate-brown Pro-Panel to absorb heat, the roof is also a solar cooler and heater.

Bob sheathed the roof with plywood. This is typical in the industry. But then he did something different: he laid down inch-thick boards in a lattice-like framework so that each channel of the Pro-Panel metal was elevated off the plywood base by one inch. This simple detail creates dozens of air channels running to the top of the roof. In the summer, when the sun cooks the roof from overhead, hot air builds up inside the channels and turns them into small chimneys. Bob opens a pair of vents at the end of his gables, and the heat is exorcised into the outdoors. In the winter, he can close the vents and trap all the warm air from the roof to create a heat pocket for his space below. He needed to drill holes at the top of the roof, however, to make sure it didn't build up any pressure and warp the building.

We walk out the east door to where Bob has dug up the dark earth as though planning another excavation, where he will put in a flagstone patio and a hot tub heated by a snorkel heater made from cast iron.

Now Bob gets excited. He takes me to see the invention he brought back from Bolivia.

We wander to the edge of the dilapidated barn. Bob lifts a roll of tar paper draped over a long object barely larger than an engine block.

"This is going to change everything," he says. A metal frame holds a pair of rollers set on axles so they run on top of each other. It looks like the manual wringer on an old washing machine. But these wringer rollers are ribbed with welded steel paddles running the length so they resemble extremely wide cogwheels. Bob grabs the simple crank on the other end, made from welded plumbing pipe.

"The mouth is sized to the standard roll of chicken wire. You just place the end of the chicken wire into the mouth there and it just feeds itself. I can do about fifty feet with a minute of cranking."

This little machine—invented and built by Ron Davis in La Paz, Bolivia—creates a corrugated chicken wire. The reason Bob had the rollers shipped up from Bolivia and refabricated in a machine shop while he was living with his daughter in Atlanta is that this chicken wire that gets formed into waves by the machine now has *dimension* that allows it to be strung around the inside of a pit and layered with cement. The wire acts like a flexible matrix that creates more triangulated tension than rebar inserted into the concrete. This means you can dig a cylindrical pit on your property and create a one-inch thick, one-thousand-gallon cistern to catch rainwater to help you grow a garden or tap into your own drinking water. And you can do that for about $150.

"It also works great for repairing acequias damaged by gophers," he says.

He gazes off toward the southern mountains. Bob mentions he's in contact with different business people about marketing rolls of pre-waved chicken wire. He has a particular millionaire who's most interested.

"Look down in that field. That's where you'll see another amazing use for this wavy chicken wire. It's just going to change so many human lives."

Down in the field stands a small greenhouse that Bob plans to revive and line with wavy chicken wire. "It'll be way better than those thick, awkward concrete sleeves they just drop in. And a mere fraction of the price."

Next to the wellhouse is Bob's little invention. It's a plastic outhouse, like the kind you'd see outside a rock concert or a construction site.

"Do you know the leading cause of child mortality in the developing—ah, no, I wouldn't say that—in the *developed* world?" Bob asks. "Deep-pit latrines. People digging those deep gauge pits and as soon as you let that shit mix with urine, that's where you get the pathogens building up. Most of the people I met who lived out in El Salvador would just go wherever. But when people would live in tight villages, the pathogens would get plunged by gravity down into the earth and infect the water table. I talked with this woman who is interested in this work I'm doing. She says to me, 'I lost three brothers to sickness from a pit latrine outhouse.' This was in rural southern Illinois. And this woman is a millionaire today. It's a pretty simple set up. I created the bottom of that outhouse with the wavy chicken wire. So it's super light and very strong. I took some boards and attached them to the bottom as skids. This way you can just dig a shallow pit. Once it's full, you just move the outhouse, bury the stuff, then by the time you've filled the other hole, the crap has dried out and it's free of disease. You can just move the outhouse back. Then back again. It solves everything."

We head back in to finish our coffee at the table.

Bob had lived in Bolivia for nearly four years and produced a documentary called *Bolivia Beyond Belief* that you can easily find on YouTube. In the film, he praises the traditional coronation of the president, Evo Morales, and the dictates of a truly collective, socialist society.

"True wisdom is a collective thing," Bob says. "It's not an individual thing. It's like salvation."

He saw this play out in an old man in one of the villages who was able to keep his potatoes from spoiling much longer than anyone else.

Bob went out to study what the old man was doing. The old man had dug a fifty-foot-wide pit and had put down a layer of leaves from the forest. Then he would lay the potatoes. Then he would lay down the leaves. And the bugs wouldn't eat the potatoes.

Bob learned after talking with the old man that the leaves had a type of insecticide in them and that his ancestors had always used them as a way to bug-proof their food reserves.

"There's no way he could have learned that all by himself," Bob said. "His ancestors laid all that down, one brick at a time."

He had a friend in Bolivia who had developed pulmonary edema. It would have cost him at least two thousand dollars to take care of the problem in America. In Bolivia, it cost him $3.60.

"That's socialism," Bob says. "Illnesses don't bankrupt people there. It's people before profit."

That rule reversed when Bob came back to live in America.

He and Julie moved to Atlanta to be close to their daughter. Bob was sickened by the place. The congestion. The cramped space. There is no country when the land becomes a succession of backyards. And slavery left a lot of anger in the air. Julie and Bob bought a house in Louisville, Kentucky, built out of the way of the Mississippi River flood plain, where he planned to retire. He would be close to the Presbyterian Church headquarters in Louisville. He thought they could volunteer and design curriculum to help the mission staff avoid some of the mistakes people made in the field.

Bob saw the Presbyterians giving inappropriate technology to the people. The Presbyterians might go in and build a new clinic, but they didn't involve the community. They didn't bring in local talents or municipal government to ensure the staffing and maintenance so the clinic would remain a viable option. As soon as they left, most of it was ripped out and destroyed. The people from the community would come in and replace the equipment with local products that could be maintained there in that country.

Bob knew that the Presbyterians or any sort of NGO down there had to be very careful about who they were going to put in charge of the new water plant or the hospital. In that society, the people have relatives who are electricians, plasterers, and carpenters who weren't able to participate in creating the building because the gringos brought in their own people.

"Julie and I got in trouble with the church when we noticed some of their own people were making some really bad decisions down there," Bob says. "We had one pastor down there who used eighty thousand dollars to rent an office in the capital of La Paz. He had a secretary there who turned out to be his mistress. And then she started blackmailing him. His wife didn't know where the hell he was."

"We sort of blew the whistle on him. And the church did very little."

This hurt Bob, since he holds the Presbyterian Church in high regard. He reminds me that the Presbyterian Church is one of the founding churches of this country. The writers of the Constitution—many of whom were congregants in the Presbyterian Church—based the bicameral legislature on the deacons-and-elders structure of the church.

We sip coffee.

"It's really a shame," he says. "But that mindset has been around a long time. My dad was a missionary in Brazil, where I was born. And he could tell the people when he went to them, 'You know, I'm here for *you* to evangelize me.' He didn't see savages running around in a jungle. He saw a creative, vibrant, faith-filled people who created samba, bossa nova, capoeira, and *carnaval*. My dad would go to these assemblies and people would ask, 'How many souls did you save down there this year?' He would say, 'I would say at least one. Me!'"

One soul is all it takes. And once that one soul meets other like-minded souls, they can work toward a better world here on Earth. Over more sips of coffee, we talk about his new project: a bioregional council in Rio Arriba county. The way Bob sees it, the world that could freely burn carbon fuels, exhaust the soil, and pass on the costs to the next generation is over. Period. If we want to survive as a species. If we want to be able to talk to House God.

But the majority of money and capital in America is invested in corporations that have no incentive to reverse carbon fuel use, preserve soil, or think long-term. Bob thinks we should wrest control from corporate forces using councils focused on regional issues. These councils could then combine with other councils and put together votes on the long-term, biological issues of land, water, soil, and energy, whose consequences long outpace the thinking abilities of a corporate board fantasizing in quarterly economic cycles. It is a vision in the essence of House God, of Strength, Wisdom, Good Health, and Integrity.

This all leads to Bob's political treatise: "The Great Mandate." It is a document with the essence of House God. If the United States federal government actually followed the Great Mandate, it would return much of the power to the people.

"We need to give the power to the people," Bob says. "That's the only way we're going to get out of this mess: when local people start making wise, long-term decisions about their water and soil. People will no longer say, 'Oh, just let the market solve the problem.' That's a way of thinking that isn't designed to heal anything. For example, if a guy is bottling water from an upper mountain stream and selling it, he probably doesn't care about making sure his neighbors have clean drinking water downstream. In fact, it's not in his interest to do so. That way, more people will buy his water. He's driven by the profit motive."

Bob saw this profit motive destroying people's souls in Latin America. Tribes living far out in the jungle had to have their water trucked in. Bob went to them and asked how their ancestors got clean drinking water before Europeans showed up. The people had never had a foreigner come in and actually ask them about how they had lived before European colonialism. A man raised his hand and led Bob into the jungle. He picked up a big stone bowl with three holes chipped in underneath where you could insert sticks as legs to hold it up. Bob saw it was a bowl of pumice.

"You'd pour water into the top and collect what dripped down underneath," Bob says. "And I was amazed. That pumice took out giardia and bacteria just fine. But that's working *through* the people. That's what I was especially good at: going into an area, listening to what the people needed and could do on their own, and then helping with that. Otherwise, the people don't do it. Nothing lasts."

During his travels, Bob never pretends to be a technical expert.

"What I am an expert at is drawing out the indigenous wisdom there.

That's what's more important. That's hope. Having a vision. It's not about the mind. It's about the heart. In a way, it helped that I didn't have a technical agenda. It's important to not even set an agenda. They've all been told what to do by the white man for decades and decades."

Bob saw this when he traveled twice to India to help with food production and to teach them how to use solar heat to maintain biogas digesters.

He also helped the people figure out how to use waste rice hulls to preserve their potato crop. The hulls did what Bob thought they would do: they worked like a natural cellulose insulation and trapped the heat so the potatoes lasted months longer and farmers made more money and avoided drowning in their competition with big, tax-welfare agribusinesses in the United States.

Bob also worried about trees in El Salvador. During his seven years in that country, Bob wrote his autobiography because he wasn't sure he was going to leave the country alive during the late 1990s. Family and political vendettas chewed through communities and left corpses in shallow holes in the jungles. Workers and aid workers were kidnapped, extorted, and sometimes killed.

Bob asks if I'm hungry for lunch. I almost check my watch to see the time. But I've given up watches.

Last Christmas Day, I had visited Taos Pueblo for the Deer Dance. The young men and women of Taos Pueblo paraded in the skins and erect heads of deer, elk, buffalo, and mountain lion. The young women— many of them my students from the high school—shook gourd rattles and waved blue and red macaw feathers. The black-and-white-streaked clowns entered the dance with hawk wings tied in their hair. They were thanking the animals for their lives. And they were welcoming them back to the world of the living, where they would give up their lives again in order to feed the people through the winter.

The people were asking for life. The air was less than ten degrees. My feet were blocks of ice, and I shivered under my winter coat. The women danced in sleeveless, woven dresses. Under their deerskins, the men danced in loincloths and their naked skin shined with black, white, and red clay paint. Their breath made clouds in the air.

Had Joseph Campbell been standing next to me, he would have said we were in the "dream-time." It is a way of seeing that understands *Haashch'ééhoghan*, House God. We were looking thousands of years into the past. I had bought a new watch when I moved to Taos, a nice, reliable Timex Expedition. After the dance, I looked down to check it. The face was dead gray crystal. It never worked again. I haven't worn a watch since.

I keep Bob company while he cooks uncured hot dogs in a cast-iron skillet at his stove. We talk about his two surviving kids. His son is a financial advisor who just moved to Aurora, Colorado. He and his wife had a baby a few days ago. Today they named her Anagene.

"I'm not sure where his math ability came from," Bob says, stirring the hot dogs. "I can't even balance a checkbook."

His daughter is a full-time mom in Atlanta. Her husband is a manager for a liquor distributor in the city.

"A few years ago, during the financial crisis, around 2008, he said to me, 'You know, these times of depression are really good for business.'" Bob has to laugh and shake his head. His eyes hold an aware sadness. He stirs the hot dogs.

He mentions how he's got to watch his feet and how he's had to contend with planar fasciitis the past few years. I mention how my neck had been giving me trouble since I tweaked it escaping a guillotine choke while training jiu-jitsu.

Bob sets the spatula aside. "I can help you," he says. "What side of your neck was it?"

I indicate the left side.

"Can I have your hand?" He cradles my left hand in his thick fingers. He places his big thumb over the flesh that sits an inch from where the thumb attaches, the hinge point from which our ancestors launched their fool's quest for global domination.

Bob places the thumb over the skin and pushes lightly, pinching beneath with his index finger. "Is it sore there? Feels a little tight?" I nod. He angles his thumb down into my skin, like a carpenter pushing an awl into a block of wood. "I'll hold it here for half a minute."

My hand slackens and I accept Bob's compression. A warm seep of blood pushes up into my limbs, like I've been stretching after a hard training session.

"Feel better?" he asks.

I turn my neck to the left. It's the first time I've been able to do that in almost two weeks.

Bob tells me he's been doing reflexology for decades. "I first learned about it when I was having back problems. I would just have this intense pain. I would wake up crying in the middle of the night. I had gone to a doctor and they'd referred me to a surgeon. A friend of mine heard what was going on and he said, 'Nope. You're not doing that surgery. Come see this reflexology person.' And that was it for me. One treatment and I was already feeling better. Of course, I found out it all went back to one of my past lives, where I'd fallen from the roof while laying tile on the Denver capital building. And that trauma got awoken when I fell out a one-story window when I was a baby in Brazil."

Bob repositions his thumb and forefinger. He pushes down again. The blood flows up like sap. Bob turns the hot dogs in the skillet. His thumb and forefinger pinch down over my other hand. I hardly noticed I'd offered it to him.

"I forgot to balance it out," he says. "You should always balance out whatever you're doing."

We sit and eat the hot dogs with romaine lettuce and some ketchup. No buns. Bob's watching his carbs. My neck pounds with energy.

Bob gets to talking about ORMUS—the white powder made from gold that was supposedly in the Ark of the Covenant. It was apparently a semiconductor. Some say it was manna. Bob explains that the ORMUS powder is a technology developed by an alien civilization that inhabits a planet in our solar system that orbits the sun once every 3,300 years. They came here to retrieve vital particles of gold that they've used to build an atmospheric shield that circles their planet and protects their atmosphere from dangerous radiation.

"It sounds rather 'out there,'" Bob says, forking in a slice of hot dog. "But after reading this stuff for several years, I'm pretty convinced."

A part of me wants to dismiss Bob as a crank. But I also know that our dreams and imaginations are powerful. Isaac Newtown—who sought the laws of the universe by rational observation, invented calculus to help explain planetary motion, and divined for the force of gravity by explicit adherence to scientific method—also believed that lead could be turned into gold and that the Bible held numerological secrets that predicted Armageddon. He wrote far more essays about religion than science.

We rise and stretch. I help Bob wash dishes. The beams and rafters overhead have that distinctive roughness that tells me they were probably cut in some lumber mill not too far away. They are often labeled "rough-sawn lumber" and most people don't use them in a house because they still have those little fibers poking out that can catch a spark or invite flame.

The phone rings. Julie's voice is light and pleasant on the other end. She asks if we'd like to come down and see the community center. I say sure.

Bob gathers his shoes. I ask him how he was able to build with rough-sawn lumber, remembering what Ted Elsasser said about how you can't use rough-cut lumber as a building material. Timber actually doesn't even qualify as a building material under the current standards. It's just something we've inherited.

"You know, the building inspector walked in here and said the same thing," Bob says. "'You can't build with rough-cut lumber. But . . . I guess we can let it slide.' He was impressed. He actually believed it better to build with local materials. But then there are laws, too."

I remember Paul O'Connor's building inspector. It's just how things work out here.

The lumber was cut at a local mill. This was part of the reason Bob's house only cost him thirty-five dollars per square foot to build.

We walk out to the car. Bob admires my Prius.

"Julie and I had to spend thousands of dollars just last week to get this gravel put down in our driveway," Bob says, nudging one of the small gray stones. "Our car kept scraping bottom without it. But I wouldn't give up that Prius. It's saved me at least ten thousand dollars these past years."

We get in my car and drive down toward the bridge. A dented GMC

Suburban pulls up next to us. It seems to have rolled off the assembly line just before the doomed American adventure in Vietnam that Bob spent his college years protesting against. I recognize the handsome, mustachioed driver; it's Servio, the contractor who had helped during the solar collector workshop in Ojo Caliente.

Bob waves and smiles. "Servio drives slow," he says.

I wait and follow him. He drives slower than I walk. No big deal in El Rito. The electric engine of the Prius runs quiet. Servio's chubby, brown-and-white Staffordshire bull terrier pants and wiggles from the passenger seat. We follow him over the one-lane bridge, turn left at the Catholic church, and pull up to the side of a small adobe community center that was once the mercantile. The old adobe had run bolts of cloth, bags of coffee, metal tools, and leather horse tack to the people of El Rito, who had committed their bodies to distilling the skyward essence of the ponderosa pine to viga and the split, plumb timber of the rough-sawn board.

The sun drops to the edge of a granite spur. The golden hour is upon us as we walk into the cool of the small library. It is all there: a dusty globe, Michael Crichton paperbacks, James Michener hardcovers, newer matte trade paperbacks of Naomi Klein's *This Changes Everything*, the antique map of northern New Mexico in Spanish. Boxes of books wait to be shelved. Julie has been certified as a community librarian and has received over fifteen thousand dollars in funding from the state to renovate the small center.

"We've been making a go at it here," Bob says. "It was rough when we first got here. There was an attic in this building that someone had converted to a leaky greenhouse. We went up there and found about twenty marijuana plants. Some hippies had sort of just moved in and were squatting in the place."

Bob walks me back under the vigas and the *latillas* to the *tracienda*, the room that would have stored the *yodí* (soft goods). The bars are still on the windows from when the building needed to be locked up. We walk into the book room. Servio's pudgy bull terrier catches up with us and I am well-versed in how to properly pet a pit bull. After twenty seconds, Servio's dog can't leave me alone.

We walk outside and meet up with Donald, a thin man with a rusty-blond beard who once ran a shop in Ojo Caliente. We step carefully through mud along the small, shaded south-facing porch. A handsome, green-painted sign reads, "El Rito: Est. 1776." Bob points to the Forest Service map on the wall. He notes how the community center is an important stopping point for cyclists on the Continental Divide trail.

"We have burritos and snacks and water," Bob says. "We're their angels." He stoops slightly with his hands raised in playful prayer.

Bob points down the hill to a port-o-potty he has mounted on wooden skids so that he can move it. No shallow-pit latrines allowed. "I ripped the bottom out of it. Whoops. Don't tell anybody. They also love that outdoor shower."

Bob points to a large steel garbage can that he had painted black that sits on top of a timber frame. The sun heats the black container and gravity drives down the water. It is a simple affair.

We say our goodbyes, I give Servio's dog one last deep rub on the neck, and I drive Bob up the hill to the water tower for El Rito. Bob has rigged a meter plate to the side of the tower made from an old railroad sign tied to an air-filled milk jug floating inside the large water tank. Bob is currently the man in charge of El Rito's water system and it's his job to report on how much water is in the tank. Right now, the meter plate is hanging near the bottom. This means the tank is full.

We walk down the hill and Bob's dark soil yields to our feet as we approach the creek.

"This would be a great place for the key-line plow. This guy in Texas has run it across his acreage. All sorts of seeds sprouted just from him slicing the soil and allowing it to breathe. The deer and elk are just

---

*   The key-line plow—or yeoman's plow—is a system designed in Australia that uses the "key line" in the landscape. The key line is the spot on the slope of a landscape where the farmer can cost-effectively keep water in the soil. The key-line plow supposedly creates trenches in the landscape that awaken seeds, slow or eliminate erosion, and retain water in the clays of a soil. Some in Australia and Texas say the yeoman's plow can deliver agricultural and biodiversity miracles. Others who have studied the plow have seen no benefits to its use.

flocking to that land there. There is abundance. So who knows what seeds are hidden down in the soil until we invite them up? That's just a different way of thinking. The demand for abundance. It's in the Great Mandate."

It goes back to Bob's vision of reorganizing the country around small regional councils that create laws and mandates locally and speak their power to the state-level leaders. They will speak for House God. Bob helps organize a Rio Arriba Council from all the points along the Rio Arriba county line, from Tres Piedras down to Estancia. They have been using the talking stick* and Bob is impressed with its effectiveness.

Through these councils, many people would make many demands; this would come forward in a Northern New Mexico council. Then those demands would go forward into a state council, where everybody would vote with a cellphone. Then it would go forward to a national council.

"But I understand the great irony in all this," Bob says. "For goodness sake, we're talking about councils and direct democracy and just over the mountain sits Los Alamos labs, where a national government that doesn't answer to the people forged in secret a weapon that they used to kill hundreds of thousands of people. And they didn't even bat an eye. I mean, here we are in Rio Arriba county. We're one of the poorest counties in the country. We've got the highest per capita heroin usage in the United States. And we're right next to Los Alamos County, which is the wealthiest county in the state. And one of the wealthiest in *the country*. So I understand what we're up against."

I tell Bob I'm aware of the strange stories of the land. I share the story of the dog hit beside the road while driving through La Madera, how it's one of the saddest things I've seen in years.

"Oh, I've got a sadder story for you," Bob says. His hazel eyes look over the dark soil, still green in some places with the last grass able to

---

* The talking stick was commonly used in East Coast tribes to mitigate democratic debates. In a simple gesture, the person holding the stick in a council can speak. Those not holding the stick can listen. Everyone is in attendance to hear each other's words.

withstand the frost. But he's also looking nowhere but to the fires of his memory. Willy Groffman would say he's juggling.

Bob tells of a friend who ran over his own daughter three weeks ago. He was getting into his van to go to work and his daughter came running around the back. He didn't see her. He backed up. And.

Bob motions with his hand. His hand goes up. His hand drops down. It is a tire running something over.

And.

The man was in Bob's driveway a few days ago in the middle of the night. High on painkillers, heroin, and who knows what else. Calling out that he just wanted to die, to have it all end.

Bob tells me I've met the man. It is Santiago.

Santiago. The solar electrician who helped us mount the solar air heater to the side of the trailer during the workshop that fall. Santiago, who moved easily through the crowd with his well-combed, wavy blond hair and white cotton shirt. His daughter—who had inherited that wavy blond hair—drifted behind him in a pink My Little Pony T-shirt.

I see his crucifix shining against his white shirt. I see the alcove plastered in micaceous earth shining behind the picture of Bob's son, Aaron Eli, that dark-haired young man, twenty years old, glasses, with Bob's nose and smile. They are no longer here. They are fed to the altars of the automobiles. What does House God say in consolation?

"He just wanted it to end," Bob says. "And I can't blame him. There's not just the pain of the loss. There's the greater pain of having to keep living. I know that pain. And here I am," Bob sighs, running his big hands back through that snowy hair. "Here I am about to cry again."

Santiago has another child, a son.

"It's hard," Bob says. "I had to do the same when my oldest son died. I knew I had these two other beautiful children right in front of me. But the other part of me was, like, 'Just take me out of this world.' But my kids are why I sat down and wrote that autobiography. That's why I'm doing all this. I know it can go away so easily. Life. That's why I'm promoting the Great Mandate online on the website. For almost two months, I was removed from this place, from this house. I was up in Colorado, in the San Luis Valley. I went back and visited those springs at the hippy commune where I lived when I was younger. I had gone up there into the mountains and really thought to myself and I realized that I had to further the causes in the Great Mandate. I would work for the better world. I would do that for Malaya."

Let me tell you about Malaya. You can find her online. Bob recorded a video of her speaking and posted it on YouTube. She is one of those students from the Montessori school in Española where Bob volunteered. He helped them build a greenhouse and wrote a curriculum centered around the four elements of earth, fire, wind, and water. The students broke into these four groups and used problem-solving methods to rid themselves of the serious problems affecting the planet. They learned about what was in the soil and how the soil worked. They learned about the air and how wind was born from the solar energy of the sun. But then the No Child Left Behind Act took hold in New Mexico. In came the standardized tests and the fearful laws written to enforce it. The school administrators, like many others in the state of New Mexico, folded and complied. Out went earth, fire, wind, and water.

Malaya sits in a school library. Her smooth features, short dark hair, and intelligent eyes bring to mind a young Natalie Portman. She speaks from the anger that most girls stepping into puberty know all too well. But hers seems a righteous anger.

"We, as humans, we can change the world," she says. "If you just stop for a second, and look at the mess, you can change it. You have the chance to change it. You don't have to rely on others to change it. Get a solar panel or two. Or maybe wind energy . . . renewable resources instead of using the fossil fuels or natural gases. That's not right. It's resource depletion. Use the solar energy! Wind energy! It's all renewable. You need to stop destroying *my* planet because I live here. I want a clean world. I want to be able to go outside and not smell disgusting KFC or see a giant Walmart bag or a telephone pole. I want to be able to experience nature as it was meant to be. We have to clean up the mess that *you made*. We didn't want this. I want a clean world. I don't know what other people want, but you should want a clean world, too. Just do *something*, because if you were to stop for at least a *second* and think about what you're doing to this planet and think about what you're doing to my generation and the next generation . . . because without a clean world, there is no *you*. There is *no life*."

When you see someone like Malaya talk, you can't help but wonder whether the children are all our children. Whether House God might talk to all of them.

Bob turns to the portrait of Aaron Eli, set into the altar of the straw-bale wall on the north side of the house. In the *Diné* understanding, the north is the place where all things travel out of this world. It is a place of endings. But a place of reverence. The mica in the plaster on the wall glitters like something of another world. It is a skin made of earth and sand and rock. Human hands glided it over those stalks of straw, cut and killed to reap the barley that the Coors brewery in Denver will distill to make beer to lubricate the fun of the American affair, and though some people will follow the flow of that beer toward ditches and contortions of flaming metal on the highway, I am asked to believe it is somehow all just good times.

The north wall gives you a view of that cruelty. Plants tamed for thousands of years build their bodies to the sun. We cut them as the cold months and the solstice approaches. The strawbale is a compression of these many deaths. A pulling together of what was once life. And we make from it a wall that keeps us warm to live through the winter. To breathe the essence of House God in the doorway. In the Christian tradition, this might be called a resurrection.

"The Buddha sacrificed the heart to achieve the mind," Bob says. "Jesus sacrificed the mind to achieve action. I do not call myself a Christian, because that means you believe salvation comes through Jesus. But Jesus didn't want that. He wanted salvation from God *within*. It's our program. I can't rely on other people to do it for me. I describe myself as a disciple of Jesus. I feel he's accessible, a brother who will walk with me through this kingdom of Heaven. I can talk with him, just like I know I can talk with my son. I know my son walks with me through my troubles, my testings, and my rejoicings."

"You know, he once said to me, 'Dad, I think people have the Golden Rule all wrong: Do unto others as you would have them do unto you. I don't think that's it. It should be: Do unto others as *they* would have done unto *them*.'"

Aaron Eli's face watches from the wall. It speaks nothing of cruelty. If the children are watching from the wall and they can never really die, what do we say back? And what kind of life do we owe them?

Bob has to remind me to grab my jacket when I leave his house. It's cold outside.

Bob Dunsmore's strawbale home in El Rito, New Mexico. Photo by Jim Kristofic.

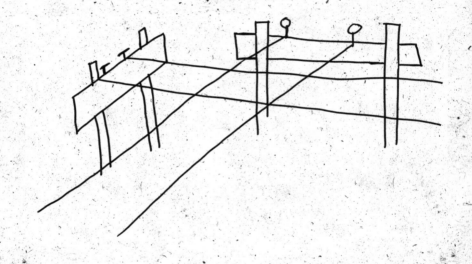

THE MOUNTAIN SPEAKS

In Taos, they say the mountain either sucks you in or spits you out. They say it is an easy, hard place to live. This is true. I can tell you why.

In February, I pass into my thirty-fourth winter. I have outlived Jesus of Nazareth, that Judaic lay-rabbi. That carpenter. That builder. I still hold the vision of finding some way to find that design, that method, that will help my relatives in *Diné Bikéyáh*—Navajo country. I don't want people living in trailers or Weather Kings as the climate breaks down and gasoline prices climb. That *hoghan*—that house—that will keep people from burning coal and burning down their forests to make it through the winter is shimmering ahead in the distance. It is made of adobe or cordwood or Earthship tires or compressed earth block or strawbales. It runs on solar power or it just doesn't need it. It is going to keep the *cháoł* (pinon trees) and *gad* (juniper trees) growing on the mountains and mesas. It's going to preserve the soils that the trees create year after year. It will all speak to and speak of *Haashch'ééhoghan*. House God.

Maybe.

I take these ideas to my relatives around Ganado, Chinle, and on Black Mesa. They point out new ideas. They give suggestions. They dismiss some ideas. They say, "What about this?" I write down what they say. I remember Bob Dunsmore.

I won't do this with the love of Jesus. I'm no savior or messiah. Our buildings are our doom. But they are our survival. And building them the right way can take us down off the cross and put us back on the earth. And that earth can easily be heaven. If we understood this, we'd be less of an endangering species, whose fangs leave no scars upon our kin. Rather than loose the wolf that will eat the sun and devour the sky, we might find a kind of wolf who can sit before us, raise its head, and there we might rest our hand. It is a wolf that will guard us as we sleep.

Some stone is laid inside the trench of a foundation. It finds the earth as surely as the bluebird finds the fencepost on the road to Willy Groffman's house in Mora. It is a beginning. I feel a pull to buy land. I lick my teeth. The American writer and naturalist Henry David Thoreau felt this same pull in his thirties. In his eddied classic, *Walden*, Thoreau wrote how men in a certain season of their lives are "accustomed to consider every spot as the possible site of a house." Thoreau had surveyed the country on every side within a dozen miles of where he lived. I do the same now.

I drive west toward the Río Grande Gorge, to the mountains toward Colorado, toward Arroyo Hondo, that valley where the rocks bear the petroglyphs of human hands, where hippies with hip replacements have called forth with drums some spiritual power I'd never seen advertised on television. I shake hands with real-estate agents, check well logs, sniff sagebrush in my fingers, collect soil in jars to test for the right clay content for making adobe bricks, measure angles of sunlight for solar gain, and scan for signs of bad neighbors.

I always come back to the first piece of land, just south of *Arroyo Hondo* (Deep Wash). The acre slopes north toward the base of a maroon hill that could have been uprooted out of the Ganado valley. The melted snow feeds ground lichen spread in bright, scaly green. The *cháʼoł* (piñon trees) stand fragrant and flexible with every succulent needle shining with that pale winter light.

I talk with the real-estate agent. I cannot afford this land and he knows it. But we are both thinking of the future, of what money I might save. He is a kind Taoseño, a boy who grew up speaking only Spanish, joined the Air Force, and became an engineer while ascending to the rank of colonel. We are men at ease with each other. We seem to understand that sacred quality of Purpose in the air. We each seem to know something of House God. We shake hands and he drives to his next client.

I stay and the *cháʼoł* (piñon trees) sway in the winter breeze. The broad head of *Dził Shash łitsoí* (Yellow Bear Mountain) stands helmeted in snow, staring off to *Diné Bikéyah*, to the West. I stare back until the flash of blue from the east.

And there he is. A mountain bluebird—who is all the blues of all the mountain skies of the world—perches in the closest piñon tree. A gray flash and his mate perches next to him. They look West. Two bluebirds sit in that tree above the snow. And the place becomes sacred forever. That is it.

Still, I have questions. I do not feel close enough to *Diné Bikéyah*. I must ask myself the hard question: *Are you really ready to live in a place where you won't teach Navajo students every day? Could you really do that? Let's find out.*

During my spring break, I travel to school districts in Crownpoint, Gallup, and Farmington. My last stop is in Cuba, New Mexico, that small village at the crest of the Naciamento mountains. I have been here before.

I had been with my stepdad in Kayenta for the night. Then over the Chuska Mountains, past Sheep Springs, through Shiprock, Farmington, and finally cutting the air on the highway near Chaco canyon. I passed *Dził Naʼoodiłii* (The Traveler's Circle Mountain), where the Hero Twins, those Monster Slayers, endured their training and became men with the help of the gods to make them worthy to endure a journey to the Sun, to receive the weapons and knowledge that would save their people. The white shell of the moon emerged in the purple sky like a glowing mountain. This was the night of a lunar eclipse. As I drove north along the Naciamentos, the moon was already turning the red-purple from the shadow of our Earth.

I try not to watch too much. The *Diné* say if you stare at the moon, it will start to follow you. I knew many *Diné* who thought it was wrong for people to ever travel to the moon. They enjoyed their *Star Wars*, but they never wanted people to travel to the stars. They thought it was a waste of time. When you keep your mind too much into the stars, you stop looking into the eyes of the people around you.

J. R. R. Tolkien described how the great civilizations of his imagined world rotted from within when their kings began obsessing over the stars and planets. They took their eyes off the earth and the water and the growth of the plants. Their people starved and their spirits shriveled. Even today, some Americans live on a world that is not the ground of *Nahasdząán*. It is not a place where House God waits. They don't know how to plant the corn or the bean or the squash. They watch movies about traveling to Mars or jumping through wormholes to some other New World in the heavens. They no longer need to dream of leaving the earth. They are already gone.

So. Eyes on the road. Coffee from the Apache Nugget Casino near the turnoff to Gallina, New Mexico. Within twenty minutes, I was glad I wasn't watching the moon when two smaller green stars flashed at the edges of the road. I hit the brakes before the *dzeeh'* (elk) had time to turn. Two cows grazed in the sagebrush at the edge of the road. A tall bull walked the yellow center line toward the Prius with the commanding calm of a state police officer asking me to pull over at a checkpoint. The bone lines of his eight-point rack of antlers stood etched in the red moon. I rolled down the window.

"*Yá'át'ééh Hastiin Dzeeh,*" I whispered.

He cocked his chin back, sniffing, as though to say, "License and registration, sir."

Then he caught my scent. He chirped and the rest of the herd bounded into shadows and sagebrush. The bull was gone before I could get out of the car.

The *Diné* roamed all over this country, far more than we think. Around the canyon created by the Chama River (that canyon is now Abiquiú Lake), people have found rings of stone corrals and foundations for what appear to be early forms of *Diné hoghans*. Curtis Schaafsma describes them clearly in his book, *Apaches de Navajo*. So I went out to find them. The lake had mostly ground the homesites away. But I did find some of the seventeenth-century stone corrals, believed to have been built by the ancestors of the Apachean people who would emerge from their sojourns and weavings with Tewa people as the "Apaches de Navajo" or the *Diné*. As I walked past one of the corrals, I noticed that black shine in the sand that speaks of obsidian. And there it was. I brushed the sand and found six more thumb-sized shards of the volcanic glass arranged in a perfect ring. I took enough to make an offering to *Dibé Nitsaa*, the sacred mountain of the North. Maybe someday.

I pull into the Cuba Middle School parking lot, where the archery range borders the National Forest boundary. I speak with one of the custodians, who is pouring dog food into a steel bowl for a female stray who had given birth to puppies five weeks ago. He has laid an old army blanket next to the space heater in his shed for them.

I walk inside and meet the principal. I do a model lesson with a seventh-grade class. The kids look like my younger *Diné* sister and brother. Most come from the chapters at Torreon, Star Lake, and Pueblo Pintado. I pull a bandana from my pocket as one of my props for the lesson on writing a paragraph. The bandana is covered in the red, white, and blue of the stars and bars of the American flag. One of the Navajo kids at the back of the class whispers, "This guy's probably a *racist.*"

I smile. My kind of place.

Paperwork fills an hour, then I drive back to Taos and write my letter of resignation. I do not need Taos. I do not need *Dził To'woł* (Taos Mountain). I will build toward the sun on the ragged edge of Navajo country in Cuba, New Mexico. Land is cheaper and they sell *The Navajo Times* at the local gas station. Deal sealed. I had my say.

But I am not the only one talking. Nobody thinks this is a good idea. This does not sit well with Ryan Daly, the owner of the Defendu Academy in Taos, where I train jiu-jitsu. Ryan is my teacher, a modern samurai, and his lack of faith in this new enterprise to Cuba gives me pause.

Ryan grew up with a military father, and so enlisting in the military was part of his destiny since his ninth birthday. He served three combat tours in the Army Special Forces with Airborne before he was twenty-one years old. He spirited away people's heads into a pink mist while a sniper in Iraq. He intubated collapsed lungs of his comrades, had both eardrums blown out by IEDs and mortar rounds, was exposed to Sabo depleted uranium anti-tank rounds while clearing the barrels of Iraqi tanks after the conquest of Baghdad, put his hands into bullet wounds and saved lives. He has hunted men to their death. He often jokes, "What does not kill you gives you a dark sense of humor and unhealthy coping mechanisms."

He has seen things.

He brings these things with him into the Defendu Academy.* The

* "Defendu" was the name ascribed to jiu-jitsu by Col. William Fairbairn, a British Royal Marine who adopted its use after World War II and gave it to the US Special Forces.

academy started with Ryan and his brother and me fighting on small mats in an indoor climbing gym he owned at that time. Many a spindly climber in sandals and reggae T-shirts raised many an eyebrow at Ryan and me in our Japanese kimonos and bare feet, rolling around on a mat and trying to choke each other unconscious.

That was the start. Now we have more than thirty students who train three days a week. Ryan loves it. He loves staying a warrior.

"I'll tell you, Jimmy," he tells me one night after class while we stand around in our sweat-soaked rash-guards and sweatpants, "there are four reasons people join the military. There's the Captain America-apple-pie types who want to serve their country. Some want to get out and travel and see the world. Some want money for college. And some people just really want to hurt somebody. And I'm not sure which one I am."

"One thing I do know is that most people just want to be comfortable, stick with the herd, and not cause any trouble," he says. "They're sheep. But there are wolves out there, ready to come in and gut the sheep with their fangs. Slaughter them and *eat their ass*. That's just how wolves are. And the only thing keeping the wolf from killing the sheep is the sheepdog. The sheepdog *is* a wolf. He's a type of wolf. But he's got a purpose, a feeling like he should protect that flock. He wants to use his fangs to defend, not to kill. The problem is that there's a lot of wolves out there. But there's only one or two sheepdogs. So the sheepdog's got to be a *bad motherfucker* if he's going to keep the flock safe."

I contemplate that Rainey is part border collie, a superb sheepdog.

Ryan lets us know during training sessions that his job is to make us bad motherfuckers. He laughs and jokes, but he takes that job seriously.

Mark Myers's words pass by: "This is what the new warrior needs to look like."

Ryan doesn't laugh or joke when I tell him I'm leaving Taos. His tears don't come easy. But they are here for me. He says he loves me like a brother. He says he needs me to help build the school. He says he wants to give me a purple belt, to make me a coach and a teacher. He says my decision to leave is going to hurt me.

I know I will be losing much by leaving Taos. But I practice losing all the time. Losing is an art for me. I believe in losing.

For me, the art of losing began in the basement of a health club back in Pennsylvania on the tatami mats of a jiu-jitsu school, where I walked in barefoot in my old river-guide shorts and a dirty T-shirt and a guy with a shaved head and cauliflower ears showed me how to defend a punch and escape a headlock. I drove home that night chugging water and fell asleep on the floor.

This was my first day in learning the art of losing. Elizabeth Bishop once poetized of how "the art of losing is not hard to master." But, like most poets, she was being ironic. Learning how to lose is a constant problem. Those warrior-servants, the Japanese samurai of the medieval world of the horse and the battlefield, used jiu-jitsu as a way to answer the problem of losing their sword, losing their balance, losing their advantage, losing their minds in a fight. For them, jiu-jitsu (the Way of Yielding) became a method of bending with the fight and maybe—just maybe—turning the fight around.

I came to another class. Then another. Three nights a week. I learned to control a man with my legs, how to break a man's arm with a turn of my hips, how to stretch a bruised rib, how to treat a staph infection, how to reset a dislocated shoulder, how to choke a man with my arms and my legs, and how to breathe before my own mind could choke me.

I learned to sweat comfortably, to submit by tapping my training partner's arm or chest before my bones broke or my blood cut off from my brain.

When you begin training in jiu-jitsu, your teacher gives you a white belt. Your job is to tap out when your partner puts you in a choke hold or a shoulder lock. You learn how to lose. And you learn that losing is a way of learning. And learning is a way to survive.

I brought my white belt with me to Taos. I used it for the winter, until my black belt instructor threw me on the floor and tried to kill me.

He reached in to choke me. He tried to break my shoulders and arms. I struggled. I kicked and escaped. I survived. When he presented his arms, I attacked in return. After five minutes, he pulled me up from the mat. He slapped my back and untied my white belt. He made me hold out my hands and tied a blue belt around my waist.

But in that blue belt, I learned that the fight is sometimes as illusory and shifting as the force of life itself. I learned that the fight is sometimes only survival. And to survive you have to learn. And to learn, you have to be willing to lose. Even the things you love most.

If you want to understand this more, come down to the academy, to the mats. Come join us. We are all down here, losing. There is no one here but the losers. And the fighters.

I turn in my letter of resignation.

That night, I join the fighters at the academy. Ryan demonstrates a technique. He weights his fist over my blue belt and pops my legs apart. When he does this, he gives me the gift of pain. When I was twenty-one years old, my summer of hauling gear and fifty-pound gas cans on boats on the Colorado River ended with my diaphragm tearing into a hernia. A year later, a surgery corrected the problem. But I still have the scar.

When Ryan drives his knuckles over the scar, he hears my flesh pop and give. I walk off the slight pain. My body is warm and the adrenaline flows. But when I wake up in the morning, it feels like Ryan has shoved a knitting needle in my groin and left it there. During the school day, I have to keep my hand up against my scar to keep the pain from throbbing. Sometimes during class, I have to sit down for five minutes because I think I'm going to throw up. There is something in this.

Word gets around the school that I'm leaving. My fellow teachers are not happy. I call one of my close friends from Navajo country, looking for support in my decision. He doesn't give me any.

"Do you have friends in Taos?" he asks.

"Yeah," I say.

"So why do you want to leave your friends so you can go live with strangers? Do your friends all have to be *Navajo*? Isn't that a form of racism?"

The next day, my principal pulls me into his office after school and we meet for over an hour. He speaks to me like an uncle. You belong here, he says. The mountain chose you. He doesn't have to tell me that. He owes me nothing. He is from old Taoseño blood. His grandfather was a silversmith. Most older Hispano administrators have flatly told interloping Anglo teachers that if they don't like the way things are, they can simply get the hell out of town. Just leave. But he doesn't want me to. The wound in my groin forces me to limp that night.

My superintendent calls me in my classroom. I limp beside her as we wander the halls of the middle school before a school-board meeting. She wants to tear up my letter of resignation. She hasn't even processed it. She asks why I'm leaving. I say I want to help on the Navajo Reservation. I also don't feel like I'm able to get anyone excited about solar technology at Taos High.

"That doesn't matter," she says. "*You* are excited. The rest will fall into place with time."

She tells me I belong here. She says she'll fund anything I want to do. She wants me to keep working, to keep building to the sun. She asks me to call her tomorrow if she wants me to tear up the letter of resignation. They'll have to decide on it next week.

Perhaps the final decision comes from *Tsiyaalzhahí*, who comes to hunt my bird feeder while the snow still freezes to the piñon boughs that afternoon. The chicken hawk with blood-colored eyes perches in the back yard near the bird feeder. I had held one like him in my hands twenty years ago in Navajo country.

They say the *Diné* have been here in this Taos country many times. They would ride out of the mountains to the west or secret themselves along the washes of the Río Chama to take the horses and sheep for their small settlements on the other side of the Chuska mountains. It was all a heist in a larger war of attrition against the *Nakaii* (Mexicans). The *Diné* came with sinew-backed bows they'd used to dominate the Hopi in the West and drop the Utes from their mounts and put them under the earth. They slung arrow quivers made of mountain-lion hide across their shoulders. The young men believed it good form to leave the tail of the lion on the skin so that it stretched behind them and gave them stealth and balance. It was a warrior's prayer to say to a young man before he went off to fight: "We want to see you, in our mind's eye, among the enemy, your war club swinging, your shield tight against your body, with your tail wagging out behind you." Many of these men grew up hearing this phrase at dawn: *Bił na'ahxidíí'diiltóhii niniyo ninalwo.* "The one you will trade arrows with someday is out there running in the morning." And they would go run before the sun came up, sometimes with water or rocks in their mouths to build their endurance. That way, when the Apaches or the Utes showed up, you wouldn't be a coward.

These were the kinds of men who rode into the gorge at Arroyo Hondo to cross into the country and raid the Tiwa people at *Tówoł* (Taos pueblo) and the village of Don Fernando de Taos. One of my students from Taos Pueblo had gone through the initiation rites in the kiva. He said that before the Spanish arrived, the Navajo came in war against the Tiwa. They were led by a war chief and a medicine man with red hair tied back in a *tsiyeeł*. By the end of the day, some Taos pueblo warriors had killed him with arrows, and the *Diné* dragged back his body. The next day, the fight continued and the medicine man with red hair was back. He had come back to life. He killed many Taos warriors, but finally fell to many arrows. The Navajos dragged back his body. The next day, there was his red hair shining in the sun, and he killed more Taos people. Then they killed him. The next day, he was there again. He could not die.

Finally, the Taos pueblo warriors dropped him with arrows. They dragged his body away. They scalped him. Then he stayed dead. They still have his scalp. My student touched it in the kiva.

At Taos Pueblo, they say that scalp is red as a hawk's eye.

Those red eyes of *Tsiyaalzhahí* are talking to me now. "You," they say, "you are the scout. You stay here and keep watch. *Ákódí.* I have spoken."

My leg twitches with pain as I walk out and sit on the boulder next to the adobe cabin. Rainey licks my face and whines. I raise the tennis ball and playfully act like I'm throwing it. Every dog I've had would run at least ten yards looking for the ball that is not there. Not Rainey. She stands alert and watches my arm. She cannot be fooled. There is something to be learned from an animal like this. There is something to be learned from this land that expects things of warriors. That they respect House God.

I throw her the tennis ball, she tears up the gravel road, and I call the doctor's office to make an appointment about my hernia. Then I call my mom. Mom says it sounds like I have a lot of doubt going into my decision. "When in doubt," she says, "just do nothing."

The setting sun lays scarlet and gold light over the mountains. That light is the bluebird's song coming with the dawn. It reminds me to juggle, to stay *chingón*, to build to the sun, to walk in Beauty. *Hózhóningo naniná.* To find that good essence of *Haashchʼééhoghan*, that Strength, Wisdom, Good Health, that Integrity. You move through it. You breathe it in. You take in his essence. And that becomes your character. Your actions. You step through the door and you are made into something every day. Something that can live in your home—your *hoghan*—and on the Earth. Forever.

I listen to House God. I decide to stay and scout Taos. It is not yet time to leave.

The next morning, I wake from my floor mattress next to the wood stove, where I sleep with Rainey. I walk out into the blue darkness at 4:30 a.m., and I feel like I am on heroin. My body sails in euphoria to the line of dawn. The pain in my groin is completely gone. I could jump and click my heels and I do. I thank House God.

In the Prius that morning, I drive through Taos with a mind free of pain. The sun lights the clouds pink and fire orange above the town. Rain splashes the windshield. I look up and a dawn rainbow spans directly overhead, pointing the way to Taos High. Of course it does. The mountain speaks. House God speaks. Message received.

I was going to leave to show that I didn't need any of this. I didn't need these people. I didn't need Taos. But maybe Taos needed me. It *wanted* me. When do you leave something like that?

There are still questions. Willy Groffman said he's always interested in the questions. Perhaps the Southwest is the Land of Questions rather than answers. Who are we? What do we really want? If we really want to build to the sun, if we really want to meet House God, what will we be willing to lose? Or to fight for?

In Taos, they say the mountain either sucks you in or spits you out.

In Taos, I hoped I would find out why.

Offering made to House God.
Lobo Peak, Taos County.
Photo by Jim Kristofic.

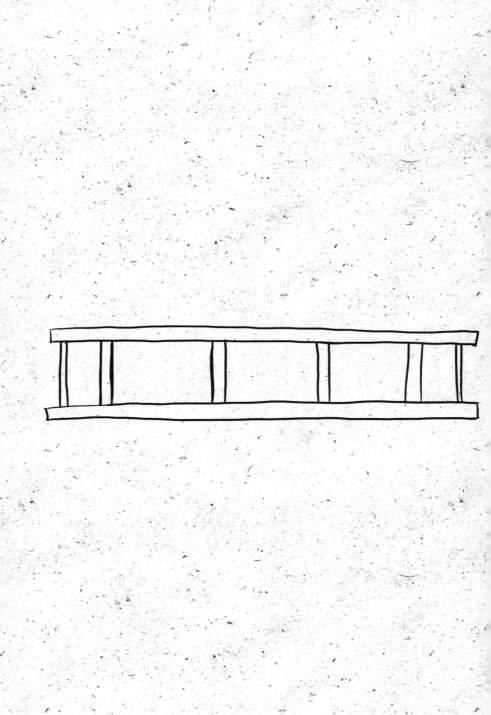

GOOD ADOBE DIRT

The spring passes into the summer and all the high school kids go home. The cottonwood leaves rattle over the Wired Café. Coyotes trot through fields popping with grasshoppers. The bluebirds sing in the dawn from the telephone wires. My wood stove squats silently and its red mouth quiets.

I arrive at Stacy Diven's house on a hot summer day. A jackrabbit the size of a small dog lopes between sagebrush. A bluebird dives off a power line and snags a robber fly from the top of a year-old piñon tree. I pull up the gravel drive and Stacey's wife, Lisa, directs me to the east side of the L-shaped pumice-crete home.

Stacy walks out with his long-sleeved purple shirt tucked into his jeans. His sunglasses hide his blue eyes ever darting to new ideas and suggestions. His faded University of Arizona Wildcats baseball cap has seen many summers working outside.

He waves. I wave back. I slap my desert camouflage work hat against my jeans and join him. I have come today about Stacy's planters built from adobe mud that he uses to catch rainwater to feed plants.

Next to the planter, Stacy introduces me to a mustached, dark-skinned Méxicano man named Louís Reyes, working trowel and hawk effortlessly on the edge of the planter. His strong shoulders bulge beneath his long-sleeved T-shirt and flannel work shirt. An athletic, handsome Méxicano young man works beside him. The older man pauses for a moment to shake my hand. Stacy explains in Spanish that I am *el maestro á la escuela*. The man nods approvingly. He introduces the young man next to him as his son, Rámon, or "Ray." Stacy explains that Ray is in college right now. He is studying to be a dentist.

Louís smiles with admiration at his son when he hears the word *dentista*. Four of his teeth are metal. Metal fillings glint silver along the edges of all of his molars. Ray smiles. His teeth are perfectly straight and white.

The planters face south to the sun. They swoop in the crescent shapes of the Pueblo Bonito houses at Chaco canyon, of the moon that will be rising tonight over Taos Mountain.

These planters do their own quiet kind of talking as they invite the rain to the soil. People talk about catching rainwater. But it can be expensive to bury cisterns, buy and service pumps, filter water, and run the plumbing. Stacy is letting the water and the sun do the work.

It is all part of a sacred ceremony, infinitely random but intensely purposeful. It all starts with the dust—those particles of *Nahasdzáán* (Earth) floating through the air, thousands per square foot, smaller than the red blood cells in our bodies—that take in the vaporized water from the upper reaches of air. Rain clouds carry millions of pounds of water. But that water clinging to the dust will only swirl as vapor in the wind. It will not fall as rain until it has condensed to ice. Only then can the force of *Nahasdzáán* pull them back to the ground where the washes, rivers, lakes, the soil, our bodies all chant to be filled.

Every living thing twenty-six thousand feet below the clouds hopes for this shapeshifting of vapor to ice. This transformation is not easy. I was taught in my science class at Ganado Intermediate School that water freezes at thirty-two degrees Fahrenheit. But in the sky, the water droplets on a dust particle won't freeze even at thirty degrees below zero. We do not know why.

But we're learning that many of the clouds in the Western United States can transform the vapor to ice with dust rich in iron and titanium. Dust scientists have tracked the chemical signature of this rain-chanting dust back eight thousand miles to its origin: the Taklamakan desert, a six-hundred-mile-wide eye of sand and glacier-pulverized granite, ringed by twenty-four-thousand-foot mountains in northwestern China, near the Kyrgyzstan border. It is the second-largest desert in the world. Local people call it the Sea of Death. But it is our Sea of Life in the West, the drumskin from which the rhythm asking for rain is beaten. In this rhythm, begun in the winds generated by the sun, meet the particles of *Nahasdzáán* (Earth Mother) and *Yádiłhił* (Sky Father). Rain is male and female. The *Diné* have always known this. And we *Nohokaa' Diné* (Five-Fingered Earth Surface People)—and the *gałbáhí* (rabbit), *tsétah dibé* (bighorn sheep), and *mą'ii* (coyote)—are the beneficiaries of this ceremony.[*]

Like the clouds made sacred to rain, the adobe bricks need that ceremony of earth, sand, and straw meeting with water. The water leaves and what is left behind is that object, that *bis tsédaazt'eego kin bee 'ádaal'inígíí* (adobe brick), that can make the walls that bend and flex with the expansion and contraction of the sun-heated day and the moon-cooled night that Christopher Columbo has seen gnaw apart so many houses.

Stacy builds his planters to benefit from this rain. The adobe is simple. It is old.

The planters rise from adobe. Dig a four-foot-wide pit into the ground about a foot deep. Get a pile of sand (less than nine dollars for a truckbed load at Taos Sand & Gravel). Get a pile of adobe dirt (earth with at least a 12 percent clay content). Get a bale of straw. Put them near each other. From here it is all *siete y siete* work, *tsosts'idi adoo' tsosts'idi.* Seven shovelfuls of dirt into the pit. Seven of sand. Mix them with a chopping motion of the shovel, holding the shovel out like a canoe paddle and angling downward. Add water. Mix again until the mud becomes thick enough to hold in a clump in your hand. Then add two slices out of the strawbale. Stab the straw into itself and rub the fibers together so they rip into each other and shred apart into pieces about as long as your finger. It is the same mixing method that built the walls of my cabin.

Mix with the shovel in that same canoe-paddle motion, up and down the pit. In the old days, when New Mexico was a Spanish colony, the settlers would dig a long pit, run water into it, and trot horses back and forth to mix the adobe with their hooves. Pick up a handful of the mud.

---

[*]   All relevant facts related about the sacred ceremony of rainfall are related by the brilliant Douglas Fox in his article "The Dust Detectives" in *High Country News*, December 22, 2014.

Form it into a little football. This is America, damn it. It should hold its shape. Hold out the shovel head. If you can throw the mud football at the shovel blade and it sticks, the adobe is ready.

You have to keep adobe off the ground if you want it to last. The erosion of snowfall, ice-cracking, snow melt, and water flow during a rain will carry away the outer plaster in the way that acid will eat away the enamel on your teeth. Stacy lays out the foundation for the planter with concrete blocks, buried just an inch into the ground. Then you start laying in the adobe. You do it shovelful by shovelful, *poco y poco*, and shape it with the shovel blade. Pieces of straw will stick out at odd angles. It doesn't matter. It's all getting covered over with a finish of plaster.

The plaster. Ah. It is all simple, something people used to do with baskets in their hands. You take a wooden frame with a metal screen over it. Throw the adobe dirt over it, and the larger rocks and stones will hit the screen and fall away. You don't want any rocks thicker than your plaster.

Gather the screened earth from your pit or your wheelbarrow and it is all back to the *siete y siete* work, *tsosts'idi adoo' tsosts'idi*. Seven shovelfuls of dirt into the pit. Seven of sand. Back to the canoe-paddle movements of the shovel. Add water. Add less straw than before. Now you will use the hawk and the trowel, just as Louís Reyes is doing here at the planter. Scoop and smooth, no different than spreading peanut butter on a slice of bread or icing on a cake. Let the sun cook it. Then do it again. Now the plaster is holding everything together and will weather the winter and need to be patched in the spring. But this is easy. You scoop what ran off and remix it and replaster it back on. Some say this sounds monotonous. But what else are you going to do with your mornings? Watch television? Update your social media? Film yourself doing the plaster. Put that on social media. Talk to House God.

The adobe eases a plant's survival in the summer. Drought, heat, and grasshoppers strip plants of life. But so often it is the wind. I have seen hot wind evaporate moisture out of a field within an hour of being watered by the flow from an acequia. The water needs to seep into the roots, but instead it spirits to vapor and will not return until it has frozen to ice in the sky and the cycle repeats. The adobe blocks much of the wind when the plants are fragile shoots emerging into the air. The mud also absorbs heat during the day and stabilizes temperatures at night. The adobe absorbs moisture and keeps the plants preserved in that stable state while they unfurl their roots and pulse forth the flowers that make the beans and squash for our stomachs.

Your roof gathers the rain for the planters. This works. Just look along the highway anytime you are driving through the Southwest in the summer. All the scarlet globemallow, yellow sunflowers, white daisies, blue chickaree, and tall grass are there for the gathering. Why? They are fenced from the cows and sheep grazing along the road, true. But most importantly, asphalt does not absorb water. So the rainwater runs off to the sides, and these plants have put their seeds next to a long ribbon of rain-catch on purpose. Your roof works the same way.

Every square foot of roof space collects 0.6 gallons of water in a one-inch rainfall. So a roof space that is ten feet by thirty feet will fill 180 gallon jugs if the sky drops an inch of rain in a night. The water flows into the downspout off the roof and through a flexible pipe that guides the water into a 90-degree street PVC elbow that takes the water a foot down through a perforated length of sewer pipe that slowly releases the water under the sand and dirt, where no wind can vaporize it and call it back to the sky.

So you put them in place: the concrete block, the adobe, the pipe. Now the rain will come. It fills the planter with water. It will overflow from beneath. So you build a second planter to catch the runoff. Plant what you like. It will grow.

We walk the southern wall of Stacy's pumice-crete house. The pumice is the gift of volcanos that sleep on the Taos plateau and beyond. The pumice-crete house was innovated in the late 1970s, when contractors mixed pumice (sometimes called *scoria*) with conventional concrete. It created a wall more than fourteen-inches thick filled with small pieces of pumice rock pocketed with dead-air space. That is the key to any insulation: a place where temperature can barely conduct and does so slowly at that. So you mix the pumice bonded with concrete. You pour it down into forms that create windows, doors, walls, everything to the ceiling line. There it is. You have your walls up in a day.

Stacy points to the solar collectors along his wall. Copper lines run through these rectangular metal frames coated in glass so they collect heat. The glass and metal create what meteorologists call a "solar pocket," where air movement can't affect the temperature. As in the pumice, in this dead-air space between metal, insulation, and glass, the temperature expands to over four hundred degrees Fahrenheit. Even on a thirty-four-degree winter day. As long as the sun is shining. The air outside is thirty-four-degrees. It doesn't matter. The voice of Bob Dunsmore is reminding me: the sun doesn't heat air. It heats *mass*. It heats *you*. That's the magic of the solar pocket.

Water coils through these copper lines under the glass and heat to more than 150 degrees. The lines run through the pumice-crete walls into Stacy's garage, which currently functions as a shop, recreation room, and entertainment room. The copper lines move to the central utility room, where the heart of the hot-water tank absorbs the copper veins and arteries. The in-running copper artery runs from the top of the tank and around the insulated water tank. The artery continues down into the concrete floor to create radiant floor heating. The other set of copper pipes run down and through the core to give hot water to the house. A small on-demand propane heater kicks up the temperature when needed.

We walk to the west side of the building and look out across the gorge dropping to the Río Grande, *Tóóh Ba'áád*, toward Mark Meyers out at Two Peaks, toward Navajo country, to the Chama River valley, to where the *Diné* had begun to emerge from the circles of the rock foundations of their *hoghans* built at the cliffs of the canyons. Where they spoke with House God and encountered his essence.

We walk to Stacey's "adobe set up," as he calls it.

"Now this here is how to make the adobe," he says. "You take the mixer. And you want to fill it with the screened earth that falls back with the rocks. That's the good stuff for making the adobe."

Stacy walks over to the screen. It's a simple set up. He's taken the metal joint pieces from old sawhorses and fastened them to eight-foot 2×4s to make a steep surface that can catch the adobe thrown from the shovel. The one-quarter-inch hardware cloth screen is stacked over itself and spread so one can easily run a wheelbarrow into the space. The rocks and thicker dirt that roll back from the other side serve as thick mass to make the adobe bricks. They have more aggregate and can take the expansion and contraction that are the ever-spinning war between day and night.

Stacy points to his simple adobe brick form lying in the dirt. A pair of 2×4s run parallel with six ten-inch boards running between them to create the standard-size adobe brick form that has been 10×14-inches since the Americans invaded New Mexico. Each end is stabilized with cut pieces of rebar that function as handles, but I can see that Stacy has also attached a pair of drawer handles at a more convenient length for picking up the form.

"My brother-in-law built this for me," Stacy says. "It's a real simple form. The standard adobe size is 10×14 inches. So you take this form and you really soak it. If you don't, the adobe sticks to the frame. Once you get the adobe mixed with a little bit of straw, you just start to fill the molds. Once they're packed, you have to lift it out quick or else it will stay stuck in there. And then you just repeat, repeat, repeat. I used this form to build almost all the adobe buildings you see here."

We walk under a raven sailing the blue summer sky. The raven lands atop the timber building Stacy is raising as a greenhouse with double-walled plastic. To the west is his utility shed.

"That place is a *mess*," Stacy laughs and shakes his head as though remembering a roguish yet reliable friend. To the left of the shed sits the trailer where he and his wife lived for two years while building their place. In the winter they would rent a nearby house for a thousand dollars per month. To the right of the greenhouse stands a large post-and-beam, gabled *ramada* shade house larger than some of the houses I've lived in. Stacy bought the pine beams from a sawmill in Colorado. The long *ramada* hosts a brick grill and large tile plates for a floor. The west and south side is set with a large strawbale wall, coated with an adobe plaster Stacy made here in his yard.

"You have to get the adobe up off the ground if you want to have any success with it," he says. "You also can't let snow pile up on it. That'll also get you in trouble."

He examines the northwest corner of the building. The adobe has worn away from a small flagstone stoop. Stacy has recently bolted a small gutter to the lip of the roof. He has hung this gutter only in this spot. It is only as much as he needs to redirect the energy of water.

Stacy has built over a thousand adobe bricks in his mold. He used them to build his tack shed for his two horses. We walk to it.

The interior of the shed is calmly warm, even though the night before dipped below freezing. Western saddles rest on wire mounts. Framed art of the southern Rockies hangs under the trusses above. Stacy has left the walls exposed on the east side of the building so people can see the adobe bricks pressed down by the concrete bond beam floating at the top. Stacy hadn't planned to build the tack shed, but when his wife and he were building their pumice-crete house, the trusses for their roof were incorrectly dimensioned and the order came out wrong. Stacy decided to use the trusses to build the tack room. But he theorizes that the tack room could be made into a livable structure by simply insulating the roof and installing a wood stove.

"It's about the size of a typical frontier cabin," he says. "It would probably work just as well."

We walk out to see the post-and-beam horse barn. We then walk back to help with the adobe plaster at the planters. We help mix and apply with Ray.

As we work, we talk. Sometimes in English. Sometimes in Spanish.

Stacy would travel down to Mexico every winter for seven years. He studied at a language institute his first year and his Spanish developed.

"What really taught me Spanish was when I spent the year walking around in the Sierra Madre with a man named Filipe Rosas," he says.

The men had a donkey and they would walk through the mountains. During the day, they gathered firewood and put it on the donkey's back. At night, they walked by someone's house or cabin, as though two visiting gods in disguise.

"We'd offer them our firewood and they'd feed us and let us sleep there," he says. "And the next day, we'd keep walking and gather firewood. That night, we'd give it to someone and they'd give us food and a bed. And we just did that for a whole winter."

"That's when I didn't have a place to be," he says. He moves his foot across the earth. "Now I have this place. This place is a *great* place to be. This here is good adobe dirt."

Stacy Diven's adobe rain planters. Photo by Jim Kristofic.

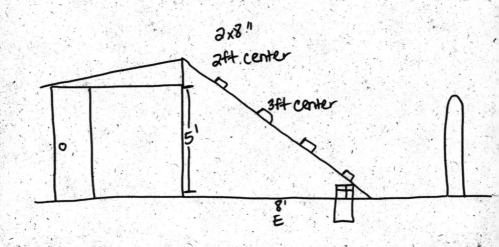

2×8 "
2ft. center

3ft center

O

5'

8'
E

HEY BRO, YOU MISSING A DOG?

The heat pounds in this second summer in Taos when I think about getting another dog. I do not know if Rainey is ready. She has nearly been in fights. She hunts the woodpile with Molly's partner, Ken. She eats her fill of mice and sagebrush lizards.

Rainey and I play fetch. We hike together. She sleeps with me every night. But whenever she is not with me, she is alone. This is not right for a dog.

I have taken her to Stray Hearts animal shelter in Taos. I have taken her to the Santa Fe animal shelter. It is all the same. If the dog outsizes her, she starts shaking and tries to attack. If the dog is smaller, she plays too rough.

One day, I return from Navajo country and I stop in Santa Fe at the animal shelter. I do my walk-through and see a little black dog rooming with two Chihuahuas. He sits on a cot in the middle of the room and the Chihuahuas lean on either side of his shoulders. He supports their weight. The small black dog is shaped like a small beast that survived the Pleistocene. His front legs are wider than his back legs. His hip is deformed on one side, so he runs slightly crooked. But he runs as hard as he can. He is likely a mix of dachshund and terrier. He sometimes resembles a little black fox.

He has survived things. He understands camouflage. The women at the shelter explain that he was found wandering the streets of Albuquerque and was transferred up to Santa Fe. He'd been living on the streets for two years. That means he'd been hunted by coyotes for two winters and he survived. The little black dog has strong medicine.

He understands that the world is out to kill him.

The Chihuahuas shiver. The black dog droops his ears back as though accepting his fate. His large eyes against his long snout make him look like a goblin fruit bat.

I ask that he and Rainey be allowed to meet in the yard.

She sniffs him with tolerable indifference. She tries to sniff his butt, but his hackles go up. He snaps at her. Here it is. The moment of death. My hand is on her collar. But she doesn't strain. He ambles to the fence, where a dog barks in the next yard. Rainey follows him. They both stand with their tails raised. Still, he is too small, less than half her size. If they start to play, she'll probably break his deformed, crooked hip.

I leave the shelter without him. I have to return to Santa Fe at the end of the week. If he is at the shelter, I will adopt him.

At the end of the week, the little black dog is there. The people at the shelter say that he is so skittish that no one has really warmed to him. I pay the fee and take him. He gets in the car, finds the darkest corner, and lays down with his tail in front of his face. The little black fox. I name him Ricky, after one of my best friends. I buy him a bright-green collar. He farts nervously the entire drive home. He stinks up the Prius.

I bring him home to Rainey. I cup Rainey's chin in my hand and look to her eyes.

"If you ever hurt him," I say, "I'm going to kill you. I'm going to take you into the arroyo and shoot you in the back of the head. And that will be that."

Rainey greets Ricky with kisses to his face. He licks her mouth. I feed them. She wanders to his bowl. Ricky growls and snaps at her. She backs off. He can defend his ground. Rainey wanders back to her bed next to the wood stove. By the end of the night, they are playing on the wood-block floor, Ricky tussling and attacking Rainey from underneath like a harassing weasel. They end with Ricky licking Rainey's face as she lays on her back. I weep in the corner from the relief.

Ricky sticks to his survival routines. He finds the darkest corner of the cabin—the space behind the wood stove—and lays against the adobe wall quietly until something disturbs the territory. Then he will run out and bark at intruders. At night, he hunts mice and leaves a chewed carcass in front of the wood stove each morning for three days. You might think he is a shut-in. But he can smile and tilt back his head like the most optimistic soul in the world while we walk toward the mountains. Ricky, the little dingle.

Rainey will not tolerate any dog to bother him. An eighty-pound dog growled and lifted his lip to Ricky in a crowded kitchen. Rainey shot across the room, bit him through the ear, and nearly ripped it off before I pulled her clear.

For her, Ricky is the puppy she lost.

So I know I can take them to the mountains. That October, I drive to one of my favorite spots near Coyoté, New Mexico. In that ponderosa-pine forest that reminds me of the country around Willy Groffman's cabin, I hike to a canyon choked to darkness by willows, aspen, and alders. You find lion tracks here. You find rocks overturned by bears. Rainey and Ricky and I walk to this canyon, about four miles from where I have parked the Prius.

When we reach the edge, I pour water for Rainey and Ricky into the small metal bowl I found in the backyard of my old adobe house in Ganado. Rainey drinks her fill. Ricky does not come.

"Ricky! Come here, boy!" I call and whistle. I do this for three hours. He is lost.

It is enough time to imagine how Ricky has been killed by a coyote or hawk or other ambush predator, how he has been caught in a rancher's clamp trap set for bobcats, how he has run the wrong way, how he will wander until dark when he will be murdered by a great-horned owl, how all I will find is his bloody bright-green collar. I search every small grove of aspens, every rock crevice, every hollow log. I find bear hair caught in fence wire, rabbit droppings, mountain-lion tracks in a temporary lion den, but no Ricky.

I make plans to walk back to the road, follow it to the car, drive the car down to a place where I can stay near the canyon, and search until dark. I have two flashlights. I will drain their batteries.

I walk to the road with Rainey. We reach it when a 1970s Cadillac convertible veers back and forth down the road. Inside, four old men in dirty camouflage with open beers salute one another. They pull up beside me.

The driver swigs from his beer. "Hey, bro! You missing a dog?"

"Fuck yeah, I am!" I wheeze.

"A little black dog?"

"Yeah, a little black dog with a green collar?"

"Yeah, we saw him about a half-mile on the road back that way." They point the opposite way from the car, where the road goes deeper south into the ponderosa forest. Toward the sun.

"Thank you and your mothers!" I grin. They laugh. They salute me with their beers and on they drive.

I drop my pack and start running. Rainey jogs beside me, excited. The hunt is on.

Jiu-jitsu practice—like wrestling—is some of the best cardio training. I am still fresh after the first mile. I know this because there are green mile markers posted alongside the forest road. My throat grows grated and swollen. I have been calling Ricky's name for hours.

The sun drops lower in the sky. It is the golden hour. Let's hope there's enough magic.

A Toyota Tacoma rolls down the road, pulling a flatbed trailer. On the trailer lies a freshly killed elk poorly concealed beneath a tarp. It is not elk season yet.

I flag down the poacher. It is easy to approach any *Norteño* New Mexican who drives a truck. They understand we are all in this suffering together.

"Hey, man, have you seen a dog on this road?"

"Yeah, a little black dog?" the driver says.

"Yeah," I pant.

"Yeah, he was near the road about a half mile back that way," he says. "But he wouldn't let us get near him."

"Thanks." And I run on. Rainey runs beside me as I tire. I struggle to keep up the pace and close the distance. Ricky is running in the wrong direction.

Please just let him stick to the road, I think. Rainey runs next to me like she is enjoying the hunt. She wags her tail and prances and is thrilled.

This is so great! her body says. *We never really run like this enough!*

After a mile, Ricky does not emerge from the pine and oak forest along the road.

Nearly halfway through the second mile, a new Toyota Tacoma V6 pulls up.

I ask the driver if he's seen a dog on the road.

"Yeah, a little black dog. With a green collar."

"Look, man," I say, taking out my wallet. "I'll pay you twenty bucks if you just let me hop in the back of your truck and you drive me back to where you saw that dog."

The man shakes his head. "I don't think it's really going to matter, bro. We kept trying to call him to the truck, but he wouldn't come. I don't think he wants to be found."

"Thanks," I say. I run and Rainey follows. Ricky is scared and on the move. And he's running in the wrong direction. I only hope I can find him before he gets deeper into the forest. Too deep to find.

The light fades to the gloaming, that time when the eyes of mountain lions and bobcats work much better than the eyes of small dogs.

But as Rainey and I jog up the hill, I have enough light to see the small outline of a black tail at the edge of the road. There it is. The black tail. The black outline. I sprint up the hill and call to Ricky, my missing dog, as he comes into view.

And it's the wrong dog.

It's a black lab, taller than Rainey. Those drunk fucking motherfuckers in the goddamn Cadillac convertible.

I call to this dog, but he keeps a far distance. He probably belongs to one of the loggers who lives on this forest road. He trots on into the gloaming darkness.

Now Rainey and I must walk through the afterglow of twilight to the car. Four miles.

It is an overturning of everything. Pound as many tires as you want. Burn as many sticks at the end of as many drum circles and ceremonies as you want, you fucking hippie. You cannot rid yourself of cruelty when cruelty is the way of the universe. It is the way of every star that ignites in birth, burns away its fuel into space, pulls with ropes of invisible gravity the masses of dust that become spinning planets, and then betrays and murders those planets when the star finally collapses in a final hemorrhaging inferno of gold, iron, and titanium—the very elements that can conduct the ceremony of rain and bring the medicine of moisture to *Nahasdzáán*. Love walks on that earth and House God does not hear it. Just one more motherfucking sham. Creation is hell unleashed.

What is one dog to the universe? I am mourning the breaking of a matchstick.

The sky glows blue and black. The earth has turned away from the sun to darkness. Rainey had found a puppy, and it had been killed again. Let all the mining and burning awaken the darker world. Let the sun smother every planted field. Let salt fill every rice paddy on every delta of the planet. Spread the death shroud over this meaningless tomb, where even a small spark of love must be stamped out so as not to contradict the plan of the universe. Let the cruelty be perfect. Let House God watch.

Still, I will search tonight with my flashlights until they burn out. No matter what, I'm going to find something to bury and honor my dog.

There is just enough light to see the windshield of the Prius as Rainey and I approach the car. And then Ricky runs out from under the car. He'd been hiding behind a tire the whole time.

He probably chased a rabbit, got lost, then picked up our scent trail and followed it back to the vehicle. Then he settled in the darkest place he could find and waited.

I am laughing and crying as I gather Ricky and Rainey into my arms. I pour water for him and he drinks greedily. On the drive back to Taos, I keep putting my arm on Ricky as he sleeps in the backseat, just to know he is actually there.

Haashch'ééhoghan. House God will lead us back, whether we believe in it or not. House God speaks. The essence is there.

Even little dogs know how to find the path that leads them back to safety. Even little dogs know how to save themselves.

Do we?

Ricky, the dingle. Photo by Jim Kristofic.

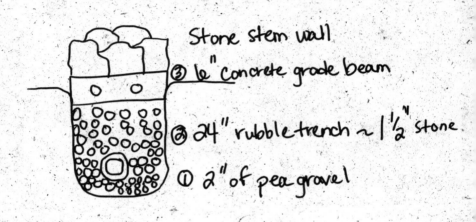

Stone stem wall

③ 16" Concrete grade beam

② 24" rubble trench ~ 1½" stone

① 2" of pea gravel

GODDESSES AND THE EARTH SERPENT

We have thrived on delusion. The land could hardly fail us since we took the land for granted, a commodity, a thing to be used and bartered and butchered and savored. We have at times flung up notions to deny this fact, we have talked about conservation and ecology and the beauties of nature, we have created temporary reserves—for surely, no one living at this moment doubts that our parks and refuges are but holding tanks for resources that will eventually be swallowed by our endless and defiant needs. Now the energy wanes, the waters recede, the temperatures rise, the trees die, the ground grows parched and hard, the wind is up and in our face. We wander lonely in the McMansions on the hill and yet out there, out on the ground where we hardly go, unless atop a bulldozer, life persists and will persist and we only get to make one more decision: do we want to be part of life? Or death?

—CHARLES BOWDEN, *TRINITY*

As the winter approaches the New Year, I move. I want to make things simpler.

Molly has decided I can rent her strawbale studio. It is a special place.

The studio began in 1992 without a building permit. There were only ten experimental permits available at that time in the state of New Mexico and Molly couldn't get one. So she went ahead with her vision for the modest rectangle with its post-and-beam corners, strawbale infill, and bamboo pins to secure the bales within their courses. Then one of the men on the project exalted his ego and destroyed the project. He got the project on the front page of the *Taos News*. People at the county zoning office read the article and ordered Molly to remove all the strawbales.

It would be nearly a decade before Molly got the building started again in November 2001 with a workshop that placed the bales and the plastering. Twenty students showed up to work for George Jackson and Molly, who taught the bale-making methods. Carole Crews taught plastering. Ed Core taught how to pin bamboo through the bales. A year later, a workshop placed the images of five goddesses on the building in earthen bas relief.

To the east is Quan Yinn, the Chinese Healing Goddess. She is a mother in China, adopted as a bodhisattva by the Buddhists, and she brings a gentleness.

On the south, on either side of the door stand the Hopi Corn Maiden and Our Lady of Guadalupe, who emerged from the image of *Tonancín*, the Great Earth Mother of Mesoamerica.

In the west, the face of Demeter pierces you from the plaster. She holds shocks of wheat in each hand. A serpent coils around each wrist, each the bringer of rain. Many remember Demeter from the myth of how her daughter, Persephone, was kidnapped into marriage by Hades, Lord of the Dead. And this is why we have six months of warm weather and six months of winter.

Whenever I see the image of Demeter plastered on the wall, I think of a different story, one of Erysichthon, the king of Thessaly. The king ordered all the trees in one of Demeter's sacred groves to be put to the ax. One of the trees had been covered with worshipping wreaths to Demeter and so the king's men would not cut it down. Erysichthon was enraged. He took an ax and cut the tree down himself and killed the dryad nymph spirit living in the tree. As the nymph died, she called to Demeter and cursed Erysichthon. Demeter heard her.

Demeter called on Limos, the spirit of unrelenting hunger, to enter Erysichthon's stomach. Limos did so. From then on, the more the king ate, the hungrier he became. He sold all his possessions and riches for food, but still he was hungry. He sold his own daughter into slavery. He was still hungry. Finally, Erysichthon found a way to fulfill his hunger. He ate himself.

That is a metaphor for our times. Demeter dances with the grain in her hands and the snakes on her wrists.

Her worshipping cult at Eleusis exposed their devotees to the Eleusinian mysteries—much like my students at Taos Pueblo were put through the kiva. There are many teachings from Demeter. Three important among them are these three commands:

Honor your ancestors.

Honor the gods with fruits of yourself.

Spare the animals.

House God could speak those words with Demeter.

On the north, the Sleeping Lady of Malta, a goddess of the Neolithic peoples from 3,500 BC on the small island south of Sicily, lounges puffed with life and fertility. The Lady was sleeping in a cave carved from the rock into a mythic womb of worship for thousands of years. It was found by accident in 1902 when workers were digging new cisterns for a housing development and broke through the cave's domed roof.

Who knows what else is sleeping beneath our feet?

The strawbale studio wasn't protected with a metal Pro-Panel roof until Joe Jensen finished the work in 2010.

It is all simple. Brick floor. Four electrical plugs. A bed. No running water. The space is smaller than some bedrooms in American houses. I have a hot plate to cook. I soon purchase an electrical pressure cooker.

I use my Christmas break to reclaim some thick, early twentieth-century planks from a fallen barn in Arroyo Hondo. I use them to build a kitchen utility table. I build a shelf that can sit directly above the college-dorm-sized refrigerator. Molly gives me a small Japanese tea table with foot-tall legs. I raise it to a kitchen table height by placing cinder blocks under each leg. I drive my truck to the mesa to cut pinon wood to feed the small wood stove in the corner.

Sponge baths with a bucket, tub, and basin become normal. I soon learn that it is a very easy thing to live without running water. Many of my friends in Taos do it all the time.

The dreams at night are good. Coyotes howl within forty feet of the front door on some nights. Quan Yinn, *Tonancín*, Corn Maiden, Demeter, the Sleeping Lady watch from the walls. The goddesses listen to the sound of my sleeping breath. If I could speak in those breaths, it would be to say a thanks to Molly.

The winter passes. Ice makes spears of crystal from the roof edges. The wood stove feeds. I greet House God and the deities with white corn at dawn. I hear rumors of new builds. The spring comes. Many of the rumors fade. But when the sunflowers grow from the edges of the roads, and the summer comes, one project emerges that may help drive my fool's quest for the most comfortable, affordable, replicable, easily maintained, sustainable home for the Navajo Reservation, one that can gather rainwater and make it easier to live with solar electricity. One that can honor House God.

Mark Goldman has drawn the plans. He knows it all lies in the concrete. Concrete flows into almost every foundation, like the slab Team Wang poured in Des Montes and like the thin trench Bob filled in El Rito. Concrete is responsible for more than 5 percent of all carbon emissions and it is expensive. The nearest place to mix and order concrete for many families is over forty miles away in Gallup, New Mexico. That's too far. That's too much pollution. That's too much money.

I hear of a building that will use no concrete in its foundation. Zero. The walls will be made of earth. The local bank in Taos is funding it. The county inspectors have approved it. I want to be part of the build and—as always—I will work for free. My kind of place.

I drive my road on the Arroyo Hondo mesa, to the west, along the paths the *Diné* raiders and warriors once took through Apache country, through the Spanish villages of Estancia, through Abiquiú, through the Chama River valley, all to see if they might be men of renown, men of prestige, men of prowess. Or they'd be dead. But perhaps they hoped they would prove they had valiant spirits incapable of dying in fear.

A bluebird sings from an electrical line overhead as I turn onto Coyote Loop.

Yáʼátʼééh Ayash Dootlʼizh. His ancestors probably watched all those *Diné* and Taos Pueblo raids and battles. Who knows if those Bluebird People or those men ever made sense of them?

The bumpy miles lead to Calle Canejo, past the five-acre lot where my friend, Doug, lives. Doug and I filled his tin-sided barn last summer with alfalfa bales we hauled from Antonito, Colorado. If you turn in a circle from his front yard, you will see the monuments of extinct volcanos glowing dark blue in the June heat. Cerro Taoses. Cerro de la Olla. Cerro Chiflo. Cerro Montoso. The Spanish used their word *cerro* to mean "hill." But these are mountains. Doug has been on all of them. He has shot elk from over 450 yards. He has trained his Walker hounds to tree mountain lion and bear on those slopes. He has never sighted down on a mountain lion or bear, though. The hounds tree these animals. Doug takes photographs. Then he leads the hounds back to the kennel in the bed of his pickup truck.

The wildlife conservationist (and former Carson National Forest superintendent) Aldo Leopold developed his thinking about the best ways to live with predators while he lived and worked in Taos County in the 1910s. If he'd shown up to the New Mexico Game Commissioners meeting at the Kachina Lodge that June, he probably would have shaken his head. He's been gone more than six decades from Taos County but he would have heard nothing new from those in power.

At that meeting, New Mexico citizens sternly cautioned the Game Commission to rethink their proposed rules on how they want hunters and private landowners to deal with mountain lions. The ranchers and trappers and hunters who commented think everything is okay.

The Game Commission wants to allow elk and deer hunters to kill mountain lions while hunting (for a nominal fee: less than the retail price of an Xbox video game from Walmart), and they want private landowners to be able to trap and mutilate mountain lions on their land without a permit. The ranchers and trappers who attended the meeting agreed with them.

Some people gave firsthand experiences in two-minute comments. One woman commented that she's kept a wildlife camera at a water trough for more than five years and had never seen a mountain lion. As she took her seat, a man whispered, "Try tying up a sheep down there."

And there's the difference. The ranchers said they see lots and lots of mountain lions. And of course they do: the ranchers live near the food.

Everyone who gave a comment had some story to tell. I have my bias. Where I grew up, on the Navajo Reservation, the mountain lion is *Nashdóítsoh*. It is an animal of wisdom and power. It is fluid movement incarnate. It stalks. It becomes the ground.

I spent my teenage years in the rural desert of southern Utah, often following mountain-lion trails. I had two dogs killed and eaten by mountain lions. I also had two dogs maimed by traps laid out by ranchers to catch mountain lions.

I teach at Taos High School. I've lived in Taos County less than four years. But I've already followed lion trails in Garrapata Canyon. I've already found their scat and fresh tracks near Jicarita Peak. I know they're out there.

But I don't know how many are out there. And neither does the Game Commission.

Our personal experiences are all limited. They only take us so far. This is why we've developed methods for thinking outside our own experiences, beyond the confines of space and time. It's called "science." Scientific thinking helps us steer away from bad decisions long before we reach them. It helps us think on longer time scales.

Aldo Leopold knew that. When he was young, he believed in killing predators in order to have a healthy landscape. But he learned that he was wrong. He had the guts to admit it. He saw how killing predators like mountain lions actually caused the range to wither as elk and deer populations exploded.

Our science has since told us stories about mountain lions: We know that they don't need to be hunted and killed to keep their populations in check. They kill each other over territory. And with territories of often more than a hundred square miles, mountain lions are naturally scarce. We also know there is a direct link between mountain lions and water. Mountain lions keep elk and deer herds moving and prevent them from mowing down the green areas around streams and causing them to erode. They also kill small herbivores like rabbits and desert rats that can overgraze grasses on the range and cause moisture loss and (over time) drought.

But stories only go so far. Data only goes so far. Data is science driven.

But culture drives what we do with the data. Aldo Leopold knew that. That's why he said it was important to think on longer time scales, which leads us to "thinking like a mountain." Which is another way to say, "Think like House God." In the meeting, I admired the rational restraint and the quiet courtesy of the commissioners. I hope they can apply that same restraint as they decide how to live with *Nashdóítsoh*.

The truth is the commission can wait for real numbers of mountain lions before they change their rules. The mountain lions aren't out in the hills arming themselves with AK-47s. There's no incoming invasion or Red Dawn approaching. We're all going to be okay. The overwhelming public comment at the meeting was clear to the commission: think like mountains.

Doug knows how to do this. He keeps an album of his photos in his glove box, next to his work gloves. One photo still holds me. A mountain lion postures in silhouette against the blue sunset, ears flattened, paw raised, hissing between her fangs as two hounds close toward her. In the next moment, she jumps to a higher rock where the hounds can't follow. This happened on Cerro Montoso.

It's one of the rare photographs that can't really be a photograph. The record of light cannot hold the momentous life of the dogs and the lion.

"I couldn't believe that cat could move so quickly," Doug said.

Now Doug is moving. His wife has had open-heart surgery. She can no longer handle the high elevation and thin air of the Taos plateau. And he is a good husband. In less than two months, I will help him load a forty-eight-foot trailer when he pulls up stakes to move to Pensacola, Florida. Taos is a place ill fit for the faint of heart. An easy, hard place to live.

The address of the jobsite is easy to find: a set of numbers painted on a plank beside the road. A white 1990s Nissan 4×4 truck sits parked next to a backhoe. Neither belong to the builder, Kenny Quinn.

"James!" Kenny exclaims from the large A-frame pavilion tent. His gray T-shirt and white khaki shorts and his easy manner make him seem a man on vacation. His Pikes Peak athletic socks and running shoes don't seem to belong on a building site. His ashy, coyote-colored hair and the weathered lines of muscle tracing his birdlike face make it hard to guess his age. His veined hands would have you guess he's been digging ditches for at least thirty-eight winters. His teenage blue eyes investigating from his tanned crow's-feet advertise that he is twenty years old once you get some good music going.

When I first called Kenny about working on the site, I asked him why he decided to jump off the grid of "normal life" and run after sustainable buildings.

"Jumping off?" he said. "It's more like jumping *in.*"

The truck is not Kenny's. His vehicle is lying on its side in the sagebrush: a Schwinn road bike. Stickers cover its lightweight aluminum frame. *Taos Cyclery. Bikes Not Bombs. Bicycles Do Not Tolerate Idealists.* A pump is mounted above the gears. When you ride a bike, you feel the wind and Murphy's Law. Kenny Quinn always rides a bike. He has forsaken ownership of any internal-combustion-driven vehicle. This is not because he is a purist. He just knows where the fossil-fuel supply chain really ends. And it doesn't lead to House God.

He saw the end of one of the lines in 2007 after he joined a group of activists and Navajo organizations led by Eloise Brown and Diné Care to oppose the construction of the Desert Rock coal-burning power plant in the San Juan basin. The coal in the San Juan basin is mined by a twelve-story machine that eats earth down to more than eighty feet, twenty-four hours a day, seven days a week, along a coal vein that runs from Gallup to Grants, New Mexico. This machine is called a "drag line."

Kenny faced the consequences of that drag line when he helped haul in a solar trailer to provide power to the resisters in Burnham chapter, near Newcomb, New Mexico. He followed the Northern Environmental Protection Agency (NEPA) and Environmental Impact Studies (EPS) hearings all over the Four Corners. At one of the meetings in Burnham, the local college graduates showed up with a PowerPoint presentation about how the NEPA and EPS were leaving out the alternative power sources of wind, solar, and natural gas. These twentysomethings could prove that the alternative energy was actually cheaper than the coal. They were about to start their presentation when the power went out in the chapter house.

So Kenny powered up the solar trailer and they ran the power in the chapter house meeting room off the trailer. When the power came back on (and this is power generated with coal), the mediator hired by the Navajo Nation grinned and said, "Let's stick with the solar energy. That's fine."

"I would go to these meetings, and the thing that really moved me was when the local doctors and their patients would show up," Kenny says. "Just listening to them, about how the effects of coal burning drive up the asthma and cancer rates in the children. That was enough to make me say, 'What are we doing?' I noticed something else. At these meetings, 90 percent of the people who showed up were against the power plant. And they were there on their own time. Only 10 percent of people supported the construction of the power plant. And they were *paid* to be there. We had over three hundred people show up to these meetings in Durango, Colorado. A hundred people in Window Rock and a hundred in Santa Fe. Fifty people showed up in Burnham. One guy showed up on his own time to support the plant. One guy. And he worked at the coal plant near Farmington.

"I would hear things at these meetings, like, how if we put a second power plant burning coal in that area, it would be like having 1.3 million cars driving around in the sacrifice zone of the San Juan basin. I couldn't understand why we would do this. So I thought, 'What about us is out of balance with the earth?' And then I realized that it was the car. So I said, 'I'm just going to let it go. Time to walk your walk. I'm going to listen to that inner voice and act on it.' So it really took a friend to get me to give up my car. I told her about these problems. And she says, 'Are you really going to do that?' So then I have to do it. She dared me. So I gave her my truck. That was it. And I've been riding a bike ever since."

"I love the feeling of biking. You're more aligned with nature. People are so much more curious and generous to you when you're traveling on a bike. Whenever I'm out there on the bike, especially on long bike trips, I'm really recreating myself. It's medicine. And you feel so much more connection to animals. They're used to people just whizzing by in cars. But when you're going past on a bike, the horses, the cows, the coyotes, they get curious about you. And you get connected."

I ask him what kind of truck he gave up.

"It was a white Nissan pickup truck," he says.

I tap the tailgate of the white Nissan 4×4 pickup parked in the dirt driveway. "Like this guy?"

Kenny smiles. "Exactly. It's a blast from the past. When I first showed up at the jobsite and saw the truck, I just laughed. Yeah. It was just like mine. But I don't miss it."

Kenny leads me down to the trenched foundation. Other dome tents lie pitched in the sagebrush below. This build was advertised as a workshop under Earth and Sun Sustainable Builders. I've been to workshops with thirty people. Twenty-seven people did the Earthship internship with me. At this workshop, one person has shown up. Her name is Madison and she is from Scottsdale. She earned her master's degree in interior architecture from the Boston Architectural College (BAC), the same school as Mark Goldman, who drew the plans for this house. We are going to build it out of earthbags, a collection of polypropylene bags tamped full of dirt, secured with strands of barbed wire.

The earthbag concept was pioneered by Iranian architect Nadir Khalili. Khalili made his reputation designing and building skyscrapers in the Middle East. He shifted his focus when two things happened: He was asked by NASA to design structures that could be built on Mars for a space colony. And he visited one of the many refugee camps in Jordan and other parts of the Middle East. With the NASA mission, he quickly realized that there was no way to import the building materials in a spacecraft. They would have to use the Martian soil. So he thought they could pack rolls of tough polypropylene bags and compact the soil into structures of "earthbags." While NASA considered the idea, Khalili visited the refugee camp and saw that people were living in tents and aluminum shacks poorly designed to handle the heat and the wind. He thought of the shelters he'd designed for Mars. He had only one question: Why aren't we doing this here *on Earth?*

So he built the structures using an earth mix with small amounts of Portland cement he dubbed SuperAdobe and founded a company, CaliEarth, that runs an institute and builds his earthbag structures in California.

I came to this project because of its innovative foundation design. It is a foundation that uses no concrete. Zero. Usually, you can cut out a lot of concrete usage when you use a "rubble-trench" foundation. Why cut the concrete? Concrete accounts for over 2 percent of greenhouse-gas emissions in the United States, much of which occurs when heating the limestone needed to create the cement. When you pour a concrete slab, you're voting for more climate change. You are refusing to speak with House God. Using a foundation without concrete is also four times cheaper than a concrete slab.

For the rubble trench, you dig a trench directly under where the walls will stand and fill it with smooth rock. The rock compacts perfectly into itself and settles with very little tamping needed, just as it did in the foundation of Bob Dunsmore's house in El Rito. Then you pour down eight inches of concrete, creating a smooth cap where you can place your walls and studs. It uses far less concrete and saves you at least four thousand dollars on the day of the pour. This way would work with House God. It would serve on the Navajo Reservation.

So I am confused when I see the foundation ditches that end half-way through their length. After a brief talk with Kenny, I learn that Kelly, the owner, had decided she didn't like the original location of the foundation. She didn't like looking through her north-facing windows and seeing neighbors. This gave Kenny a brief facial tick. I've never heard of redigging a foundation on my first day. But that's what we were going to do.

The backhoe driver, Charlee Meyers, a white-haired man who bears an uncanny resemblance to the poet Robert Frost, isn't sure he can do it. He'll have to straddle the preexisting trench while digging the new one. But he decides to try it. I jump in every now and then to clean the trench with shovels. Nick, a straw-haired teen with a loud mouth and a meaty wrestler's body, jumps in to help me.

I learn Nick likes high school, but knows he is not really pushing himself. He's a professional roofer's son, but he's thinking of college, and he has a right to. His grades are beyond your typical professional roofer. But he likes the physical labor. Once we decide to slope two of the ditches running north and south, Nick hits the dirt with the pick like he's splitting wood in a race for money. He can tell you all about laying down EPDM rubber and asphalt shingles. He liked reading *Animal Farm*. He and his family voted for Donald Trump in the last election.

Kenny is coated with dust by the time we're done. We take many water breaks. We try to pee clear. We can't.

Charlee finishes and decides to leave his backhoe. He's off to the Navajo Nation, to Fort Defiance, to install some rain-catchment tanks. He is a generous man and agrees to leave us his spinning laser level to help find our elevations.

My right wrist tweaks during the last five minutes of swinging the pick. I hit a rock and the recoil is too much. If you want to demand things of the Earth, you must do so on the point of a shovel or pick. You might not always like the answer. And you only have so much cartilage.

At jiu-jitsu that night, I am satisfied with the injury after I do twenty pull-ups. I am a blue belt now. You have to show up.

The next day, we need to dig out a hole around the well casing above the house. The well driller, Dean Cowell, says it needs to go down about four feet and "have enough room for a fat man to work."

"Exactly how fat are we talkin' here?" Nick asks from behind his shades.

"Oh," Kenny says, "real American fat, bro."

Kenny grins as he takes pick to the ground, turning in a circle at the edge of the quarter-inch-thick steel wellhead. The pipe runs quietly through those geological layers of silent violence. Through sand and gravel and water-smooth stones left behind by a giant lake that once sparkled over the Taos plateau. Through basalt from the cataclysmic violence of volcanic eruptions that have left the dark towers of diatremes standing sentry in the windy heat.

While we dig, Kenny tells the story behind the tattoo on his right bicep. A bulldog in a red, spiked collar growls and grins around a fighting knife clamped between its fangs. Above its head it reads, "Devil Dogs." Below it reads, "USMC"—United States Marine Corps.

Kenny was in the Marine reserves for seven years, but he opted out of the Corps when he made staff sergeant.

"They really work you, man," he says. "They feed you everything you need to want to join up. Those recruiters. But it really wasn't hard for me. I just didn't enjoy studying in school. And I didn't know what I wanted to do when I got out. So, the Marines just made sense. It gave me money for college."

Once he stepped out of the Marines, he worked through an associate's degree in forestry. That brought him out for a survey of the ponderosa-pine forests of Coconino County, near Flagstaff, Arizona, in 1995. He worked on fire crews, got out to see the country. He traveled through Utah and Colorado, where he saw an Earthship for the first time.

"Once I saw that, I mean, that was it for me," he says. "I had been working construction since I was eighteen years old. So I had a building background. Seeing that Earthship building. Whoa. It just all made sense. So I just came out here to Taos to really learn and work on something that was alive in me."

Kenny runs the site with the efficiency of a Marine officer and the relaxed air of a surfing instructor. When you leave someone to start a new job, you "peel off." When you go deep into a task with someone—like shoveling into the same wheelbarrow or working a two-man bucket brigade, you are "in their flow." Kenny and I are in each other's flow right now, and the well hole is two feet, eight inches deep. The sun makes dark shadows of our moving bodies. A sagebrush lizard runs to the nearest cover, his bright-blue scales shining like an azure hallucination.

A new volunteer, Antonio, shows up and Kenny peels off. Antonio works five days a week at the gas station on the north side of town. He lives behind the building in a small camper trailer that he pulls with his four-cylinder RAV4.

Antonio has a passage from the book of Revelations tattooed to the ribcage of his slim frame that is more cross-country runner than Nick's wrestler's body. A portrait of a Shawnee Indian warrior poses from his deltoid. A falcon flies over his back. He wears a large sun hat. His teeth are supremely white against his gums. He is from St. Louis. But he's happy he's broken free. He's sad that his mom works so much back there, seven days a week, and lives in a McMansion she doesn't get to enjoy.

We get down to three feet, ten inches when Dean, the well driller, arrives. Dean dug this well ten years ago. He laughs at us digging the hole.

"You know what tool would work a hell of a lot better?" He points to Charlee's backhoe sitting at the edge of the trench. Kenny laughs along the dust lines of his face and explains he isn't a backhoe operator.

Dean talks about what a great deal this well was for Kelly. Since the "Great Recession," the price for drilling a well has almost doubled because the owners of the million-dollar rigs that drill down through the layers of earth still have to make financing payments on the equipment. So now it costs fifty dollars per foot drilled, easily twenty thousand for the well Kelly has. That would be unaffordable today. This well-drilling to the Jurassic-era aquifers still happens. The pumps still run. Dean shows us the brass pitless adapter that he will drill into the side of the steel well casing. It will allow the pump to sink into the casing, descending the cold dark to 380 feet. That 380 feet is where water begins. Most wells on the Taos plateau are drilled to 600 feet. The drillers know that the water levels will eventually drop, just as they've dropped everywhere else. They know we are on borrowed time. Life is currently financed.

Dean watches us with his cocked eyebrow as we hop out of the hole. He tells us we're going to need to dig it out to twice the width so he can climb in and drill. There is no way we can dig this out by the end of the day. Kenny adjusts his tattered gray camo hat. A green dragon fetish on a thin copper chain around his neck shines in the ninety-degree heat. We are all feeling it. The trench. The water. The electrical. The compaction test where the visiting technician will strike the earth at the bottom of our trench with radioactive beams to make sure the earth will not settle. The mung beans cooking in the solar cooker. All of these spokes spin around Kenny.

"Wow," he says. "What a dance."

"I used to be a digging maniac," Dean says as I knock the dust from my work glove. "I'm sixty-three years old. Now, I don't dig *shit.*"

The next day, I bring the solar cellphone charger designed by Mark

Myers that my students in my solar club had built. Kenny is glad for the power source and plugs in his smart phone. We convene and groom the trench. We shoot ten elevations using Charlee's laser level. We track these elevations and shoot them to level the trench.

Wheelbarrow after wheelbarrow. Pick strike after pick strike. We change the edges of the ditch to a plumbed, groomed trench. It is all so careful. We cannot drink enough water.

The hair of the building inspector is all so careful and feathered. She steps out of the white Taos County Ford Ranger and walks up to the trench. Her ID swings from her lanyard in front of her sequined pink blouse. She is the head building inspector for the county. She looks at the trench and the one-foot-deep hole that Kenny has dug into it. Within three minutes, she has failed the trench.

She says that in her twenty-seven years as an inspector, she's never seen a trench like it. But if Kenny thinks it's going to work and Kelly is okay with it, then the inspector needs a letter from Mark, the architect, with his stamp and seal saying it's all on him.

"I can't have no liability on us," she says, spitting her tobacco into a Pepsi bottle.

A bit of background here. The Taos County Building Department was sued less than a year before when a two-foot, eight-inch-deep foundation heaved up from frost and nearly destroyed a multimillion-dollar hotel in the Taos Ski Valley. Now, because of what Kenny calls "global weirding"—where the pendulum of the seasons has begun to swing ever wider and more erratic, where winters have been deepening their cold into the earth and frost line has expanded ever downward, down through the skin of that apple that is mostly made of fire—now Taos County requires three feet of depth to get below the frostline. When Kenny first moved out here, it was two feet.

But Mark and Kenny know this. That's why they've taken the gravel, concrete-less foundation down to three feet, four inches. But they didn't count on what the inspector is saying.

The building inspector waves her arms out. "I mean, look, you just put your excavation back into the hole and tamped it down."

Kenny tries to explain that he's using a pre-engineered mix from the

New Mexico Department of Transportation that works best for compaction. She says she doesn't know anything about it. She will need a letter. When she has a letter, we can fill in the hole Kenny has dug.

So we turn to building what we can. It is a better option than crawling off into the sagebrush to cry. We talk of projects past. We build a barbed-wire spool. It is simple. Take five contractor's stakes. Arrange four crosswise and use plyers to tie them together with baling wire. Set the fifth stake in place and level it with a torpedo level. Widen it enough so the barbed wire roll will fit. Use 15.5-gauge barbed wire with four-point barbs.

Then we go pound the road to make it easier for the dump truck to make deliveries of gravel.

The truck shows up to deliver pit-run base course to build up the driveway. We pound it. We give our sweat to the driveway. We rake them out and create a crown so water will run off the sides. Nick and I chat about jiu-jitsu, marriage, students not giving a shit, where we're headed in school. We plant the biggest rocks in the middle of the road to lift the crown higher. Kenny sucks from his CamelBak. The sun shines hot enough to drive lizards under the rocks. We need something to do while we wait for Mark's letter.

We patch tears in the main tent. We re-tie knots where the wind has undone them. We hope the trench can be finished before the summer rains come.

Those rains will feed the Petaca canyon, running invisible to the southwest, beyond the gorge. Kenny has hiked much of the Petaca, where the melting snow off the wide shield of Bear Mountain to the north seeps down and runs through a shallow basalt canyon. Puebloan people hunted the Petaca for centuries and farmed where they could. Kenny walked there and once found a fertility shrine, where a life-size figure of a man stands carved into the crow-black basalt. Between his legs, a profound penis descends like a string of thundering cloud dropping rain to the seeds in the Earth Mother below.

The clouds darken over *Dził To'woł* (Taos Mountain). A bluebird drops to catch a white cabbage moth on a sagebrush. Thunder booms. The backhoe will be here tomorrow.

The next day begins with another "rough start," as Kenny calls it.

It doesn't feel that way. After days of digging by hand, I can see Charlee Meyers's backhoe as some yellow hydraulic god, supernatural in its steel bucket that lifts the pit rocks by the wheelbarrow load. You would have to enslave an entire village to accomplish what the backhoe does in the next four hours. Charlee has returned from the Navajo Nation, where he put down two aboveground cisterns for a community center near Lupton.

Then comes the rough start. After we excavate for the concrete bunker, the solar designer does not like the plan for running utilities into the space. Kelly had planned to use a fifteen-foot-high cement vault, buried like a bomb shelter, filled with all the electrical and plumbing entrails of modern amenities. Kelly wants to keep all electromagnetic devices out of the living space. This will help her healing journey.

I've met people who won't live under a steel roof or sleep in a building with steel studs. They believe the electromagnetism in the metal will visit them like demons in their sleep and whisper cancer into their bodies.

The solar designer worries of a plumbing piece breaking or condensing and then destroying all the mounted electrical components.

"It could totally fill up with water if a pipe breaks," he says, scratching his baseball cap against his balding forehead.

So we are waiting once again. Kenny rubs the rocky earth through his leathery fingertips. His bicep twitches. His Devil Dog shakes the knife in its jaws. We all drink water. It is not enough.

Mark Goldman pulls up in his Toyota pickup and powwows with us under the tent. I learn why Kenny seems shaken, and it's not just the vault. The building inspector has told Mark that she wants to see a way for water to drain out of the ditch so there is absolutely no frost heaving. In the first century of the American Republic, a farmer and bureaucrat from Massachusetts wrote how a trench filled with gravel and laid with a pipe perforated with small holes would guide water through the pipe to daylight and clear out any land a farmer needed to drain. This farmer's basic concept is still in use today. His name was Henry Flagg French, and they still call his innovation a *French drain*. The French drain is common in rubble trenches. But our trench and our foundation is not common.

"That drain is totally going to fuck me," Kenny grins desperately. Mark nods.

I imagine having to dig a perimeter ditch by hand to lay in the perforated pipe of a French drain. It is not pleasant.

Kelly, Kenny, and Mark finish their conversation about how to approach the building inspector. Kenny gets into the Nissan pickup truck to drive into town so he can camp-out in front of the inspector's office.

"Bummer, man," he says. He rubs the gray beginnings of a beard. "Such a bummer. I just need to have a good cry."

It is Monday. The meeting went well. We are not required to dig a French drain, but we will lay in PVC pipes with holes and screen cloth to allow moisture to travel out. We don't have to dig a new ditch. The *diyin diné*, the Great Ones, are kind, indeed.

Kenny, Nick, Madison, and I are back in the flow. Kenny shows me how to build the wooden stand that will create the foundation for the earthbag building.

It is all simple. The stand looks something like a hip-high tower built from small-dimension lumber. A cardboard concrete form tube sits inside the stand. You walk the tube over to the bag roll. The bag roll sits like a three-hundred-pound roll of toilet paper, only instead of being spooled with hundreds of feet of asswipe, it is coiled with strong polypropylene bags often used in sacking wheat or sand.

You spool out the bag and pull it down over the tube, with your hands at three and nine o'clock positions. Someone else pulls down with their hands at six and twelve, and you alternate back and forth until the tube is ribbed with solidly compacted bags. Once you have the tube ribbed, you carry it over to the stand.

You have just made the plastic and cardboard throat you will use to talk to the rocks and soil to tell them how to create a shelter for you. To talk to House God.

You place the tube into the stand. A long screw runs through the top of the tube and connects it with the stand. The throat was ready to talk. Now it will eat.

The buckets come, two by two, from the gravel pile at the northwest corner of the trench. The bag drops with the weight of the gravel and we tie off the end. The buckets come. The gravel drops down the throat. The esophagus of the plastic bags fills. A rock-filled anaconda snake— an earth serpent—gets left behind as I run the stand down the line of the trench. Nick and Kenny come behind me and fill the remaining space with loose gravel. Then they lay in the PVC drainage pipe. This is how the foundation is built.

There is no loud, spinning concrete truck. No burning and smashing of stone. No concrete stirrer or vibrator. No form work. No big crews troweling a slab. Here, gravity and stone settle the question of whether the house will be allowed to survive the freeze and thaw of winter's reckonings.

While we fill the tube, Kenny carefully keeps tension in the bag, letting gravity walk it out. "We're building the big snake," he grins. "The rock anaconda. The earth serpent."

The earth serpent grows foot by foot until it will be cinched off by spinning the last foot of the bag and tucking it underneath the edge. Then we tamp the bags down with the flat tamper. This all happens over the tendons of barbed wire. We spin these off a spool and use gloves to bend the wire straight. Two people walk the wire to the trench and lay it down on the gravel bags.

These tendons run about four or five inches from each other. As you lay the wire, you turn the spikes so they grab the bags. These keep the building from shearing. As we set the rock anaconda in place, Kenny and I chat. He tells us to drink water. We share horror stories of watching people collapse into heat exhaustion.

We talk as we run the stand, pulling on the bag at the edge of the tube, keeping the tension on. We leave two four-inch PVC pipes running through the bags. One will run to the septic. The other will run to Kelly's "illegal graywater" planter. She could run the water to a buried graywater tank. But she's just going to run the pipe straight to the outside of the house.

Kenny checks my bags. "You're crushing it!" he cheers as he dumps his gravel-filled buckets to the lip. "You're all over it, bro!"

When I'm done, Kenny checks my work. He says I went from a C- to an A+ by the end of the course."

A part of me is the grunt impressing the sergeant. I work from the edge of the outer bag and we "free tube" the rest of the bag. This allows us to neatly "hard ass" the bags, where you lift and shake the bag until it's super tight and fat at the end.

Kenny built this way in Nepal, when two NGOs requested him in the same week to go to Nepal and build a three-classroom school from earthbags.

"So it was just right there," he says. "The universe was totally vibing for me to go to Nepal."

In a small mountain village, Kenny organized about twenty people. The village was so remote they couldn't bring anything in. There were no quarries nearby. "We didn't have gravel," Kenny says. "So we had to *make* it. These people made gravel, by hand, in the village. You'd hear them all morning and through the night. They would drop and smash big rocks onto little rocks. And they'd hit the rest with a hammer. We only went down a foot with the foundation, so that didn't take long."

They didn't even have soil for earthbags in the high mountains.

"We had to *bring in* soil," Kenny says. "People literally shoveled it into backpacks and walked the clay soil a kilometer down the mountain."

Most of the workers were women and teenagers. When Kenny left, the locals had over half of the roof on the building. They finished it two weeks later.

The storm comes. Gray monuments of rain descend from over the mountain. Then the mountains are gone and the rest is hail and lightning and drumming thunder. This is a day for House God, for a roof with a door to protect you.

We secure all the tools under the main tent.

Kenny digs a trench with a hoe so water can be diverted away from the gear. The rain persists. We have to call it a day. Kenny will probably hike down into the Río Grande Gorge to the nearby hot springs.

Running out the earth serpent. Photo by Kenneth Quinn.

The next day we get after the trench. We work in the gravel bags and create the earth serpents filled with two-inch washed gravel. We set up a flow of gravel buckets, carrying them two buckets at a time, to the trench edge.

We keep loading until Kenny has cut himself.

"There is now blood on the bag, Kenny," I say.

"Yours or mine?" Kenny laughs. "You know, I'm thinking my clotting abilities are actually diminishing as I get older."

Kelly comes by and offers to bandage Kenny's leg and arm. He says he's fine. He is calm as any boy flung from his bicycle. Kelly reminds us to place her shard of quartz at the northeast edge of the foundation.

Kelly places an "energized gem" at the corners in order to run good energies through the house. She's not placing any of the utilities in the house. Her breaker box is actually going to run outside the house. I ask if that's normal.

Frank, Kenny's older brother, says, "Well, I got those kinda meters on my rental properties back in Fayetteville. Course, a neighbor could just walk by and shut yer power off!" He laughs and we laugh with him.

Thunder chants in the East. Lobo Peak vanishes in the mist of an eleven-thousand-foot storm. We call it a day.

The next day, I run the stand with new metal rubes that Kenny and Frank ordered from a local contractor. The cardboard concrete tubes kept wearing out.

"These are just bomber, man," Kenny says. "It's fucking expensive. But we have bags in the air, gentlemen! We are not fucking around now." He smiles. He is the shop student who has just outsmarted the test. I run the crusher fines into the tube. Danny, a fourteen-year-old kid with Down's Syndrome, is here with Rachel, a young woman who had worked in Nepal building earthbag houses. She lays barbed wire on the previous bag course with the care of a woman setting a loom.

"In Nepal, with Kenny, if we had a problem, you just sent the teenage girls after it. Not the men," Rachel says.

Kenny chimes in as he and I lay barbed wire. "Oh God, the men were just the *worst*," he says. "You can't keep track of their time. And where *are* they? Now it's time for their smoke break. It's just totally not productive."

We feed the earth serpent the crusher fines. But we have also mixed in buckets of clay adobe dirt from a local spot on the Hondo Mesa. Kenny slightly wets the mix before we load it by the bucketful. The run is hard going today. The metal tube has no give as I pull the bag. After forty feet of bag, my skin rips from my right ring finger in a perfect circle the size of a leather punch.

Kenny will be talking tomorrow with Rebecca about setting up a build for a school where the dirt road from Two Peaks meets the highway.

"I really see myself as a community builder," he says. "I'm all about getting people together. That's how I built my place out at STAR.* I

* STAR (Social Transformation Alternative Republic) is the first Earthship community established by Michael Reynolds under what was then called "Solar

would host these work parties out there. And a lot of it toward the end would turn into drinking parties. But before the drinking started, we would knock out a shit ton of tire work."

We run the tube. Certain spots are marked with "+" marks where we need an "extra-fat schlong" and "-" marks where we will have a "skinny schlong."

I reply to Kenny's adolescent penis humor with an even more juvenile joke made by a six-year-old I overheard talking in the grocery store the week before. "What if," the boy asked his mother, "a piece of poop farted on its own pee?"

Kenny laughs. "It sounds like something Ted Elsasser would say."

Survival Architecture, LLC." The former community of around three hundred people is established on the western slopes of the 7,950-foot volcanic mound Tres Orejas, often called "Three Peaks" in Taos.

Demeter, an earth goddess, shaking the serpents and the wheat, speaking from the earth plaster in New Mexico. Photo by Whitney Nieman.

Epilogue | *The Voice of Grandfather*

The summer moves toward an end. The earth tilts and the days grow shorter. The storms come and the mountains become dark fantasies in the mist. The earth serpent rises. It coils Demeter's wrist. More blood spatters the bags. The roof spans by the autumn and Kelly occupies the house before Thanksgiving. The first house in Taos county—inspected by the building department and financed by a bank, with no concrete in its foundation or walls—rises from the earth into the sky. We have fed it all. We have made it a place. House God has spoken.

The snows fall and the woodsmoke fills the valleys in the morning.

In the *Diné* way, winter is the time to tell stories. The snakes sleep. The fire cracks over the juniper logs. In Fort Defiance, Arizona, the Navajo Nation Tribal Council gathers for their winter council. During that session, I bring the feathers of bluebirds to give to certain council members to thank them for helping me with a writing project. A council staffer passes around an attendance sheet for the meeting. I pass the clipboard to the nearest attendee. He is a short-legged man with uncommonly good posture, strong shoulders, and long, braided black hair. There is something about his face. He signs his name to the clipboard. Caleb Yazzie. I know him.

Caleb was my first martial-arts teacher. He ran Kung Fu classes in the Ganado Middle School woodshop, where he taught carpentry and electrical wiring. He hung heavy bags and speed balls next to the bandsaws and drill presses. We learned the forms that teach the body movements—the *kata*—and to imitate postures of the tiger, the horse, the snake, the panther. We learned to sweat, to punch, to kick, to throw, to be unashamedly violent and brashly disciplined. I learned that I loved these things.

At this winter council, it is an honor to shake the hand of the man who has given me these teachings and started me on the path to Muay Thai, to jiu-jitsu.

"You train jiu-jitsu?" he asks. "What belt are you?"

Over the two years I've been in Taos, I trained at least two nights a week at my jiu-jitsu academy. I've torn tendons in my elbow no less than three times, dislocated my knee twice, nearly broken my hand, broke my foot, and ripped my hip flexor. I trained through the injuries until it was time for my purple-belt test that spring.

In jiu-jitsu, a white belt is a person who walks in off the street. They know nothing. They advance to blue belt, a person who can defeat a larger, untrained opponent. A purple belt is someone who can defeat the average jiu-jitsu blue belt. They have begun a journey of jiu-jitsu that will likely lead them to mastery. To receive a purple belt, it means your teacher sees the teacher in you. The black belt.

For the ceremony of my purple-belt test, I memorized five pages of techniques, became CPR certified, learned basic first aid, and performed ten hours of community service. I had to write my own code of ethics and my own philosophy of training.

Then I showed up in the academy in the middle of the day. Ryan Daly and his brother lit the incense on the altar where they'd hung the portraits of Carlos and Hélio Gracie—those brothers from Brazil who innovated the art of Brazilian jiu-jitsu. These brothers of mine kneeled with me on the white mats while I demonstrated the techniques. Then they kicked my ass for an hour. We fought four fifteen-minute matches. I escaped, endured, and finally submitted. Hélio and Carlos Gracie watched from their framed photographs on the wall. They seemed to approve. Their portraits had watched this ceremony hundreds of thousands of times all over the planet.

When it was over, my teacher had to keep reminding me that I'd earned it. He tied the belt around my waist.

"I'm a purple belt," I said.

"Ah, so you're a coach," Caleb said. "You should get your brown belt and come out here to open a school."

"You never know," I smiled. "The fight is always worth it."

That summer, Caleb invites me to a Tipi Way. This is also called a peyote meeting or Native American Church (NAC). I didn't know what to say.

I knew *'azee' dei'aałí* (peyote, the Chewed Medicine)—the soft bodies of the cactus known also as *Lophophora williamsii*—had migrated up from Mexico and emerged in the Plains tribes, whose ceremonies had scarified and prepared one for the excruciating pain and ecstasy of survival. People call it Medicine. It carries truth. Caleb's family was willing to be arrested by their own Navajo Nation government outside their own tipi by Navajo police officers after the tribe declared it illegal in the 1950s. I knew many *Diné* people who attended NAC and attended traditional ceremonies and believed both. By the 1980s, the peyote meetings were no longer illegal.

When I arrive at Caleb's house at Hunter's Point, Arizona, he asks me to lay down in the tipi and rest before the sing that will go all night. A blue flicker passes through the boughs of a large piñon tree. A *dólii'* (bluebird) watches me from a pole set against the tree as I walk into the canvas tipi, spread in its circle that had so reliably parted the winds of the Great Plains those few centuries ago, just as it parts the winds at Standing Rock, where water protectors make encampments to stop the Dakota Access Pipeline that could put their children at risk and bring the life of the Missouri River to shambles. I lay opposite the entrance. I rest my head near a pole where a rope coils to where it ties to the connection of poles at the sky hole.

I flutter in and out of sleep. I'd driven out to *Dził Dah Si'ání* (Fluted Rock) earlier that day. I walked that sacred site, found a flicker's nest under a grove of pines, picked *dah yiitįhídąą'* (Indian paintbrush), and held a hawk feather from the grass in front of the Fluted Rock. The sun glinted in the summer leaves of the oaks. Rainey ran far and drank deeply from her water bowl.

The sun warms my bare feet. Someone in the tipi whispers my name to gently wake me. I sit up. No one is there. I walk outside, looking for who called my name. There is only the bluebird watching from the pole set next to the piñon tree. Someone spoke. Might as well have been him.

He is as beautiful as any bluebird who could land on a fence post along Willy Groffman's road in Mora. He could land in any piñon tree in Arroyo Hondo.

The sun walks down the West while I visit with Caleb's wife, Janice. She was my eighth-grade science teacher and has forgiven my many in-class torments. She will prepare food for the morning, after everyone has sat up praying all night. The old people show up as the sun sets. They have their blankets for sitting. Some of them have thick cushions for their knees. They are not hippies with hip replacements, but they are something like elders. This is not their first night sitting up.

We pray outside the tipi before we enter. Caleb tells me that I don't have to take the peyote into my body if I don't want to. Many people attend and don't ever take anything. A local man named Wilfred says the medicine is good for you, though. It will come as a powder, as a sliced raw button, and as a tea. It will show you things you need to see.

"The peyote is like a direct antenna to talk with the Creator," Caleb says. "That's why we call the peyote 'Grandfather.' It has wisdom. It's for broadcasting the signal to directly connect with the Creator who is above us and inside us."

We enter and circle to the south to find our seats in the ring of people. One of Caleb's sons comes in last and checks on the long poles of aspen, piñon, and cedar stacked for the fire. He has already set up the fireplace at the center of the tipi. A crescent moon of white sand runs south to north. In the sand sits the powder, the buttons, and a jar of the dark-yellow tea made from Grandfather Peyote.

We take our seats. Caleb's daughters sit under the pole with the coiled rope. They had birthdays recently, and this sit-up tonight is for them, to help them go forward with what they need to do in a good way. One daughter will decide if she travels overseas to finish her PhD. The other daughter will decide if she finishes her college degree. These are not bad choices to make. It is a celebration time, to decide the path one will choose and the other paths they will have to look back on with a sigh so many years hence.

I know the feeling. The mountain spoke for me. I've tried to not be a burden to *Dził To'woł* (Taos Mountain). I started the Solarado Solar Club at Taos High School. I helped the students build solar cellphone chargers. I've started a jiu-jitsu club at the high school, and I've trained young women how to choke-out a misbehaving date. I've used a thousand-dollar grant from Facebook to build worm composters and placed them in every classroom in Taos High School so that students don't have to throw away their food into the trash. Instead, they toss it into a small bin where thousands of earthworms chew it down to some of the richest soil on the planet.

That fall I helped design and build a greenhouse on the Taos High campus that will use one of Bob's solar collectors to heat air and blow it into a buried concrete air chamber that will heat the insulated foundation and keep it from freezing even in the coldest of Taos winters. I've tried to juggle. I've tried to do Willy Groffman proud.

These are all acts to promote life. To empower people. To talk to House God. To use that good essence.

Mark Meyers and I are in the business of empowering people. The coyote who sniffed the door handle of Mark's Toyota 4Runner seemed to agree.

It is so easy to feel righteous in my actions. But am I doing the right thing? When do I bring these things back to the Reservation? How?

Maybe Grandfather Peyote will tell me. The mountain spoke. What it will say tonight?

Caleb's son, Steven, brings in the first poles to create the fireplace. He lays the poles in the way the Plains people have built them for centuries. It is still the best way to make a fire in the West. He builds the fire as an arrowhead opening to the East. The poles interlock like your fingers or the way logs connect at the edges of the *hoghan*. The arrowhead aims to the West. You add new poles as the fire gnaws them to coals. You push the dead coals to the edge of the white sand crescent. Steven will do this all night.

Sitting opposite of the entrance is the man who will conduct the ceremony and keep things moving around in the circle. He is the road-man.

The prayers move between people. They travel in the circle. People give advice to Caleb's daughters. They encourage them. The four Anglo men in the circle talk of how the people in the tipi are their family. All the *Diné* people nod. Many whoop, "Yeah." I sit silent because I have nothing to say. I have come to listen.

The road-man asks someone to sprinkle cedar on the fire whenever anyone returns from outside the tipi. The road-man passes the mountain tobacco and corn husks for people to make smokes. I pull mine deep from the embers. There is no pleasure in this. My legs—those birthrights from my standing and running ancestors—have become numb from sitting. My ass is on the ground and there is only the pain of belonging to the Earth.

Maybe tonight Grandfather can give us another and a wiser and perhaps a more mystical concept of humans. Something that turns us from being the endangering species. Something that helps us feel *Haas-hch'ééhoghan*, House God.

The fireplace cracks and glows with embers.

Caleb's son fits a water drum and ties down the leather head. He drums and sings until it becomes a heart we share. The road-man gives the first of the peyote. It circles in powder. Then raw buttons. Then the tea.

The road-man speaks in measured, calm patterns. He speaks of how "we're going to take care of this medicine, going to take care of it" or how "we're going to take care of this water, going to take care of it."

Grandfather Peyote circles. We take care of him. He takes care of us. I take as much as Wilfred and Caleb. They sit back with the medicine and quietly pray. I do the same. I pray the kinds of prayers without words.

The Rain Dog is sniffing north through the fence of the animal shelter. She is trying to catch the scent of those puppies given up to murder.

Willy Groffman is reaching for a St. Pauli Girl beer after he has finished watering the tomatoes in his greenhouse.

Mark Myers takes up the hose and flips the switch on his outdoor solar pump and the hummingbirds scatter as water showers over his sunflowers. DeLynn weeds the spinach.

Molly and Ken feed the chickens and water my pumpkins while I am gone. Ken flies people into the gorge and watches for *tsétah dibe'* (bighorn sheep)

Ted Elsasser is fitting glass to a south-facing window and making penis jokes.

Christopher Columbo clicks his tongue so his mules will pick up the pace as he rides the rim of the gorge.

Mark Goldman tests the tension of his new adobe mix in his workshop behind his house. His fingernails are black with dirt.

Bob Dunsmore looks to the alcove in his wall where his son watches. Sometimes Aaron Eli speaks. Bob's strawbale walls keep the place quiet enough for Bob to hear him.

Thunderstorms over Arroyo Hondo tear apart the nests of magpies. When it is finished, a rainbow spans the sky. The magpies rebuild.

The rain flows from Stacy Diven's roof and gurgles silently into the adobe planters on the south side of his pumice-crete house.

Dogs get lost in canyons. People put up posters and hope for the kindness of strangers. Some of the dogs save themselves.

Kenny Quinn drums the tamper into the skin of the great earth serpent running its coils around the foundation.

They have all walked into the tipi with me. They sit in the ring with Caleb's neighbors and relatives, who are now my relatives. They say so.

After the second circling of the medicine, I am thinking of my sister, Yanabah. She and I met in southern Utah the summer before. We hiked a slot canyon near our house that a woman had once driven her car down into after falling asleep at the wheel at night. The woman remained pinned in her car between the smooth, rippling sandstone walls of the canyon for two days while cars screamed past. Some local hikers heard her blaring the horn. She was only twenty yards from the highway. They say she stayed alive in the desert heat by peeing into her hand and drinking it.

Rainey followed us panting in the searing heat. We followed the tracks of a coyote to Wahweap Wash, where we watched that *mą'íí*—that little wolf—navigate between the tangled, clay-rich waters. Rainey ran for the water.

"I hope Rainey doesn't get in the mud." I turned to Yanabah. "That would ... oh shit."

Rainey stood bathed in clay mud. Dog and earth had become one. We laughed as we combed it out of her to get her back into the car. Rainey smiled and panted with relief.

At sunset, after we'd cooked for the night, I caught a *diyóósh* (bull snake) sliding between four-wing saltbush and brought it to Yanabah.

"I remember how you used to catch them all the time," she said, taking it carefully from my hands. "You never hurt one. Not once."

"Look at its head," I said.

The yellow and brown scales on the snake's head formed a perfect pattern of a grinning human skull.

Now Grandfather Peyote has guided that snake into my guts. The snake crushes my insides with the coils of its body with more force than an earthbag filled with gravel. I never fear falling asleep as I sit-up. Everything is pain now. I breathe through it.

The peyote cactus grows no spines. It seems to want to be eaten. But it also swells with alkaloids. These are poison. The poison does its work.

Some people step outside to vomit. This happens. The fireplace wavers with its coals. People pray quietly. I pray quietly.

I don't expect to see anything with my eyes. And I don't. We understand the world with our five senses. I am understanding something with a sense that is not one of those.

It all comes with the dawn, after we eat the three foods: the *naadą́ą́'* (corn), the *béégashii bitsį́'* (meat), and the *didzé* (berries). *Jó'honaa'éí*, the Sun, has walked back up with his crystal shield. *Haashch'ééhoghan*, House God, waits at the door. It is time to walk out and be counted as one of his children. Some people stay in the tipi. I walk out to see the white line of dawn over the piñon trees.

That's when Grandfather speaks with a voice that is not a voice.

What we do here in our ceremonies is important. But it is not where the ceremony begins, he says. The ceremony begins with what we *bring with us*. The ceremony is not inside here. It's *out there*.

Everything is ceremony. Everything is ritual.

This ritual in this tipi has spoken, he says. And it is this: you are on the right path. But *your* rituals are out here. *Your* prayers are your good actions. Go do them. Sit by a fire when you need to remember, when you need to rest.

Everyone walks out to eat the breakfast Caleb's wife has prepared. I cannot imagine eating. The snake remains down in the guts, twisting, teaching me to breathe.

Walk to that piñon tree next to the tipi. The *dólii'* (bluebird) is there again. He whistles as I crumple to the earth. I sleep in the shade for four hours. I wake with black ants crawling through my hair and over my neck.

In that place between waking and sleep, the sun makes a scarlet and gold light with my eyelids that is neither the blood of Christ nor the light of angels, but the splendor of the energy, the juggle between light and dark, that first bluebird at dawn that travels in a path to keep everything *chingón*. Where House God walks. I hear that voice that is not a voice. Grandfather Peyote is still at work.

It is the black wolf talking. It can be tamed because its jaws kill but not with any cruelty. And we have tamed it and called it a dog, and we evict from our midst those who would betray this animal.

The politicians are at the priests' throats. They have no answers. Perhaps they will soon be strangled.

We can take our time to grock things. Our cellphones can talk with the sun.

Take our worst impulses. Our cruelty. Take the betrayers of children. Make the ceremony that lets us burn them away in the fire.

We can demand our sovereignty from our buildings. We no longer need to work below the waterline and continue the dark witchcraft of our nuclear prowess. We can play for Team Wang.

We can trust that children who learn to walk in prison can grow to become builders who are willing to sleep in the backs of their trucks so that their buildings will safely house homeless teenagers.

The sun strikes the earth like a drum. It makes a sound so sacred we can't hear it.

The dead children are talking. Their voices are the straw rustling.

The dogs find their way home. The dead return to life.

The foundations don't need concrete. It will all flow like the earth serpent. It always ends with a ceremony. And it begins that way. The taste is bitter. But it is medicine.

The bluebird watches from the pole. He turns his head. His eye shines black.

What a dance. To the sun. To House God.

Dance it. Build it.

Say, *Yes.*

A face of House God, who speaks from the West, Taos County. Photo by Jim Kristofic.